Advancing Foundational Skills *for*

English Language Learners

By Silvia Dorta-Duque de Reyes

Table of Contents

Word Study

Overview

Advancing Foundational Skills for English Language Learners

Foundational literacy skills – which primarily address print concepts, phonological awareness, phonics and word study, and fluency – are critical for English Learners at all ages who need to learn basic literacy (August & Shanahan, 2006; Riches & Genesee, 2006) skills in English. These foundational skills are the same for all students, including English Learners. Furthermore, current research shows that English Learners can transfer native language literacy skills to English literacy learning (August & Shanahan, 2006; Riches & Genesee, 2006). Thus, it is recommended that foundational skills instruction for English Learners be adapted based on:

- the student's age and level of schooling,
- the student's previous literacy experiences in his or her native language,
- the student's level of oral proficiency in the native language and in English,
- the native language writing system used, and
- how closely the student's native language is related to English.

Therefore, students' language and literacy characteristics need to be taken into consideration and individualized instruction may be needed in order to provide the appropriate foundational skills instruction. The following are general guidelines:

Student Language and Literacy Characteristics		Considerations for Foundational Literacy Skills Instruction	Common Core State Standards for ELA Reading Standards: Foundational Skills
Oral Skills	*If students have…* No or little spoken English proficiency	*Then…* Students will need instruction in recognizing and distinguishing the sounds of English as compared or contrasted with sounds in their native language (e.g., vowels, consonants, consonant blends, syllable structures).	*Therefore, provide instruction for…* **Phonological Awareness** 1. Demonstrate understanding of spoken words, syllables, and sounds (phonemes).
	If students have… Spoken English proficiency	*Then…* Students will need instruction in applying their knowledge of the English sound system to foundational literacy learning.	
Print Skills	*If students have…* No or little native language literacy	*Then…* Students will need instruction in print concepts.	*Therefore, provide instruction for…* **Print Concepts** 2. Demonstrate understanding of the organization and basic features of print. **Phonics and Word study** 3. Know and apply grade level phonics and word analysis skills in decoding words. **Fluency** 4. Read emergent-reader texts with purpose and understanding.
	Some foundational literacy proficiency in a language not using the Latin alphabet (e.g., Arabic, Chinese, Korean, Russian)	Students will be familiar with print concepts, and will need instruction in learning the Latin alphabet for English, as compared or contrasted with their native language writing system (e.g., direction of print, symbols representing whole words, syllables or phonemes).	
	Some foundational literacy proficiency in a language using the Latin alphabet (e.g., Spanish)	Students will need instruction in applying their knowledge of print concepts, phonics and word study to the English writing system, as compared or contrasted with their native language alphabet (e.g., letters that are the same or different, or represent the same or different sounds) and native language vocabulary (e.g., cognates) and sentence structure (e.g., subject-verb-object vs. subject-object-verb word order).	

Adapted from "Foundational Literacy Skills for English Learners," in Chapter 6 of the California English Language Development (CA ELD) Standards (Education, 2014b, p. 180)

Who should participate in the Advancing Foundational Skills for English Language Learners component?

English Learners who are newcomers to English or enter school after or at the very end of the primary grades need to develop English foundational skills **in an accelerated time frame** so that time teaching foundational skills is warranted and efficient. *Advancing Foundational Skills for English Language Learners* positions English Learners who are already literate in their native language as competent and capable of quickly achieving academic literacy in English.

For students enrolled in an alternative bilingual program (e.g., dual immersion, two-way immersion, developmental bilingual, etc.), foundational skills are taught along with the CCSS-aligned primary language standards, in order to develop foundational skills in both the primary language and in English.

Advancing Foundational Skills for English Language Learners **is specifically designed for identified English Learners in grades 3 through 6 who already possess some spoken English proficiency and some foundational literacy skills in their home language or English.**

It is recommended that, after consideration and assessment of a student's language and literacy characteristics, he or she participate in **one** of the following:

> *Benchmark Advance English Language Arts/English Language Development program and individualized or small group instruction using the Advancing Foundational Skills program.*

> *Benchmark Adelante Spanish Language Arts/English Language Development program and individualized or small group instruction using the Advancing Foundational Skills program.*

What is an Accelerated Program?

Accelerated instruction is not about racing through the curriculum. Rather, it is about the maximal use of instructional time for each individual student in order to accelerate learning (Levin, 1988; Levin & Hopfenberg, 1991).

Advancing Foundational Skills for English Language Learners is a series of highly engaging lessons designed to build upon English Learners' existing literacy knowledge in their home language and to promote a deeper understanding and working knowledge of print concepts, phonological awareness, phonics, word study, and fluency in English. While organized systematically and sequentially following a continuum from simple to more complex skills, teachers, in collaboration with individual students, can make programming decisions by adapting or compacting learning as they define learning goals and maximize the outcomes of a given segment of instruction. The idea is to enable students who have already mastered a skill to move on to what they need to learn.

In order to implement accelerated foundational skills instruction, teachers must first carefully assess students in both English and their primary language, to determine the most appropriate sequence and type of foundational skills instruction each individual student may need. Each of the foundational skills components in *Advancing Foundational Skills for English Language Learners* has an informal pre-assessment that can be used to determine if the student would benefit from participating in the lessons in that component, with the ultimate goal of mastering all the foundational skills strands to support the student's development of high levels of proficiency in English. With multiple entry points and an assessment for each foundational skill to inform placement decisions, the *Advancing Foundational Skills for English Language Learners* is designed to identify and build upon their linguistic strengths and develop their area(s) of linguistic need and provides maximum flexibility for both teacher and students.

Benchmark's *Advancing Foundational Skills for English Language Learners* includes 15-20 minute lessons for each of the four foundational skills that are designed to accelerate the students' development of proficiency in English. Each lesson makes a direct connection to the students' prior knowledge and experiences, valuing their home language, and connecting what is being taught in the lesson to what may transfer to their native language.

Accelerated lessons are designed to capture students' interest, and rather than slowing down instruction until each skill is mastered, skills are presented and compacted whenever possible. Pre-assessments, formative assessments, and spiral reviews are important tools that are provided to guide and reinforce instruction (Burris & Garrity, 2012).

The Foundational Skills in Advancing Foundational Skills for English Language Learners

Print Concepts

Print concepts include the organization and basic features of print. Among these are that English is read from left to right, top to bottom, and page by page; spoken words are represented in written language by specific sequences of letters; words are separated by spaces; and sentences are distinguished by certain features, such as capitalization of the first word and use of ending punctuation. English Learners in grades 3-6 who are already literate in their native language may or may not be familiar with the type of writing system or with the Latin alphabet. Therefore, this component includes explicit instruction in alphabet recognition, the alphabetic principle, and text features for those who may need it.

Phonemic Awareness

Phonological awareness is the awareness of and ability to manipulate the sound units of spoken language. Phonemic awareness is crucial for developing an understanding of the alphabetic principle, which is that individual sounds in spoken words can be represented by letters in print. English Learners in grades 3-6 who are already literate in their native language will need instruction to recognize and distinguish sounds in English as compared to or contrasted with sounds in their native language. Lessons in phonological awareness include recognizing onset and rimes, recognizing and producing rhyming words, and recognizing compound words.   Phonemic awareness lessons are integrated with phonics lessons and taken to print through shared writing.

Phonics and Word Study

Phonics and word study standards include knowledge of letter-sound and spelling-sound correspondence, recognition of irregularly spelled words, and knowledge of word parts (syllables and morphemes). English Learners in grades 3-6 who are already literate in their native language will need instruction in applying their knowledge of the English sound system and to recognize and distinguish sounds in English as compared to or contrasted with sounds in their native language.

The instruction in letter-sound and spelling-sound correspondence is explicitly and logically sequenced and applied to meaningful text. It includes consonants, consonant blends, consonant diagraphs, short and long vowel patterns, vowel diagraphs, and r- influenced vowel patterns. Phonics elements are taken to print through shared writing and brief spelling activities. Word study lessons include inflectional ending as well as common Greek and Latin prefixes, suffixes, and derivatives.

Fluency

Fluency is the ability to read with automaticity, accuracy, and expression at an appropriate rate. Automaticity refers to effortless, virtually unconscious, accurate identification of words. Prosody, or expression, includes rhythm, phrasing, and intonation. Prosodic reading suggests that the reader can identify words quickly and accurately and comprehends the text. Rate of accurate reading of connected text is a common measure of automaticity and although rate is important, the goal is not speed for its own sake. The goal is automaticity with print so that meaning-making can occur. All lessons in the *Advancing Foundational Skills for English Language Learners* program include a Shared Reading section, where students read, practice, and apply the skills in context. This Shared Reading section is multi-purpose in that it can be used for fluency practice through repeated readings once comprehension has been confirmed. Teachers first model and read the text with appropriate pacing, expression and intonation and encourage students to echo read, choral read, and read independently, pausing and changing the intonation in their voices as appropriate.

Foundational Skills Assessment

Students' progress in acquisition of the foundational skills of print concepts, phonological awareness, decoding and word recognition, and fluency should be monitored carefully.

Screening assessments and identification of students' existing skills and knowledge drives the placement, instructional planning, and lesson compacting in the *Advancing Foundational Skills for English Language Learners* program. Screening assessments include information related to a student's literacy experiences in his or her native language, level of schooling, level of oral proficiency in his or her native language and in English, and how closely a student's native language is related to English as well as the type of writing system used.

A balanced approach to assessment includes both assessment of learning and assessment for learning. Assessment of learning usually involves a tool or event after a period of learning, while assessment for learning is a process that occurs concurrently with learning. Each lesson provides formative assessment options to inform instructional decisions in the moment and in subsequent lessons. Any evidence-gathering strategy used during formative assessments yields information that is timely and specific enough to assist the teacher by informing his or her instruction and thus will affect the students' learning. It is important to note that pronunciation differences due to native language, dialect influences, or regional accent should not be misunderstood as decoding or comprehension difficulties.

Active student involvement in the assessment process is a vital element in the development of student self-direction in learning. Feedback is key to student assessment because it is a critical factor in the development of students' insight into their own learning and understanding (Council, 1999; Development, 2005)

Instructional Sequence

The instructional sequence in the *Advancing Foundational Skills for English Language Learners* program reflects an interactive approach to learning.

Each lesson introduces the standards-aligned objective, skills, and concepts. The teacher elicits prior knowledge and acknowledges each student's native language by asking them to use their metalinguistic awareness to recognize how concepts introduced in the lesson are the same or different than in their native language.

The teacher then teaches and models the skills and guides students in practice. Each lesson contains a Shared Reading section where students apply the learned skills. This Shared Reading section, which is analyzed and deconstructed, is also used for fluency practice.

Each lesson includes a concluding section where students are prompted to review and reflect upon what they have learned and consider how the concepts will be applied or generalized to other contexts.

Student are encouraged to bring their work home to share what they have learned with their families, affirming the value and advantages of bi-literacy.

Maximizing Student Capacity

There are three main considerations at the forefront of foundational skills instructional planning for English Learners: transfer, fluency and meaning making. To this end, teachers should:

- carefully assess which skills students already know in their primary language and which of those skills are transferable to English so valuable instructional time is not wasted.

- be aware that pronunciation differences should not be considered decoding or accuracy errors.

- should actively and frequently model and read the text with appropriate pacing, expression and intonation and encourage students to echo read, choral read, and read independently, pausing and changing the intonation in their voices as appropriate.

As stated in the overview of the California ELD Standards, English Learners possess cognitive abilities appropriate to their age and experience. In order to communicate about their thinking as they learn English, they may need varying levels of linguistic support depending on the linguistic and cognitive demand of the task.

English Learners come to school possessing a wide range of competencies in their native language appropriate for their age. They may have varying levels of literacy in their native language, depending on their prior experiences in the home, community, and school. As they are learning English as a second or subsequent language, they gain metacognitive awareness of what language is and how it is used and apply this awareness in selecting and using their language-learning strategies, including drawing upon knowledge of their native language.

In *Advancing Foundational Skills for English Language Learners*, students are encouraged to become increasingly aware of the similarities and differences between their native language(s) and English and how to intentionally and purposefully apply the language skills learned.

Metacognitive Strategies

Students take charge of their own learning by applying metacognitive learning strategies, which are executive processes that enable students to plan, monitor, and evaluate their learning. Since metacognitive strategies are mental processes, it is difficult to tell whether a student is applying them or not. Teachers can help by making strategy instruction explicit by thinking aloud as they model and perform a task similar to what students will be required to do and to remind students at the beginning, middle, and end of lessons:

- At the beginning of each lesson, students are reminded and encouraged to use selective attention to focus on specific letter patterns, words, or phrases.

- As the learning activity transpires, students interact and are reminded to self-monitor to determine whether or not learning goals are being met.

- At the end of each lesson, students are prompted to reflect on the learning and check on their success in accomplishing their learning goals.

Metacognitive Learning strategies instruction can help students by showing them techniques for how to learn and by developing their awareness of their own thinking and learning process (Chamot & O'Malley, 1994).

Corrective Feedback

Corrective feedback is an essential feature of language development instruction. In both behaviorist and cognitive theories of language acquisition, feedback is seen as contributing to language learning. In both structural and communicative approaches to language teaching, feedback is viewed as a means of fostering learner motivation and ensuring linguistic accuracy (Ellis, 2009). The purpose of the feedback is to close the gap between the student's current learning status and the lesson goals (Sadler, 1989). Students can receive feedback in three ways: from their teachers, from peers, and through their own self-assessment. The feedback information can consist of any one or all of the following:

(a) an indication that an error has been committed,

(b) provision of the correct target language form, or

(c) metalinguistic information about the nature of the error.

Corrective feedback in the form of negotiating for meaning can help learners notice their errors and create form-meaning connections, thus aiding acquisition (Ellis, 2009). Corrective feedback can be:

- Explicit: Teacher overtly draws the learner's attention to the error made.

- Implicit: Teacher attracts the learner's attention without overtly informing the learner that he/she has made an error or interrupting the flow of interaction.

It is important to emphasize that language learners can only self-correct if they possess the necessary linguistic knowledge (Ellis, 2009). Therefore, it is suggested to conduct corrective feedback as a two-stage process: first, encourage self-correction and then, provide the correction immediately and check for understanding. (Doughty & Varela, 1998).

Motivation and Encouragement

Students who are motivated to engage deeply in literacy tasks are most successful in developing literacy and language at high levels. The National Research Council (Pellegrino & Hilton, 2013) cites the importance of "motivational factors (engagement, interest, identity, and self-efficacy)" (p. 19) and "dispositional factors (conscientiousness, stamina, persistence, collaboration)" (pp.111-112) in supporting deeper learning.

In addition, motivation and engagement are fostered with culturally and linguistically diverse students when teachers and the broader school community openly recognize that students' native languages and cultures are resources to value in their own right and also to draw upon in order to build proficiency in English (De Jong & Harper, 2011; Lindholm-Leary & Genesee, 2010).

Enthusiasm and feedback are both vital parts of the effective teacher's repertoire. Effective teachers have positive mindsets that guide their behavior in the classroom and their interaction with students (Gregory & Chapman, 2012). They respond to students' successes and earnest attempts using feedback prompts that encourage or validate achievement, as shown in the table below (p. 14):

Feedback for Success	Feedback for Encouragement
Your practice paid off! You did it! – I knew you would. Great effort! You succeeded.	Try one more time, you are getting it. Don't give up – you are on the right track. Keep going, you are almost there.

The process of setting goals allows students to take responsibility and control of their learning and achievements. Knowing what they want to achieve helps students plan and develop short- and long-term goals. Teachers guide students in setting goals, plan learning strategies, monitor their progress, and celebrate success.

All students need to be supported to invest personally in literacy—to see the relevance of the content for their lives and to sustain the effort and interest needed to learn skills and gain competence.

Home Connection

Intimately tied to one's identity, language is first learned from a child's parents, family members, and caregivers and is used to accomplish all aspects of daily living. Strong bonds between home and school are essential if the educational process is to be effective (Ada, 1990). Students are encouraged in *Advancing Foundational Skills for English Language Learners* to share their work at home. The goal of these suggestions is to affirm the understanding that productive struggle towards literacy in English and bi-literacy is a worthwhile endeavor. By sharing their work students can prompt meaningful dialogue with family members directly related to an aspect of the lesson the student may have found interesting. Parents are positioned as funds of knowledge (Moll, 1992) as they affirm home language and culture. Students sharing their work at home encourages metalinguistic awareness as students can relate the similarities and differences of foundational skills learned in English to their native language. It is important provide time between lessons for students to share back information conveyed by family members.

References

Ada, A. F. (1990). *A magical encounter*: Santillana.

August, D., & Shanahan, T. (2006). Executive summary: Developing literacy in second-language learners: Report of the National Literacy Panel on   Language-Minority Children and Youth. *Retrieved February, 16,* 2009.

Burris, C. C., & Garrity, D. T. (2012). *Opening the Common Core: How to bring all students to college and career readiness*: Corwin Press.

Chamot, A. U., & O'Malley, J. M. (1994). *The CALLA handbook: Implementing the cognitive academic language learning approach*: Addison-Wesley Publishing Company Reading, MA.

Council, N. R. (1999). Improving student learning: A strategic plan for educational research and its utilization. Washington, DC: National Academy Press.

De Jong, E. J., & Harper, C. A. (2011). Accommodating diversity: Pre-service teachers' view of effective practices for English language learners. In T. Lucas (Ed.), *Preparation for linguistically diverse classrooms: A resource for teacher educators* (pp. 73-90). New York: Routledge/Taylor and Francis.

Development, O. o. E. C. a. (2005). Formative assessment: Improving student learning in secondary classrooms. Paris, France: Centre for Educational Research and Innovation.

Doughty, C., & Varela, E. (1998). Communicative focus on form. *Focus on Form in Classroom Second Language Acquisition*, 1, 114-138.

Education, C. D. o. (2014a). English language arts/English language development (ELA/ELD) framework

Education, C. D. o. (2014b). *English language development standards for California public schools: Kindergarten through grade twelve*. Sacramento, CA: California Department of Education.

Ellis, R. (2009). Corrective feedback and teacher development. *L2 Journal*, 1(1).

Gregory, G. H., & Chapman, C. (2012). *Differentiated instructional strategies: One size doesn't fit all*: Corwin Press.

Levin, H. M. (1988). *Structuring schools for greater effectiveness with educationally disadvantaged or at-risk students*. Paper presented at the American Educational Research Association, New Orleans, LA.

Levin, H. M., & Hopfenberg, W. S. (1991). Don't remediate: Accelerate! *Principal Magazine*, 70, 11-13.

Lindholm-Leary, K., & Genesee, F. (2010). Alternative educational programs for English language learners *Improving Education for English Learners: Research-Based Approaches*. Sacramento: California Department of Education. Sacramento, CA: *California Department of Education*.

Moll, L. C. (1992). Bilingual classroom studies and community analysis. *Educational Researcher*, 21(2), 20-24.

Pellegrino, J. W., & Hilton, M. L. (2013). *Education for life and work: Developing transferable knowledge and skills in the 21st century*: National Academies Press.

Riches, C., & Genesee, F. (2006). Crosslinguistic and crossmodal issues. *Educating English language learners: A synthesis of research evidence*, 64-108.

Sadler, D. R. (1989). Formative assessment and the design of instructional systems. *Instructional Science*, 18(2), 119-144.

List of Learning Strategies
by Anna Uhl Chamot and Michael O'Malley

Strategy Name	Description	Definition
Advance Organization	Preview, Skim, Gist	Previewing the main ideas and concepts of a text; identifying the organizing principle
Organizational Planning	Plan what to do	Planning how to accomplish the learning task Planning the parts and sequence of ideas to express
Selective Attention	Listen or read selectively Scan Find specific information	Attending to key words, phrases, ideas linguistic markers and types of information
Monitoring Comprehension	Think while listening Think while reading	Checking one's comprehension during listening or reading
Monitoring Production	Think while speaking Think while writing	Checking one's oral or written production while it s taking place.
Self-Assessment	Check back Keep a learning log Reflect on what you learned	Judging how well one has accomplished a learning task
Fix-up Monitoring	Re-Read to clarify Stop and think about what you read Ask questions Read ahead Talk about what you have read	Using a strategy to clarify understanding when comprehension breaks down.
Make Connections	Make a personal connection with the text Make a connection between a text that one is reading and one that has already been read.	Making personal connections to the learning
Summarizing	Say or write the main idea	Making a mental, oral or written summary of information gained from listening or reading.
Deduction/Induction	Use a rule or make a rule	Applying or figuring out rules to understand a concept or complete a learning task
Imagery	Visualize Make/draw a picture Reference a picture	Using mental or real pictures to learn new information or solve a problem
Auditory Representation	Using your mental tape recorder Hearing it again in your mind	Replaying, remembering a word, phrase, or piece of information Rehearsing language mentally
Making Inferences	Use context clues Guess from context Predict	Using information in the text to guess meanings of new items or predict upcoming information
Resourcing	Use reference materials	Using reference materials such as internet, dictionaries, textbooks, maps, charts
Grouping	Classifying ideas, constructing graphic organizers	Classifying words, terminology, quantities or concepts according to attributes
Note-Taking	Annotation, listing, Cornell notes,	Writing down key words and concepts in abbreviated, verbal, graphic or numerical form
Elaboration on Prior Knowledge	Use what you know or background knowledge to learn or connect to new ideas or information. Make analogies	Relating new to known information and making personal associations with new information.

Advancing Foundational Skills for English Language Learners

Corrective Feedback Strategies

Adapted from: Corrective Feedback and Teacher Development, Rod Ellis (2009). L2 Journal

	Implicit Attracts learner's attention without overtly informing the learner that he/she has made an error or interrupting the flow of interaction.	**Explicit** Tries to overtly draw the learner's attention to the error made
In-put providing: Correct form is given to students	**Recast** The corrector incorporates the content words of the immediately preceding incorrect utterance and changes and corrects the utterance in some way (e.g., phonological, syntactic, morphological or lexical). L: I went school T: You went **to** school?	**Explicit Correction** The corrector indicates an error has been committed, identifies the error and provides the correction. L: We will go on May T: Not on May, in May T: "We will go in May."
Output prompting: The student is prompted to self-correct	**Repetition** The corrector repeats the learner utterance highlighting the error by means of emphatic stress. L: I will showed you. T: I will **show** you. L: I will show you.	**Metalinguistic Explanation** Corrector provides explanation for the errors that have been made. L: two duck T: Do you remember how to show more than one duck? L: ducks T: Yes, you remember that we need to add "s" at the end of a noun to show the plural form.
	Clarification Request The corrector indicates that he/she has not understood what the learner said. L: on the it go T: Can you please tell me again? T: Do you mean "it goes in your desk?"	**Elicitation** The corrector repeats part of the learner utterance but not the erroneous part and uses rising intonation to signal the learner should complete it. L: I don't think won't rain T: I don't think it ...... (will) rain
		Paralinguistic Signal The corrector uses a gesture or facial expression to indicate that the learner has made an error. L: Yesterday I go to the movies T: (gestures with right forefinger over left shoulder to indicate past)

L = Learner   T=Teacher

PRINT CONCEPTS

Recommendation for English Learners

	Student Language and Literacy Characteristics	Consideration for Instructions
Oral Skills	No or little spoken English proficiency	Students will need instruction in recognizing and distinguishing the sounds of English as compared or contrasted with sounds in their native language. • Use visuals and gestures to convey that in English, letters are symbols that represent sounds and that words are a sequence of letters that make up a word that conveys meaning. • Convey the understanding that in a logographic language each character represents a meaning unlike an alphabetical language where each character represents a sound.
	Oral skills: Spoken English proficiency	Students will need instruction in applying their knowledge of the English sound system to foundational literacy learning. • For students who have been taught to use the logographic system, an introduction to the alphabet is necessary and the instruction needs to include the sound-symbol relationship (Chinese languages, Korean) • For students who use an alphabetic language other than the roman alphabet an introduction to the alphabet is necessary and the instruction needs to include the sound-symbol relationship (Greek, Arabic, Russian).
Print Skills	No or little native language literacy	Students will need instruction in print concepts. As students develop an understanding of the organization and basic features of print, the need to simultaneously understand that spoken words are composed of smaller elements of speech and that letters represent these sounds (alphabetical principle). Instruction systematically includes: 1. Following words from left to right, top to bottom, and page by page. 2. Recognizing that spoken words are represented in written language by specific sequences of letters. 3. Understanding that words are separated by spaces in print. 4. Recognizing and name all upper and lowercase letters of the alphabet. 5. Recognize the distinguishing features of a sentence (e.g., first word, capitalization, ending punctuation).
	Some foundational literacy proficiency in a language not using the Latin alphabet (e.g., Arabic, Chinese, Korean, Russian)	Students will be familiar with print concepts, and will need instruction in learning the Latin alphabet for English, as compared or contrasted with their native language writing system (e.g., direction of print, symbols representing whole words, syllables or phonemes). For students who have been taught to use the logographic system, an introduction to the alphabet is necessary and the instruction needs to include the sound-symbol relationship. (Chinese languages, Korean) For students who use an alphabetic language other than the roman alphabet an introduction to the alphabet is necessary and the instruction needs to include the sound-symbol relationship (Greek, Arabic, Russian). Compare and contrast directionality and print orientation: • Left to right, top to bottom: Greek, Russian, Barhmic, Thai • Right to left orientation, top to bottom: Arabic, Hebrew, Persian, Syriac, Urdu
	Some foundational literacy proficiency in a language using the Latin alphabet (e.g., Spanish)	Students will need instruction in applying their knowledge of print concepts, phonics and word study to the English writing system, as compared or contrasted with their native language alphabet (e.g., letters that are the same or different, or represent the same or different sounds) and native language vocabulary (e.g., cognates) and sentence structure (e.g., subject-verb-object vs. subject-object-verb word order). • Most languages that use the roman alphabet have the same line direction (left to right) bottom) and same block direction (top to bottom). (English, Spanish, French, Portuguese)

Benchmark Education

PHONEMIC AWARENESS

Recommendation for Spanish Learners

<table>
<tr><th></th><th>Student Language and Literacy Characteristics</th><th>Consideration for Instructions</th></tr>
<tr>
<td rowspan="2">Oral Skills</td>
<td>No or little spoken Spanish proficiency</td>
<td>Students will need instruction in recognizing and distinguishing the sounds of Spanish as compared or contrasted with sounds in their native language.

Teachers can enable phonemic awareness in English for ELLs by understanding the linguistic characteristics of students' native language, including the phonemes that exist and do not exist in the native language.

Some phonemes may not be present in English Learner's native language and, therefore, may be difficult for a student to pronounce and distinguish auditorily, as well as to place into a meaningful context.

For English Learners, as with all students, it is important that instruction have meaning, so that the words and sounds students are manipulating are familiar.

It is necessary for ELLs to have knowledge of the English vocabulary words within which they are to understand phonemes.

Teachers can teach phonemic awareness while also explicitly teaching vocabulary words, their meaning, and their pronunciation to ELLs.
- Use visuals and gestures to convey that in English, letters are symbols
- that represent sounds and that words are a sequence of letters that make up a word that conveys meaning.
- Use visual to ensure students understand the meaning of words in lesson
- Use visual to show rhyming pairs
- Use visuals and manipultives such as puzzle pieces or folded paper to represent compound words and word parts.</td>
</tr>
<tr>
<td>Oral skills: Spoken Spanish proficiency</td>
<td>Students will need instruction in applying their knowledge of the Spanish sound system to foundational literacy learning.

Scientifically-based research suggests that ELLs respond well to meaningful activities such as language games and word walls, especially when the activities are consistent and focus on particular sounds and letters. Songs and poems, with their rhythm and repetition, are easily memorized and can be used to teach phonemic awareness and print concepts to ELLs (Hiebert, et al., 1998). These rhymes exist in every language and teachers can ask students or their parents to share these culturally relevant and teachable rhymes with the class, and build phonemic awareness activities around them.

Take an inventory of student's oral vocabulary. Draw upon student's known and familiar oral vocabulary to:
- Clap syllables in known words
- Segment and blend syllables of known words
- Listen to the sequence of sounds in known words
- Enjoy rhyming words in context of illustrated short songs, poems, and rhymes</td>
</tr>
</table>

Benchmark Education

PHONICS and WORD STUDY

Recommendation for Spanish Learners

	Student Language and Literacy Characteristics	Consideration for Instructions
Oral Skills	No or little spoken Spanish proficiency	Students will need instruction in recognizing and distinguishing the sounds of Spanish as compared or contrasted with sounds in their native language. • Use visuals and gestures to convey that in Spanish like in English, letters are symbols that represent sounds and that words are a sequence of letters that make up a word that conveys meaning.
	Oral skills: Spoken Spanish proficiency	Students will need instruction in applying their knowledge of the Spanish sound system to foundational literacy learning. • Take an inventory of student's oral vocabulary. Draw upon student's known and familiar oral vocabulary to: • Clap syllables in known words • Segment and blend syllables of known words • Listen to the sequence of sounds in known words • Use visuals to insure comprehension
Print Skills	No or little native language literacy	Students will need instruction in print concepts. As students develop an understanding of the organization and basic features of print, they learn that in both the Spanish and the English languages spoken words are composed of smaller elements of speech and that letters represent these sounds (alphabetical principle). Instruction systematically includes: 1. Following words from left to right, top to bottom, and page by page. 2. Recognizing that spoken words are represented in written language by specific sequences of letters. 3. Understanding that words are separated by spaces in print. 4. Recognizing and name all upper and lowercase letters of the alphabet. 5. Recognize the distinguishing features of a sentence (e.g., first word, capitalization, ending punctuation).
	Some foundational literacy proficiency in a language not using the Latin alphabet (e.g., Arabic, Chinese, Korean, Russian)	Students will be familiar with print concepts, and will need instruction in learning the Latin alphabet for English, as compared or contrasted with their native language writing system (e.g., direction of print, symbols representing whole words, syllables or phonemes). For students who have been taught to use the logographic system, an introduction to the alphabet is necessary and the instruction needs to include the sound-symbol relationship. (Chinese languages, Korean) For students who use an alphabetic language other than the roman alphabet an introduction to the alphabet is necessary and the instruction needs to include the sound-symbol relationship (Greek, Arabic, Russian). Compare and contrast directionality and print orientation: • Left to right, top to bottom: Greek, Russian, Barhmic, Thai • Right to left orientation, top to bottom: Arabic, Hebrew, Persian, Syriac, Urdu
	Some foundational literacy proficiency in a language using the Latin alphabet (e.g., Spanish)	Students will need instruction in applying their knowledge of print concepts, phonics and word study to the English writing system, as compared or contrasted with their native language alphabet (e.g., letters that are the same or different, or represent the same or different sounds) and native language vocabulary (e.g., cognates) and sentence structure (e.g., subject-verb-object vs. subject-object-verb word order). • Most languages that use the roman alphabet have the same line direction (left to right) bottom) and same block direction (top to bottom). (English, Spanish, French, Portuguese) • Please note that each phonics lesson contains transfer support information relating to the explicit sound-spelling taught.

Benchmark Education

FLUENCY

Recommendation for English Learners

	Student Language and Literacy Characteristics	Consideration for Instructions
Oral Skills	No or little spoken English proficiency	Students will need instruction in recognizing and distinguishing the sounds of English as compared or contrasted with sounds in their native language. The Center for the Improvement of Early Reading Achievement (CIERA) states that ELLs should learn to read initially in their first language. CIERA recommends that ELLs participate in read-alouds of big books, read along with proficient readers, and listen repeatedly to books read aloud in order to gain fluency in English (Hiebert et al., 1998). Rhymes, poems, stories and songs are innate in most languages and cultures. The act of repeated listening to rhymes, poems, stories and songs will help students become familiar and internalize the sounds and rhythm of the English language. The particular language of rhymes, poems, stories and songs will encourage and motivate English Learners begin to produce both the familiar and unfamiliar sounds of the English language. Using visuals, gestures, emphasized rhythm and varied voice intonation are used to convey and negotiate meaning.
	Oral skills: Spoken English proficiency	Students will need instruction in applying their knowledge of the English sound system to foundational literacy learning. Rhymes, poems, stories and songs provide English Learners the opportunity to practice and build on the English language they already know. The repetitious and playful language in rhymes, poems and songs motivates English Learners and helps them to feel confident and successful as they produce English fluently, with intonation, and expression.
Print Skills	No or little native language literacy	Students will need instruction in print concepts. Fluency practice includes basic print concepts such as tracking from left to right, return sweep, top to bottom, and page-by-page sequence. It also includes recognizing and naming all upper and lowercase letters of the alphabet and understanding that letters represent sounds and most importantly, that print carries a message.
	Some foundational literacy proficiency in a language not using the Latin alphabet (e.g., Arabic, Chinese, Korean, Russian)	Students will be familiar with print concepts, and will need instruction in learning the Latin alphabet for English, as compared or contrasted with their native language writing system (e.g., direction of print, symbols representing whole words, syllables or phonemes). Beyond the directionality of print, and the relationship between phonemes and graphemes, engaging in meaningful repeated readings will help English Learners gain familiarity with the Latin Alphabet and the sounds it represents as well as building their foundational proficiency in English reading comprehension. Using visuals, gestures, emphasized rhythm and varied voice intonation and relating those specifically to words and phrases in the text will underscore that print whether logographic or alphabetic is the expression of thought and carries the message that can be voiced.
	Some foundational literacy proficiency in a language using the Latin alphabet (e.g., Spanish)	Students will need instruction in applying their knowledge of print concepts, phonics and word study to the English writing system, as compared or contrasted with their native language alphabet (e.g., letters that are the same or different, or represent the same or different sounds) and native language vocabulary (e.g., cognates) and sentence structure (e.g., subject verb object vs. subject-object-verb word order). Familiarity with the Latin alphabet affords students the opportunity to availthemselves of their primary language skills to transfer their knowledge to English. Repeated purposeful readings will enable students to construct meaning as they develop and produce the English language with fluency, intonation and expression.

Benchmark Education

Common Informational Text Feature

Purpose	Feature	Ideas or Implications for Teaching
Organization of Text	Table of Contents Index Glossary Page Numbers References	**Provides resources and help students navigate the text.**
Organization of Ideas	Titles Chapters Headings Subheadings Conclusion	**Provide the main ideas and essential concepts.**
Graphic/Visuals	Illustrations Photographs Diagrams Charts and Tables Maps Key / Legends	**Provide visual to scaffold main ideas and essential concepts**
Content Emphasis	Captions Bold, italicized or highlighted font Footnotes Margin notes Text boxes (vocabulary, skills, strategies)	**Emphasize key concepts and focus on targeted skills.**
Elaboration or Extension	Questions Activities	**Provide differentiated extension for learning and test preparation.**

Silvia C. Dorta Duque de Reyes

Print Concepts

1 Recognize and Name All Uppercase and Lowercase Letters of the Alphabet

Lesson Objectives

- Recognize and name all the letters of the alphabet
- Distinguish between consonants and vowels

Metacognitive Strategy

Selective attention, resourcing, advanced organization

Academic Language

letters, uppercase, lowercase, capital letter, consonants, vowel, print, cursive,

Materials

Print Concepts Lesson 1 Practice Pages 1 and 2

Pre-Assess

Student's ability to recognize and name the letters. Notice if student can accurately distinguish between vowels and consonants. Students whose home language is other than one that uses the Roman alphabet may need more practice and reinforcement. While students may already know how to read in their home language and English, they need to know names of letters and to distinguish vowels from consonants.

Transfer Notes

In all printed languages, have symbols or characters.English uses the Roman alphabet, each character is a letter which represents a sound. A series of characters together represent a word. Each character has a name and it is written in several forms:Uppercase and lowercase, printed and cursive.

Introduce the Lesson

Say: *Today we will learn the name of each letter and recognize each uppercase, or capital, and lowercase form.*

We identify which letters are vowels and which are consonants. There are 26 letters in the English alphabet.

The English word **alphabet** comes to us, by way of Latin, from the names of the first two letters of the Greek alphabet, **alpha** and **beta**. The Roman alphabet reached England during the fifth century (5c) and the continent of America in 1492 with Columbus's voyages. About 100 world languages use the Roman alphabet.

Elicit Prior Knowledge

Reference students to Section 1 of the Practice Page.

Say: *How do you say, alphabet or letters in your home language? What is the equivalent of a writing system in your home language? Do you use Roman letters or something different? Write it in section 1 the practice page.*

Recognizing Letter names

Reference students to Section 2 of the lesson practice page.

Say: *There are 26 letters in the English alphabet. Name and pronounce each letter as you point to it. Have student repeat as they point to each letter. Have students recognize capital and lower case pairs.*

Say: *Five of the 26 letters are vowels. The other 21 are consonants. Have student circle the vowels. Name and pronounce each vowel as you point to it. Have student repeat. Say vowels are important letters in the alphabet. Each syllable in a word includes vowels.*

Model

Point out Section 2 of Practice Page 1. Model singing alphabet song and invite student to sing along with you.

Say: *This very famous song helps students of all ages memorize the names of the letters. Most people who know English have learned this simple song to practice learning the names of the English alphabet.*

Practice

Students work with their partner to practice recognizing and naming all letters of the alphabet. *Say: It is now your turn to name each letter of the alphabet.* Have student pairs take turn naming the letters of the alphabet. Then, have them take turns spelling and dictating each other's first and last names. Afterwards, have students take inventory of letters they know and don't know. Refer to the practice page and ask students to practice the naming and writing the alphabet letters.

Apply

Refer to section 2 of Practice Page 1 and complete with students.

Say: *Uppercase, or capital, letters are used for four main purposes:*

1. To begin a sentence

2. To write the pronoun I

3. To write the names of proper nouns (names of people, animals, and places)

4. To write titles, such as the title of a book, a chapter, a person's profession or a piece of artwork

Extend Knowledge: Make Meaning

Refer to the first portion of section 3 of Practice Page 1. Have students work independently then confirm answers with partners.

Say: *Using what we have learned today, work with a partner to fill in the blanks using the words in the word bank, below.*

1. The English alphabet has _____ letters, _____ of them are vowels.

2. This pronoun is always capitalized: _____

3. The _____ of books has capital letters.

4. Proper name of people or animals always begin with a _____ letter.

I   26   5   capital   title

Reflect and Review:

Refer to the first portion of section 3 of Practice Page 1.

Say: *What did we learn today? Discuss with your partner.*

We learned to identify the names of the letters in the alphabet. We learn about the history of the English alphabet and we learned how Mozart composed the tune of the song. Turn to your partner and tell them why this is important to know the name of each letter and how you are going to use this knowledge.

✓ Formative Assessment

If the student completes each task correctly, precede to the next skill in the sequence.

Did the student...?	Intervention 2
Respond to prompts asking for letter names?	Take an inventory of the letter names and shape student know and does not know. Have students Establish a learning goal to learn letter names.
Match capital letters to lower case?	Have students practice a few letters at a time, starting with letters in his or first and last name. Establish a learning goal to match capital and lower case letters. Use letter card manipulative to match upper and lower case letters.
Distinguish consonants from vowels	Provide practice in context. Have student read a word and call out vowels in words. Point out that each syllable in a word contains a vowel.

2 Distinguish Between Letters and Other Printed Symbols

Lesson Objectives

- Recognize and name all the letters of the alphabet
- Distinguish between letters and other symbols

Metacognitive Strategy

Selective attention, resourcing, advanced organization

Academic Language

letters, uppercase, lowercase, numbers, keyboard, symbols, mathematical,

Materials

Print Concepts Lesson 2 Practice Pages 1 and 2

Pre-Assess

Pre-assess students' ability to recognize and name the letters. Students whose home language is other than one that uses the Roman alphabet may need more practice and reinforcement. While students may already know how to read in their home language and English, they need to know names of letters and to distinguish letters from other print symbols.

Transfer Notes

In all printed languages, have symbols or characters and punctuation marks. Many of the symbols are used internationally.For example, the colon (:), the semicolon (;) the question mark (?) and the exclamation mark (!).In Spanish the question and exclamation mark are present at the beginning and ending of the sentence.

Introduce the Lesson

Say: *Today we will learn the name and function of other symbols used in print that are not letters.*

Some of these symbols are punctuation marks that help a reader read with expression and intonation. Punctuation marks help the writer communicate ideas clearly. Other symbols are used along with letters to communicate in writing and are part of the Qwerty keyboard system.

Elicit Prior Knowledge

Reference students to Section 1 of the lesson practice page.

Say: *Are there punctuation marks in your home language? What are some international symbols you know?*

Write it the following symbols on the board: [, ! ? ; : @ # $ %& - + =/]

Recognizing and distinguishing letters from other printed symbols.

Have students look at Section 2 of Practice Page 1. *Say: The most common symbols used along with letters in English are the punctuation marks and the comma. There are three kinds of punctuation used to mark the end of a sentence: A period, a question mark and an exclamation point. A comma separate parts of a sentence or phrase, and signal the reader to pause.*

Model

Create a chart to discuss the four types of sentences and their corresponding punctuation marks.

Have students take use Section 2 to take notes as you teach.

Say: *End marks signal each of the four type of sentence and help the reader read with expression and intonation. A declarative sentence or statement ends with a period. A question, or interrogative sentence, ends with a question mark. An imperative, or a command, sentence ends with an exclamation point and an exclamatory sentence, which denotes or expresses emotion, also ends with an exclamation mark.*

Symbol	Name	Function	Example
.	Period	End sentence	I learn a lot in school.
?	Question Mark	Ask question	Do I learn a lot in school?
!	Exclamation point	Command	Learn a lot in school!
!	Exclamation point	Show expression	I learn a lot in school!
,	Comma	Pause	Yesterday, I learned a lot in school.
" "	Quotation mark	Signal direct quotes	When I say "a lot" I really mean it.

Shared Reading

Refer to the first portion of section 3 of Practice Page 1. Read aloud with fluency and expression, pointing each word with your finger. Read again as needed inviting students to echo or choral read. Ask students highlight the symbols and punctuation marks as you discuss how they were used in context.

Extend Knowledge: Make Meaning

Refer to the first portion of section 4 of Practice Page 1. Have students work independently then confirm answers with partners.

Say: *Using what we have learned today, work with a partner to fill in the blanks using the words in the word bank, below.*

A keyboard contains _____ and _____ for writing.

A _____ is used at the end of declarative sentences.

Question marks are used at the end of _____ sentences.

An _____ shows command or emotions.

Qwerty is a _____ system for writing.

Letters keyboard symbols period exclamation mark interrogative

Reflect and Review:

Say: *What did we learn today? Discuss with your partner.*

We learned to recognize symbols from letters. We learned that symbols and letters appear together on a keyboard. We learned that the QWERTY system is the alphabet and symbols on a keyboard. We learned punctuation marks or symbols and their functions.

✓ **Formative Assessment**

If the student completes each task correctly, precede to the next skill in the sequence.

Did the student...?	Intervention 2
Distinguish letters from symbols	Provide practice in context. Have student read a word and call out letters and symbols using a keyboard.
Recognize the name and function of punctuation marks or symbols	Have students learn the three ending marks first. Then teach commas and quotation marks. Point out symbols by highlighting them or annotating them after reading. Relate punctuation marks to reading intonation.
Recognizing letter names	Take an inventory of the letter names and shape student know and does not know.Have students Establish a learning goal to learn letter names.

3 Organization of Text: Table of Contents

Lesson Objectives

- Identify the purpose of the table of contents and its location in a given informational text.

Introduce the Lesson

Say: *Today we will learn what text features are and the ways they are used to organize an informational text, including the table of contents and page numbers. We will learn how these text features help us locate information quickly and understand what we've found.*

Organization of Text

Say: *Informational texts are texts that are non-fiction, or true. Informational texts are organized through the use of text features. Authors include them to help the reader better understand what they are reading. Text features may provide information that is not written in the text itself, and can be found in textbooks, magazine articles, newspapers, research reports, and web pages.*

Say: *Today we will be looking at how a table of contents and page numbers help you find and understand information in the text.*

Elicit Prior Knowledge

Display and/or distribute the Practice Page and complete section 1 with students.

Say: *How do you say, "Table of Contents" in your home language? Write it in section 1 of your Practice Page.*

Model

Model how to find the table of contents in the text. Point out the page numbers on the table of contents and how they are critical to finding the information you are seeking.

Say: *The table of contents is at the front of the text, typically after the title page. It lists the chapters, or major parts, of the text along with the page number where the information can be found. It also outlines the main topics or points in the text. You can use the table of contents to help locate information in the text and see how it is organized. Let's see if you can find the table of contents in our books.*

Practice

Students work with their partner to find the table of contents in their texts. Ask the students to find a particular topic in the table of contents and have them turn to that page.

Say: *Let's all look for _____ in the table of contents. (pause) Yes, it's on page ____. Let's all turn there.*

Students turn to the page indicated. Reinforce students' location of the correct page.

Metacognitive Strategy

Selective attention, resourcing, advanced organization

Academic Language

Informational text, table of contents, page numbers

Materials

- Several classroom informational books (at least one copy per pair of students) containing a table of contents, index, glossary, page numbers, and references
- Print Concepts Lesson 3 Practice Page

Pre-Assess

Pre-assess students' ability to identify and name of basic book parts (front cover, back cover, author's name, illustrator, pages).

Transfer Notes

In all printed languages, text features in printed material are organized to convey meaning and assist the reader to locate the information in text. Good readers in any language learn how to use text features as reference to support comprehension of text and to prepare to read and to advance-organize related work.

Apply

Refer to section 2 of the Practice Page and complete with students.

Say: *Look at section 2 of your Practice Page. Take a moment to look over the Table of Contents you see there. In a few moments, I will be asking you to work with your partner to answer some questions about this Table of Contents.*

Allow students to review the Practice Page.

Say: *Let's see if you can use the information in this Table of Contents to answer the questions. You may work with a partner.*

Allow students time to answer the questions, then review their answers with them.

Extend Knowledge: Make Meaning

Refer to the first portion of section 3 of the Practice page. Students may work with a partner to complete.

Say: *Now you will have a chance to use what you have learned today to complete the following sentences, using the words in the word bank, below.*

1. The table of contents is found at the _____ of the text.
2. The _____ is the last section of the text.
3. The some of the sections of the text are called _____.
4. The _____ tell you where the chapter or section starts.
5. The _____ is second-to-last section of the text.

| chapters   beginning   page numbers   References Cited   Index |

Reflect and Review:

Refer to the first portion of section 3 of the Practice Page.

Say: *What did we learn today? Discuss with your partner.*

We learned that good readers use the _____ to help locate information in the text.

✔Formative Assessment

If the student completes each task correctly, precede to the next skill in the sequence.

Did the student…?	Intervention 2
Respond to prompts relating to text features?	Provide this lesson in primary language. Think aloud responses to prompts pointing to specific details.
Name each feature?	Have students construct a text feature visual depicting and labeling each text feature.
Relate information in text feature to the text?	Point out the relation of each text feature to the text.

4 Organization of Text: Index

Metacognitive Strategy

Selective attention, resourcing, advanced organization

Academic Language

Informational text, index, page numbers

Materials

- Several classroom informational books (at least one copy per pair of students) containing a table of contents, index, glossary, page numbers, and references
- Print Concepts Lesson 4 Practice Page

Pre-Assess

Pre-assess students' ability to identify and name of basic book parts (front cover, back cover, author's name, illustrator, pages).

Transfer Notes

In all printed languages, text features in printed material are organized to convey meaning and assist the reader to locate the information in text. Good readers in any language learn how to use text features as reference to support comprehension of text and to prepare to read and to advance-organize related work.

Introduce the Lesson

Say: *Today we will learn what text features are and the ways they are used to organize an informational text, including the index and page numbers. We will learn how these text features help us locate information quickly and understand what we've found.*

Organization of Text

Say: *Remember, informational texts are texts that are non-fiction, or true. Informational texts are organized through the use of text features. Authors include them to help the reader better understand what they are reading. Text features may provide information that is not written in the text itself, and can be found in textbooks, magazine articles, newspapers, research reports, and web pages.*

Say: *Today we will be looking at how an index and page numbers help you find and understand information in the text.*

Elicit Prior Knowledge

Display and/or distribute the Practice Page and complete section 1 with students.

Say: *How do you say, "Index" in your home language? Write it in section 1 of your Practice Page.*

Model

Model how to find the index in the text. Point out the page numbers and how they are a critical part of finding the information you are seeking through the index.

Say: *The index is at the back of the text. It is a listing, in alphabetical order, of the key names, terms, events, and topics with the page numbers where you can find them in the text. You can use the index to find pages in the text that contain the information you are looking for. Let's see if you can find the index in our books.*

Practice

Students work with their partner to find the index in their texts. Ask the students to find a particular topic in the index and have them turn to that page.

Say: *Let's all look for _____ in the index. (pause) Yes, it's on page _____. Let's all turn there.*

Students turn to the page indicated. Reinforce students' location of the correct page.

Apply

Refer to section 2 of the Practice Page and complete with students.

Say: *Look at section 2 of your Practice Page. Take a moment to look over the Index you see there. In a few moments, I will be asking you to work with your partner to answer some questions about this Index.*

Allow students to review the lesson practice page.

Say: *Let's see if you can use the information in this Index to answer the questions. You may work with a partner. Allow students time to answer the questions, then review their answers with them.*

Extend Knowledge: Make Meaning

Refer to the first portion of section 3 of the Practice Page. Students may work with a partner to complete.

Say: *Now you will have a chance to use what you have learned today to complete the following sentences, using the words in the word bank, below.*

1. The _____ is found toward the back of the text.
2. The different items in the index are _____.
3. The _____ tell you where the topic starts.
4. The index is in _____ order.
5. The index is listed in the _____.

topics Table of Contents alphabetical page numbers   index

Reflect and Review:

Refer to the first portion of section 3 of the lesson practice page.

Say: *What did we learn today? Discuss with your partner.*

We learned that good readers use the _____ to help locate information on a topic in the text.

✔Formative Assessment

If the student completes each task correctly, precede to the next skill in the sequence. If not, refer to the suggestion under Intervention 2.

Did the student...?	Intervention 2
Respond to prompts relating to text features?	Provide this lesson in primary language. Think aloud responses to prompts pointing to specific details.
Name each feature?	Have students construct a text feature visual depicting and labeling each text feature.
Relate information in text feature to the text?	Point out the relation of each text feature to the text.

---

5 Organization of Text: Glossary

Lesson Objectives

- Identify the purpose of the glossary and its location in a given informational text.

Metacognitive Strategy

Selective attention, resourcing, advanced organization

Academic Language

Informational text, glossary, key word

Materials

- Several classroom informational books (at least one copy per pair of students) containing a table of contents, index, glossary, page numbers, and references
- Pre-identify a key word in the text that is also listed in the glossary. Note the page number for the key word.
- Print Concepts Lesson 5 Practice Page

Pre-Assess

Student's ability to identify and name of basic book parts (front cover, back cover, author's name, illustrator, pages).

Transfer Notes

In all printed languages, text features in printed material are organized to convey meaning and assist the reader to locate the information in text. Good readers in any language learn how to use text features as reference to support comprehension of text and to prepare to read and to advance-organize related work.

Introduce the Lesson

Say: *Today we will learn what text features are and the ways they are used to organize an informational text, including the glossary. We will learn how these text features help us locate information quickly and understand what we've found.*

Organization of Text

Say: *Remember, informational texts are texts that are non-fiction, or true. Informational texts are organized through the use of text features. Authors include them to help the reader better understand what they are reading. Text features may provide information that is not written in the text itself, and can be found in textbooks, magazine articles, newspapers, research reports, or web pages.*

Say: *Today we will be looking at how a glossary helps you find information in the text and help you understand the information that you find in the text.*

Elicit Prior Knowledge

Display and/or distribute the Print Concepts Practice Page 7 and complete section 1 with students.

Say: *How do you say, **Glossary** in your home language? Write it in section 1 of your Practice Page.*

Model

Model how to find the glossary in the text. Point out the key words and their definitions and how the glossary plays a critical role in supporting your understanding of the information you are reading in the text. Use pre-identified key word in example, below.

Say: *What if you don't understand one of the important, or key, words in the text? What could you do?*

Accept student offerings. Then direct them to the glossary in back of the book.

Say: *Many informational texts have glossaries in the back of the text. It contains a list of key words in alphabetical order, and provides a definition for each one. It may even tell you how to pronounce the word. You may use the glossary to look up key words to learn their meaning, which will help you better understand what you are reading. I found a key word on page ___. The key word is_____. Let's see if we can find it in the glossary.*

Student locate glossary in back of text and search for key word. Reinforce students' location of the key word in the glossary.

Apply

Refer to section 2 of the Practice Page and complete with students.

Say: *Look at section 2 of your lesson practice page. Take a moment to look over the Glossary you see there. In a few moments, I will be asking you to work with your partner to answer some questions about this Glossary.*

Allow students to review the Practice Page.

Extend Knowledge: Make Meaning

Refer to the first portion of section 3 of the Practice Page. Students may work with a partner to complete.

Say: *Now you will have a chance to use what you have learned today to complete the following sentences, using the words in the word bank, below.*

The **glossary** is found toward the back of the text.

The different items in the glossary are **keywords** from the text.

The glossary gives you the **definition** for each key word.

The glossary is in **alphabetical** order.

The glossary is listed in the **Table of Contents.**

Reflect and Review:

Refer to the first portion of section 3 of the Practice Page.

Say: *What did we learn today? Discuss with your partner.*

We learned that good readers use the _____ to learn the meaning of a key word in the text.

✔ Formative Assessment	
If the student completes each task correctly, precede to the next skill in the sequence.	
Did the student...?	**Intervention 2**
Respond to prompts relating to text features?	Provide this lesson in primary language. Think aloud responses to prompts pointing to specific details.
Name each feature?	Have students construct a text feature visual depicting and labeling each text feature.
Relate information in text feature to the text?	Point out the relation of each text feature to the text.

6 Organization of Text: References

Introduce the Lesson

Say: *Today we will learn what text features are and the ways they are used to organize an informational text, including the references. We will learn how these text features help us locate information quickly and understand what we've found.*

Organization of Text

Say: *Remember, informational texts are texts that are non-fiction, or true. Informational texts are organized through the use of text features. Authors include them to help the reader better understand what they are reading. Text features may provide information that is not written in the text itself, and can be found in textbooks, magazine articles, newspapers, research reports, or web pages.*

Say: *Today we will be looking at how the references help you find information about the text and help you understand the information that you find in the text.*

Elicit Prior Knowledge

Display and/or distribute the Practice Page and complete section 1 with students.

Say: *How do you say, **References** in your home language? Write it in section 1 of your Practice Page.*

Model

Model how to find the references in the text. Point out the references and how the references play a critical role in supporting your understanding of the information you are reading in the text. Use pre-identified reference citation in example, below.

Say: *Often in informational texts, the author will share information that he or she found from another source, such as another book, article, or research report. The author will then cite, or give credit to, the author of the other source in the text where it is shared by listing the author's name and the year the other source was published. At the end of the informational text, the author lists all the sources that he or she referenced in the text.*

Say: *Let's look at a reference citation in our books. There's one on page _____. The author cites _____.*

Say: *If you wanted to find out more about what the author was talking about regarding this source, or wanted to read the source yourself, would you have enough information from the reference citation on this page to find the source?*

(Accept student offerings. Answer should be, "No.")

Say: *You're right. We would need more information. Let's see if we can find more information on this cited source in the list of references in our books. Reference lists are typically found in the back of the text.*

Students locate list of references in back of text. Reinforce students' location of the reference list.

Say: *Let's see what information is included in the reference list. What do you see?*

Accept student offerings.

Lesson Objectives

- Identify the purpose of the references and their location in a given informational text.

Metacognitive Strategy

Selective attention, resourcing, advanced organization

Academic Language

Informational text, references, cite

Materials

- Several classroom informational books (at least one copy per pair of students) containing a table of contents, index, glossary, page numbers, and references
- Pre-identify a reference citation in the text. Note the page number for the reference citation.
- Print Concept Lesson 6 Practice Page

Pre-Assess

Student's ability to identify and name of basic book parts (front cover, back cover, author's name, illustrator, pages).

Transfer Notes

In all printed languages, text features in printed material are organized to convey meaning and assist the reader to locate the information in text. Good readers in any language learn how to use text features as reference to support comprehension of text and to prepare to read and to advance-organize related work.

Say: *Yes, each listing should include the author's name, the year that it was published, the title of the book, article, or research report, and other publication information. That way, if you wanted to learn more about what any of these sources said, you could look the information up at the library.*

Say: *Did you find our citation that we were looking for? Remember, it was _____. Who has found it?*

Accept student offerings and reinforce students' location of the cited source.

Say: *So now, if we wanted to learn more about what this author had to say about the topic in our book, we could go to the library and locate the text. That is how a reference list and the references in it help you find information about the text and help you better understand the information in the text*

Apply

Refer to section 2 of the Practice Page and complete with students.

Say: *Look at section 2 of your Practice Page. Take a moment to look over the reference list you see there. In a few moments, I will be asking you to work with your partner to answer some questions about this reference list.*

Allow students to review the lesson practice page.

Extend Knowledge: Make Meaning

Refer to the first portion of section 3 of the Practice Page. Students may work with a partner to complete.

Say: *Now you will have a chance to use what you have learned today to complete the following sentences, using the words in the word bank, below.*

The References list includes the _____**author's**_____ name and the name of the _____**article**_____.

The _____**Reference**_____ list_____ is found in the back of the text.

The References list also includes the year the article was _____**published**_____, and the_____**pages**_____ where you can find the _____**article**_____.

The References list is listed in the _____**Table of Contents**_____.

The References list is in _____**alphabetical**_____ order.

Reflect and Review:

Refer to the first portion of section 3 of the Practice Page.

Say: *What did we learn today? Discuss with your partner.*

We learned that good readers use the _____ to look up the sources that the authors have cited in the text.

✔**Formative Assessment**

If the student completes each task correctly, precede to the next skill in the sequence.

Did the student…?	Intervention 2
Respond to prompts relating to text features?	Provide this lesson in primary language. Think aloud responses to prompts pointing to specific details.
Name each feature?	Have students construct a text feature visual depicting and labeling each text feature.
Relate information in text feature to the text?	Point out the relation of each text feature to the text.

7 Organization of Ideas

Introduce the Lesson

Say: *Today we will learn how text features are used to organize the ideas in an informational text, or a non-fiction text, including the titles, chapters, headings, subheadings, and conclusion. We will learn how these text features help us locate information quickly and understand what we've found.*

Organization of Ideas

Say: *Informational texts are organized through the use of text features. Authors include them to help the reader better understand what they are reading. Text features may provide information that is not written in the text itself, and can be found in textbooks, magazine articles, newspapers, research reports, or web pages.*

Say: *We will look at how some text features help you find information in the text, and how other features can help you understand the information that you find in the text.*

Elicit Prior Knowledge

Display and/or distribute the lesson practice page and complete section 1 with students.

Say: *How do you say, **chapters** in your home language? Write it in section 1 of your Practice Page.*

Model

Model how to find the title of the text. Point out the title and how the title plays a critical role in supporting your understanding of the information you are reading in the text.

Say: *The title of the text will be on the outside cover of the book, on the first page of the magazine article, newspaper, or at the top of the web page. The title tells you the topic of the text, which lets you know what you'll be reading about. That way, you can connect what you already know about the topic to the text. Point to the title of the book.*

Students work with their partner to find the title on the front of the book. Accept and reinforce students' location of the title on the front of the book.

Say: *Many books also have a page inside the cover that is called the **title page,** which will include the name of the author or authors, the illustrator or illustrators, if any, and the publication information will be on the back of the title page. Following the title page you will find the table of contents, which we studied in one of our previous lessons. In the table of contents, the titles of each chapter will be listed, along with the page number where each chapter begins. These titles also give you an idea about the topic covered in each chapter. Let's look at the table of contents in our books and see what some of the chapter titles are.*

Students work with their partner to find the table of contents. Reinforce students' location of the table of contents in the front of the book.

Say: *What are some of the chapter titles in your book? What will be the topics?*

Students work with their partner to find the chapter titles. Accept and reinforce students' offerings of chapter titles and topics.

Say: *In each chapter, there may be headings and subheadings to divide the information on the topic into sections. Each heading or subheading will tell you the main idea of that section of the text. They may be printed in large, bold, or colored font to make them be*

Lesson Objectives

- Identify the purpose of the titles, chapters, headings, subheadings, and conclusion and their location in a given informational text.

Metacognitive Strategy

Selective attention, resourcing, advanced organization

Academic Language

Informational text, titles, chapters, headings, subheadings, conclusion

Materials

- Several classroom informational books (at least one copy per pair of students) containing a titles, chapters, headings, subheadings, and conclusion.
- Print Concepts Lesson 7 Practice Page

Pre-Assess

Student's ability to identify and name of basic book parts (front cover, back cover, author's name, illustrator, pages).

Transfer Notes

In all printed languages, text features in printed material are organized to convey meaning and assist the reader to locate the information in text. Good readers in any language learn how to use text features as reference to support comprehension of text and to prepare to read and to advance-organize related work.

easier to see, and can help you locate the information you are looking for. Let's see if we can find some headings and subheadings in a chapter in your book.

Students work with a partner to find the headings and subheadings in a chapter in a text.

Say: *What are some of the headings and subheadings in the chapter in your book? How did you recognize them as headings or subheadings? What do you think will be the topic in the section under each heading or subheading?*

Students work with their partner to find the headings and subheadings in a chapter in their book. Accept and reinforce students' offerings of how they recognized the headings and subheadings as well as the heading and subheading titles and topics.

Say: *Now that you have a better idea of the ideas and topics that will be discussed in your informational text, you can see that there is a lot of information that will be shared as you read through the text. Most texts include a section, called the conclusion, where the author summarizes all the information presented. Some include a conclusion at the end of each chapter, while others have an entire chapter at the end of the text for the conclusion. Some texts even include both! Let's see if we can find a conclusion at the end of a chapter and if there is one at the end of the book.*

Students work with their partner to find a conclusion in a chapter and/or at the end of their book. Accept and reinforce students' offerings of where they find a conclusion.

Apply

Refer to section 2 of the Practice Page and complete with students.

Say: *Look at section 2 of your Practice Page. Take a moment to look over the textbook pages you see there. In a few moments, I will be asking you to work with your partner to answer questions about these pages.*

Extend Knowledge: Make Meaning

Refer to the first portion of section 3 of the Practice Page. **Say:** *Now you will have a chance to use what you have learned today to complete the following sentences, using the words in the word bank, below.*

The chapter includes __**heading**__ and __**subheadings**__.

Titles, headings, and subheadings let us know the __**main idea**__ that we will read about in each section.

Headings are related to the __**chapter title**__.

Subheadings are related to the __**heading**__ they are listed under.

The __**conclusion**__ summarizes what the chapter has said about a topic.

Reflect and Review:

Say: *What did we learn today? Discuss with your partner.*

We learned that good readers use the _____, _____, _____, and _____ to understand the topics that are presented in the text.

✓Formative Assessment	
If the student completes each task correctly, precede to the next skill in the sequence. I	
Did the student...?	**Intervention 2**
Respond to prompts relating to text features?	Provide this lesson in primary language. Think aloud responses to prompts pointing to specific details.
Name each feature?	Have students construct a text feature visual depicting and labeling each text feature.
Relate information in text feature to the text?	Point out the relation of each text feature to the text.

8 Illustrations and Photographs

Introduce the Lesson

Say: *Today we will learn how text features are used to support the understanding of the ideas in an informational text, or a non-fiction text. We will learn how these text features help us understand what we're reading.*

Illustrations and Photographs

Say: *Informational texts are organized through the use of text features. Authors include them to help the reader better understand what they are reading. Text features may provide information that is not written in the text itself, and can be found in textbooks, magazine articles, newspapers, research reports, or web pages.*

Say: *Today we will be looking at how some text features help you understand the ideas or concepts in the text, and how these features can help you link the information you are reading in the text to ideas or concepts that you might be familiar with.*

Elicit Prior Knowledge

Display and/or distribute the Practice Page and complete section 1 with students.

Say: *How do you say **illustrations** or **photographs** in your home language? Write it in section 1 of yourPractice Page.*

Model

Model how to find the illustrations or photographs in the text. Point out the illustrations or photographs and how they play a critical role in supporting your understanding of the information you are reading in the text.

Say: *There may be illustrations or photographs in informational text. The illustrations or photographs will show you some of the ideas and concepts that are found in the text, which lets you know what you'll be reading about. That way, you can connect what you already know about the ideas or concepts to what the text is telling you. Point to some illustrations or photographs in your book.*

Students work with their partner to find the illustrations or photographs in their book. Accept and reinforce students' location of illustrations or photographs in the book. Now direct the students to turn to the preselected illustration or photograph.

Say: *Let's all look at the (illustration /photograph) on page _____ together.*

Students work with their partner to find the illustration /photograph on the designated page. Reinforce students' location of the illustration /photograph in the book.

Say: *What do you see in this (illustration /photograph)?*

Students work with their partner to discuss what they see in the illustration/photograph. Accept and reinforce students' offerings of what they see in the illustration/photograph.

Say: *We know that illustrations and photographs are supposed to help us understand the ideas and concepts in the text. What is the title of this chapter, the heading, and the subheading [as applicable for this example]?*

Students work with their partner to find the chapter title, heading and subheading that pertain to this illustration/photograph. Accept and reinforce students' offerings of chapter title, heading and subheading.

Lesson Objectives

- Identify the purpose of illustrations and photographs in a given informational text.

Metacognitive Strategy

Selective attention, resourcing, advanced organization

Academic Language

Informational text, illustrations, photographs, concepts

Materials

- Several classroom informational books (at least one copy per pair of students) containing a titles, chapters, headings, subheadings, and illustrations or photographs.
- Pre-select an illustration or a photograph and note the page number
- Print Concept Lesson 8 Practice Page

Pre-Assess

Student's ability to identify and name of basic book parts (front cover, back cover, author's name, illustrator, pages).

Transfer Notes

In all printed languages, text features in printed material are organized to convey meaning and assist the reader to locate the information in text. Good readers in any language learn how to use text features as reference to support comprehension of text and to prepare to read and to advance-organize related work.

Say: *Great! Now, I want to know how this (illustration/photograph) helps you understand the ideas and concepts in this chapter, heading, and subheading.*

Students work with their partner to discuss how this (illustration/photograph) helps them understand the ideas and concepts in this chapter, heading, and subheading.

Say: *How might this (illustration/photograph) help you understand the ideas and concepts in this chapter, heading, and subheading?*

Accept and reinforce students' offerings of how this (illustration/photograph) might help them understand the ideas and concepts in this chapter, heading, and subheading.

Say: *Now that you have a better idea of how illustrations and photographs can help you understand the ideas and concepts that will be discussed in your informational text, you can see how important it is to connect those illustrations and photographs to what you already know and to what you are reading about in the text.*

Apply

Refer to section 2 of the Practice Page and complete with students.

Say: *Look at section 2 of your Practice Page. Take a moment to look over the textbook page you see there. In a few moments, I will be asking you to work with your partner to answer questions about this page.*

Allow students to review the Practice Page.

Extend Knowledge: Make Meaning

Refer to the first portion of section 3 of the Practice Page. Students may work with a partner to complete.

1. ____**Photographs**____ help the reader better understand the ideas in the text.
2. Photographs and illustrations help readers link the ideas in the text with _____ **ideas**_____ or ideas that they may be familiar with.
3. _____**Illustrations**_____ are a text feature to help the reader understand the concepts and ideas in the text.
4. Photographs and illustrations show concepts and _____**information**_____ without using words.
5. Photographs and illustrations work with the titles, _____**heading**_____, and subheadings to help teach the _____**concepts**_____ and ideas in the text.

> Photographs ideas Illustrations headings information concepts

Reflect and Review:

Say: *What did we learn today? Discuss with your partner.*

We learned that good readers use _____ and _____ to understand the topics that are presented in the text.

✔ Formative Assessment	
If the student completes each task correctly, precede to the next skill in the sequence. I	
Did the student...?	**Intervention**
Respond to prompts relating to text features?	Provide this lesson in primary language. Think aloud responses to prompts pointing to specific details.
Name each feature?	Have students construct a text feature visual depicting and labeling each text feature.
Relate information in text feature to the text?	Point out the relation of each text feature to the text.

9 Diagrams

Metacognitive Strategy

Selective attention, resourcing, advanced organization

Academic Language

Informational text, concepts, diagrams

Materials

- Several classroom informational books (at least one copy per pair of students) containing titles, chapters, headings, subheadings, and diagrams, charts, or tables
- Pre-select a diagram and note the page number
- Print Concept Lesson 9 Practice Page

Pre-Assess

Student's ability to identify and name of basic book parts (front cover, back cover, author's name, illustrator, pages).

Transfer Notes

In all printed languages, text features in printed material are organized to convey meaning and assist the reader to locate the information in text. Good readers in any language learn how to use text features as reference to support comprehension of text and to prepare to read and to advance-organize related work.

Introduce the Lesson

Say: *Today we will learn how text features are used to support the understanding of the ideas in an informational text, or a non-fiction text. We will learn how these text features help us understand what we're reading.*

Diagrams

Say: *Informational texts are organized through the use of text features. Authors include them to help the reader better understand what they are reading. Text features may provide information that is not written in the text itself, and can be found in textbooks, magazine articles, newspapers, research reports, or web pages.*

Say: *Today we will be looking at how some text features help you understand the ideas or concepts in the text, and how these features can help you link the information you are reading in the text to ideas or concepts that you might be familiar with.*

Elicit Prior Knowledge

Display and/or distribute the Practice Page and complete section 1 with students.

Say: *How do you say **diagrams** in your home language? Write it in section 1 of your lesson Practice Page.*

Model

Model how to find the diagrams in the text. Point out the diagrams and how they play a critical role in supporting your understanding of the information you are reading in the text.

Say: *There may be diagrams in informational text. A diagram is a drawing that shows or explains something. You should read all the text in the diagram, such as the titles, labels, any captions, or parts that are numbered. Diagrams will show you some of the ideas and concepts that are found in the text, which lets you know what you'll be reading about. That way, you can connect what you already know about the ideas or concepts to what the text is telling you. Point to some diagrams in your book.*

Students work with their partner to find diagrams in their book. Accept and reinforce students' location of diagrams in the book. Now direct the students to turn to the preselected diagram.

Say: *Let's all look at the diagram on page _____ together.*

Students work with their partner to find the diagram on the designated page. Reinforce students' location of the diagram in the book.

Say: *What is the information that this diagram is showing us?*

Students work with their partner to discuss what they see in the diagram. Accept and reinforce students' offerings of the information that is being shown in the diagram.

Say: *We know that diagrams help us understand the ideas and concepts in the text. What is the title of this chapter, the heading, and the subheading [as applicable for this example]?*

Students work with their partner to find the chapter title, heading and subheading that pertain to this diagram. Accept and reinforce students' offerings of chapter title, heading and subheading.

Say: *Great! Now, I want to know how this diagram helps you understand the ideas and concepts in this chapter, heading, and subheading.*

Students work with their partner to discuss how this diagram helps them understand the ideas and concepts in this chapter, heading, and subheading.

Say: *How might this diagram help you understand the ideas and concepts in this chapter, heading, and subheading?*

Accept and reinforce students' offerings of how this diagram might help them understand the ideas and concepts in this chapter, heading, and subheading.

Say: *Now that you have a better idea of how diagrams can help you understand the ideas and concepts that will be discussed in your informational text, you can see how important it is to connect these diagrams to what you already know and to what you are reading about in the text.*

Apply

Refer to section 2 of the Practice Page and complete with students.

Say: *Look at section 2 of your Practice Page. Take a moment to look over the textbook page you see there. In a few moments, I will be asking you to work with your partner to answer questions about this page.*

Allow students to review the Practice Page.

Extend Knowledge: Make Meaning

Refer to the first portion of section 3 of the lesson Practice Page. Students may work with a partner to complete.

Say: *Now you will have a chance to use what you have learned today to complete the following sentences, using the words in the word bank, below.*

1. Diagrams help you understand the __**ideas and concepts**__ in each chapter, heading, and subheading.
2. Diagrams will __**show**__ you some of the ideas and concepts that are found in the text.
3. Chapter titles, headings, and subheadings are __**related**__ to the diagrams.
4. Diagrams may help you __**connect**__ what you may already __**know**__ about the idea or concept to what you are reading in the text.

Reflect and Review:

Say: *What did we learn today? Discuss with your partner.*

We learned that good readers use _____ to understand the ideas and concepts that are presented in the text.

✓Formative Assessment	
If the student completes each task correctly, precede to the next skill in the sequence.	
Did the student...?	**Intervention**
Respond to prompts relating to text features?	Provide this lesson in primary language. Think aloud responses to prompts pointing to specific details.
Name each feature?	Have students construct a text feature visual depicting and labeling each text feature.
Relate information in text feature to the text?	Point out the relation of each text feature to the text.

10 Charts, and Tables

Metacognitive Strategy

Selective attention, resourcing, advanced organization

Academic Language

Informational text, concepts, charts, and tables

Materials

- Several classroom informational books (at least one copy per pair of students) containing titles, chapters, headings, subheadings, and diagrams, charts, or tables
- Pre-select a chart or table and note the page number
- Print Concept Lesson 10 Practice Page

Pre-Assess

Student's ability to identify and name of basic book parts (front cover, back cover, author's name, illustrator, pages).

Transfer Notes

In all printed languages, text features in printed material are organized to convey meaning and assist the reader to locate the information in text. Good readers in any language learn how to use text features as reference to support comprehension of text and to prepare to read and to advance-organize related work.

Introduce the Lesson

Say: *Today we will learn how text features are used to support the understanding of the ideas in an informational text, or a non-fiction text. We will learn how these text features help us understand what we're reading.*

Charts, and Tables

Say: *Informational texts are organized through the use of text features. Authors include them to help the reader better understand what they are reading. Text features may provide information that is not written in the text itself, and can be found in textbooks, magazine articles, newspapers, research reports, or web pages.*

Say: *Today we will be looking at how some text features help you understand the ideas or concepts in the text, and how these features can help you link the information you are reading in the text to ideas or concepts that you might be familiar with.*

Elicit Prior Knowledge

Display and/or distribute the Practice Page and complete section 1 with students.

Say: *How do you say **charts** or **tables** in your home language? Write it in section 1 of your Practice Page.*

Model

Model how to find charts and tables in the text. Point out charts and tables and how they play a critical role in supporting your understanding of the information you are reading in the text.

Say: *There may be charts and tables in informational text. Charts and tables organize large amounts of information in a very concise way. That means that they are able to tell you a lot of information in a small space. Charts and tables often are very visual, which makes them easy to understand. They present many different kinds of data, and can help you compare the information that is being presented in the text. Charts and tables will show you some of the ideas and concepts that are found in the text, which also lets you know what you'll be reading about. That way, you can connect what you already know about the ideas or concepts to what the text is telling you. Point to some charts and tables in your book.*

Students work with their partner to find the charts and tables in their book. Accept and reinforce students' location of charts and tables in the book. Now direct the students to turn to the preselected chart or table.

Say: *Let's all look at the (chart/table) on page _____ together.*

Students work with their partner to find the chart/table on the designated page. Reinforce students' location of the chart/table in the book.

Say: *What is the information that this (chart/table) is showing us?*

Students work with their partner to discuss what they see in the chart/table. Accept and reinforce students' offerings of the information that is being shown in the chart/table.

Say: *We know that charts and tables are supposed to help us understand the ideas and concepts in the text. What is the title of this chapter, the heading, and the subheading [as applicable for this example]?*

Students work with their partner to find the chapter title, heading and subheading that pertain to this chart/table. Accept and reinforce students' offerings of chapter title, heading and subheading.

Say: *Great! Now, I want to know how this (chart/table) helps you understand the ideas and concepts in this chapter, heading, and subheading.*

Students work with their partner to discuss how this (chart/table) helps them understand the ideas and concepts in this chapter, heading, and subheading.

Say: *How might this (chart/table) help you understand the ideas and concepts in this chapter, heading, and subheading?*

Accept and reinforce students' offerings of how this (chart/table) might help them understand the ideas and concepts in this chapter, heading, and subheading.

Say: *Now that you have a better idea of how charts and tables can help you understand the ideas and concepts that will be discussed in your informational text, you can see how important it is to connect those charts and tables to what you already know and to what you are reading about in the text.*

Apply

Refer to section 2 of the Practice Page and complete with students.

Say: *Look at section 2 of your Practice Page. Take a moment to look over the textbook page you see there. In a few moments, I will be asking you to work with your partner to answer questions about this page.*

Allow students to review the Practice Page.

Extend Knowledge: Make Meaning

Refer to the first portion of section 3 of the Practice Page. **Say:** *Now you will have a chance to use what you have learned today to complete the following sentences, using the words in the word bank, below.*

1. Charts and tables help you understand the _____**ideas and concepts**_____ in each chapter, heading, and subheading.
2. Charts and tables will _____**show**_____ you some of the ideas and concepts that are found in the text.
3. Chapter titles, headings, and subheadings are _____**related**_____ to the charts and tables.
4. Charts and tables may help you _____**connect**_____ what you may already _____**know**_____ about the idea or concept to what you are reading in the text.

Reflect and Review:

Say: *What did we learn today? Discuss with your partner.*

We learned that good readers use _____and _____ to understand the ideas and concepts that are presented in the text.

✔ Formative Assessment

If the student completes each task correctly, precede to the next skill in the sequence.

Did the student…?	Intervention
Respond to prompts relating to text features?	Provide this lesson in primary language. Think aloud responses to prompts pointing to specific details.
Name each feature?	Have students construct a text feature visual depicting and labeling each text feature.
Relate information in text feature to the text?	Point out the relation of each text feature to the text.

11 Maps, Keys, and Legends

Lesson Objectives

- Identify the purpose of maps, keys, and legends in a given informational text.

Metacognitive Strategy

Selective attention, resourcing, advanced organization

Academic Language

Informational text, concepts, maps, keys, legends

Materials

- Several classroom informational books (at least one copy per pair of students) containing titles, chapters, headings, subheadings, maps, keys, and legends
- Pre-select a map with a key/legend and note the page number
- Print Concept Lesson 11 Practice Page

Pre-Assess

Student's ability to identify and name of basic book parts (front cover, back cover, author's name, illustrator, pages).

Transfer Notes

In all printed languages, text features in printed material are organized to convey meaning and assist the reader to locate the information in text. Good readers in any language learn how to use text features as reference to support comprehension of text and to prepare to read and to advance-organize related work.

Introduce the Lesson

Say: *Today we will learn how text features are used to support the understanding of the ideas in an informational text, or a non-fiction text. We will learn how these text features help us understand what we're reading.*

Maps, Keys, and Legends

Say: *Informational texts are organized through the use of text features. Authors include them to help the reader better understand what they are reading. Text features may provide information that is not written in the text itself, and can be found in textbooks, magazine articles, newspapers, research reports, or web pages.*

Say: *Today we will be looking at how some text features help you understand the ideas or concepts in the text, and how these features can help you link the information you are reading in the text to ideas or concepts that you might be familiar with.*

Elicit Prior Knowledge

Display and/or distribute the lesson practice page and complete section 1 with students.

Say: *How do you say **maps, keys,** or **legend** in your home language? Write it in section 1 of your Practice Page.*

Model

Model how to find the maps, keys, and legends in the text. Point out maps, keys, and legends and how they play a critical role in supporting your understanding of the information you are reading in the text.

Say: *There may be maps, keys, and legends in informational text. A map presents information visually through a drawing of the basic shape of an area of land and other geographic, political, or historical information. Maps help you understand where something is happening and how far away it is from where you are. You should read all the text on the map, such as the titles and labels. On a map, the key or the legend tells you what all the symbols on the map stand for. Maps, keys, and legends will show you some of the ideas and concepts that are found in the text, which lets you know what you'll be reading about. That way, you can connect what you already know about the ideas or concepts to what the text is telling you. Point to some maps, keys, and legends in your book.*

Students work with their partner to find maps, keys, and legends in their book. Accept and reinforce students' location of maps, keys, and legends in the book. Now direct the students to turn to the preselected map.

Say: *Let's all look at the map on page _____ together.*

Students work with their partner to find the map on the designated page. Reinforce students' location of the map in the book.

Say: *What is the information that this map is showing us?*

Students work with their partner to discuss what they see on the map, including the information from the key or legend. Accept and reinforce students' offerings of the information that is being shown on the map.

Say: *We know that maps, keys, and legends help us understand the ideas and concepts in the text. What is the title of this chapter, the heading, and the subheading [as applicable for this example]?*

Students work with their partner to find the chapter title, heading and subheading that pertain to this map. Accept and reinforce students' offerings of chapter title, heading and subheading.

Say: *Great! Now, I want to know how this map and its key or legend help you understand the ideas and concepts in this chapter, heading, and subheading.*

Students work with their partner to discuss how this map and its key or legend help them understand the ideas and concepts in this chapter, heading, and subheading.

Say: *How might this map and key or legend help you understand the ideas and concepts in this chapter, heading, and subheading?*

Accept and reinforce students' offerings of how this map and its key or legend might help them understand the ideas and concepts in this chapter, heading, and subheading.

Say: *Now that you have a better idea of how maps, keys, and legends can help you understand the ideas and concepts that will be discussed in your informational text, you can see how important it is to connect these maps, keys, and legends to what you already know and to what you are reading about in the text.*

Apply

Refer to section 2 of the Practice Page and complete with students.

Extend Knowledge: Make Meaning

Refer to the first portion of section 3 of the lesson practice page. **Say:** *Now you will have a chance to use what you have learned today to complete the following sentences, using the words in the word bank, below.*

1. Maps and keys or legends help you understand the ____ **ideas and concepts** ____ in each chapter, heading, and subheading.
2. Maps and keys or legends will ____ **show** ____ you some of the ideas and concepts that are found in the text.
3. Chapter titles, headings, and subheadings are _____ **related** _____ to the maps and keys or legends.
4. Maps and keys or legends may help you _____ **connect** _____ what you may already _____ **know** _____ about the idea or concept to what you are reading in the text

Reflect and Review:

Say: *What did we learn today? Discuss with your partner.*

We learned that good readers use _____ and _____ or _____ to understand the ideas and concepts that are presented in the text.

✓**Formative Assessment**

If the student completes each task correctly, precede to the next skill in the sequence.

Did the student…?	Intervention
Respond to prompts relating to text features?	Provide this lesson in primary language. Think aloud responses to prompts pointing to specific details.
Name each feature?	Have students construct a text feature visual depicting and labeling each text feature.
Relate information in text feature to the text?	Point out the relation of each text feature to the text.

12 Content Emphasis

Introduce the Lesson

Say: *Today we will learn how text features are used to support the understanding of the ideas in an informational text, or a non-fiction text. We will learn how these text features help us understand what we're reading.*

Captions, Footnotes, Margin Notes, Text Boxes, Font

Say: *Informational texts are organized through the use of text features. Authors include them to help the reader better understand what they are reading. Text features may provide information that is not written in the text itself.*

Say: *Today we will be looking at how some text features help you understand the ideas or concepts in the text, and how these features can help you link the information you are reading to ideas or concepts that you might be familiar with.*

Model

Model how to find captions, footnotes, margin notes, text boxes and different types of font (bold, italicized, or highlighted) in the text. Point out captions, footnotes, margin notes, text boxes and different types of font and how they play a critical role in supporting your understanding of the information you are reading in the text.

Say: *There may be captions, footnotes, margin notes, text boxes and different types of font in informational text. Captions explain what is being shown in a picture, illustration, or diagram. They help you understand information that may not be found in the text. Footnotes further explain a point in the text that the author thinks is important.*

Say: *Text boxes may be found anywhere in the text, and contain important information to further explain the ideas or concepts in the main text.*

Say: *Different types of font, such as bold, italicized, or highlighted, draw your attention to the text and may help you see how the text is divided. Often, important, or key, words are in a different color font and in bold. Text in italics is used to help it stand out.*

Say: *captions, footnotes, margin notes, text boxes and different types of font will show you some of the ideas and concepts that are found in the text, which lets you know what you'll be reading about. That way, you can connect what you already know about the ideas or concepts to what the text is telling you. Point to some features in your book.*

Students work with their partner to find captions, footnotes, margin notes, text boxes and different types of font in their book. Accept and reinforce students' location of captions, footnotes, margin notes, text boxes and different types of font in the book. Now direct the students to turn to the preselected diagram, illustration, table, or chart with a caption.

Say: *Let's all look at the (diagram/illustration/table/chart) on page _____ together.*

Students work with their partner to find the (diagram/illustration/table/chart) on the designated page. Reinforce students' location of the (diagram/illustration/table/chart) .

Say: *What information is this (diagram/illustration/table/chart) and caption(s) showing?*

Students work with their partner to discuss what they see on the (diagram/illustration/table/chart), including the information from the caption. Accept and reinforce students' offerings of the information that is being shown on the (diagram/illustration/table/chart) including the information from the caption.

Lesson Objectives

- Identify the purpose of captions, footnotes, margin notes, text boxes and different types of font in a given informational text.

Metacognitive Strategy

Selective attention, resourcing, advanced organization

Academic Language

Informational text, concepts captions, footnotes, margin notes, text boxes, bold font, italicized font, color font

Materials

- Several classroom informational books (at least one copy per pair of students) containing titles, chapters, headings, subheadings, captions, footnotes, margin notes, text boxes and different types of font
- Pre-select a diagram, illustration, table, or chart with a caption and note the page number
- Print Concept Lesson 12 Practice page

Pre-Assess

Student's ability to identify and name of basic book parts (front cover, back cover, author's name, illustrator, pages).

Transfer Notes

In all printed languages, text features in printed material are organized to convey meaning and assist the reader to locate the information in text. Good readers in any language learn how to use text features as reference to support comprehension of text and to prepare to read and to advance-organize related work.

Say: *We know that captions, footnotes, margin notes, text boxes and different types of font help us understand the ideas and concepts in the text. What is the title of this chapter, the heading, and the subheading [as applicable for this example]?*

Students work with their partner to find the chapter title, heading and subheading that pertain to this (diagram/illustration/table/chart). Accept and reinforce students' offerings of chapter title, heading and subheading.

Say: *Great! Now, I want to know how this (diagram/illustration/table/chart) and the caption(s) help you understand the ideas and concepts in this chapter.*

Students work with their partner to discuss how this (diagram/illustration/table/chart) and the caption(s) help them understand the ideas in this chapter, heading, and subheading.

Say: *How might this (diagram/illustration/table/chart) and the caption(s) help you understand the ideas and concepts in this chapter, heading, and subheading?*

Accept and reinforce students' offerings of how this (diagram/illustration/table/chart) and the caption(s) might help them understand the ideas in this chapter, heading, and subheading.

Say: *Now that you have a better idea of how captions, footnotes, margin notes, text boxes and different types of font can help you understand the ideas and concepts that will be discussed in your informational text, you can see how important it is to connect these captions, footnotes, margin notes, text boxes and different types of font to what you already know and to what you are reading about in the text.*

Apply
Refer to section 2 of the Practice Page and complete with students.

Say: *Look at section 2 of your Practice Page. Take a moment to look over the textbook page you see there. In a few moments, I will be asking you to work with your partner to answer questions about this page.*

Extend Knowledge: Make Meaning

Refer to the first portion of section 3 of the lesson practice page. *Say: Now you will have a chance to use what you have learned today to complete the following sentences.*

1. Captions, footnotes, margin notes, and text boxes may help you _____**connect**_____ what you may already _____**know**_____ about the idea or concept to what you are reading in the text.

2. Captions, footnotes, margin notes, text boxes, and different types of font help you understand the _____**ideas and concepts**_____ in each chapter, heading, and subheading.

3. Chapter titles, headings, and subheadings are _____**related**_____ to the captions, footnotes, margin notes, and text boxes.

4. Captions, footnotes, margin notes, text boxes, and different types of font will _____**show**_____ you some of the ideas and concepts that are found in the text.

Reflect and Review:

Say: *What did we learn today? Discuss with your partner.*

We learned that good readers use _____, _____, _____, _____, and _____ to understand the ideas and concepts that are presented in the text.

✓ Formative Assessment	
If the student completes each task correctly, precede to the next skill in the sequence. I	
Did the student…?	**Intervention**
Respond to prompts relating to text features?	Provide this lesson in primary language. Think aloud responses to prompts pointing to specific details.
Name each feature?	Have students construct a text feature visual depicting and labeling each text feature.
Relate information in text feature to the text?	Point out the relation of each text feature to the text.

Print Concepts Lesson 1 Practice Page 1

Recognize and Name All Upper and Lowercase Letters of the Alphabet

1. Prior Knowledge and Home Language Connections

My home language is _____.

Today's concept compared to my home language:

How do you say alphabet or letters in your home language?	How is the writing system in your home language same or different than in English?

2. Recognize Letter names

LETTER	NAME	LETTER	NAME	LETTER	NAME
Aa	ay	J j	jay	S s	ess
Bb	bee	K k	kay	T t	tee
Cc	cee	L l	el	U u	u
D d	dee	M m	em	V v	vee
E e	ee	N n	en	W w	Double u
F f	eff	O o	o	X x	ex
G g	gee	P p	pee	Y y	Wy
H h	aitch	Q q	cue	Z z	zee
Ii	i	R r	ar		

3. Sing the Alphabet Song

A B C D E F G
H I J K L M N O P
Q R S T U V W X Y and Z
Now you know my ABCs
Next time won't you sing with me?

4. Extend Language: Make Meaning

1. The process of becoming educated. _____
2. The process of becoming informed. _____
3. Being able to respond. _____
4. Someone you can rely on. _____
5. Someone who knows two languages. _____

bilingual   responsible   education   information   reliable

Something new I learned was _____.

I now know that _____.

I will use this when ____.

Print Concepts Lesson 1 Practice Page 2

Print Upper and Lower Case Letters

A practice sheet that shows letters and dotted lines and direction arrows for drawing the letter lines.

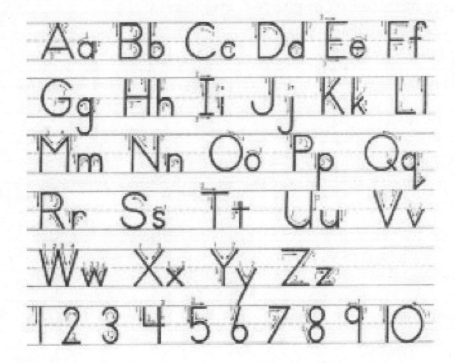

Print Concepts Lesson 2 Practice Page 1

Distinguish Between Letters and Other Printed Symbols

1. Prior Knowledge and Home Language Connections

My home language is _____.

Today's concept compared to my home language:

Are there any punctuation marks in your home language?	What are some international printed symbols you know?

2. Recognizing printed symbols

Symbol	Name	Function	Example
.			I learn a lot in school.
?			Do I learn a lot in school?
!			Learn a lot in school!
!			I learn a lot in school!
,			Yesterday, I learned a lot in school.
" "			When I say "a lot," I really mean it.

3. Shared Reading

Do you know how the keyboard was invented? Well, the "QWERTY" system was named from reading the first six letters of the top left letter row on a keyboard. The position of letters and symbols on the keyboard has evolved since its invention in 1870. Think about it, the QWERTY system refuses to get old, it just keeps getting better! It went worldwide when it became the keyboard of electronic typewriters, computers, and all mobile devices. Way to go, QWERTY!

4. Extend Language: Make Meaning

1. A keyboard contains _____ and _____ for writing.
2. A _____ is used at the end of declarative sentences.
3. Question marks are used at the end of _____ sentences.
4. An _____ show command or emotions.
5. Qwerty is a _____ system for writing.

Letters   keyboard   symbols   period   exclamation mark   interrogative

Something new I learned was _____.

I now know that _____ .

I will use this when _____.

Print Concepts Lesson 2 Practice Page 2
The QWERTY Keyboard

Print Concepts Lesson 3 Practice Page
Organization of Text: Table of Contents

1. Prior Knowledge and Home Language Connections

My home language is _____.

How do you say, "Table of Contents" in your home language? _____

2. Recognize Text Features: Table of Contents
In what chapter will you find information about:

Sight words? _____

Why kids misspell words? _____

Ideas for teaching kids how to spell? _____

What is this informational text mainly about? _____

What would be a good title for this book? _____

Table of Contents

3.Extend Knowledge: Make Meaning

1. The table of contents is found at the _____ of the text.
2. The _____is the last section of the text.
3. The some of the sections of the text are called _____.
4. The _____ tell you where the chapter or section starts.
5. The _____ is second-to-last section of the text.

chapters   beginning   page numbers   References Cited   Index

Today we learned that strong readers use the _____ to help locate information in the text.

Print Concepts Lesson 4 Practice Page
Organization of Text: Index

1. Prior Knowledge and Home Language Connections

My home language is _____.

How do you say, "Index" in your home language? _____

2. Recognize Text Features: Index

INDEX	
Bungee jumping	24
Face painting	30
Games	45
Inflatables	40
Music	49
Rock climbing	20
Super slides	42
Trains	28
Trampoline	47

On what page will you find information about:

Music? _____

Rock climbing? _____

Trains? _____

What is this informational text mainly about? _____

What would be a good title for this book?

_____

3. Extend Knowledge: Make Meaning

1. The _____ is found toward the back of the text.

2. The different items in the index are _____.

3. The _____ tell you where the topic starts.

4. The index is in _____ order.

5. The index is listed in the _____.

topics   "Table of Contents"   alphabetical   page numbers   index

We learned that strong readers use the _____ to help locate information on a topic in the text.

Print Concepts Lesson 5 Practice Page
Organization of Text: Glossary

1. Prior Knowledge and Home Language Connections

My home language is _____.

How do you say, **Glossary** in your home language? _____

2. Recognize Text Features: Glossary

Glossary

air pressure the weight of the air at any particular point on Earth

anemometer a tool used to measure wind speed

atmosphere the blanket of air that surrounds Earths

axis the imaginary line around which an object, such as Earth, rotates

barometer a tool used to measure air pressure

climate the long-term weather conditions in a region

drought a period in which less precipitation than normal falls

forecast a prediction of weather conditions in the near future

front a region where two air masses of different temperatures meet

greenhouse effect the warming of Earth due to gases in the atmosphere that trap heat near Earth's surface

humitdity the amount of water vapor in the air

meteorologist a scientist who works to understand, explain, and predict weather

orbit the path of one object, such as Earth, as it moves around another object, such as the sun

precipitation any form of water, including rain, snow, and sleet, that falls from clouds to Earth's surface

season one of four yearly patterns of weather that include spring, summer, autumn, and winter, that results from Earth's tilt and orbit

solar radiation energy, including light and heat, produced by the sun

temperature a measure of how hot or cold something is

thermometer a tool used to measure the temperature of a substance

weather the condition of the atmosphere at any given time in a particular location

wind the flow of air from a region of high pressure to a region of low pressure

According to the Glossary,

What does **precipitation** mean? _____

What does **temperature** mean? _____

What does **drought** mean? _____

What is this informational text mainly about? _____

What would be a good title for this book? _____

3. Extend Knowledge: Make Meaning

1. The _____ is found toward the back of the text.
2. The different items in the glossary are _____ from the text.
3. The glossary gives you the _____ for each key word.
4. The glossary is in _____ order.
5. The glossary is listed in the _____.

key words   Table of Contents   alphabetical   definition   Glossary

We learned that strong readers use the _____ to learn the meaning of a key word in the text.

Print Concepts Lesson 6 Practice Page

Organization of Text: References

1. Prior Knowledge and Home Language Connections

My home language is _____.

How do you say, **References** in your home language? _____

2. Recognize Text Features: References

References
Badran, A. A., Yousef, I. A., Joudeh, N. K., Al Hamad, R., Halawa, H., & Hassouneh, H. K. (2010). Portable solar cooker and water heater. Energy Conversion and Management, 51(8), 1605-1609.
Halacy, B., & Halacy, D. (1992). *Cooking with the Sun. How To Build and Use Solar Cookers*. Morning Sun Press, PO Box 413, Lafayette, CA 94549.
Löf, G. O. (1963). Recent investigations in the use of solar energy for cooking. *Solar Energy*, *7*(3), 125-133.
Panwar, N. L., Kaushik, S. C., & Kothari, S. (2012). State of the art of solar cooking: an overview. *Renewable and Sustainable Energy Reviews*, *16*(6), 3776-375.
Tucker, M. (1999). Can solar cooking save the forests?. Ecological Economics, 31(1), 77-89.

According to the References List,

Who was the author of the article, "Recent investigations in the use of solar energy for cooking"? _____

What year was "Can solar cooking save the forests?" published? _____

"State of the art of solar cooking: an overview" can be found on what pages? _____

How many authors are there for "Portable solar cooker and water heater"? _____

What would be a good title for this book? _____

3. Extend Knowledge: Make Meaning

1. The References list includes the _____ name and the name of the _____.

2. The _____ is found in the back of the text.

3. The References list also includes the year the article was _____, and the_____ where you can find the article.

4. The References list is listed in the _____.

5. The References list is in _____ order.

Table of Contents   published   alphabetical   pages   article   author's   References   list

We learned that strong readers use the _____ to look up the sources that the authors have cited in the text.

Print Concepts Lesson 7 Practice Page
Organization of Ideas

1. Prior Knowledge and Home Language Connections

My home language is _____.

How do you say, **text features** in your home language? _____

2. Recognize Informational Text Features: Organization of Ideas

In this informational textbook,

What is the title of the chapter? _____

What are the three headings?_____, _____, and _____.

What are the subheadings under "What to Plant"?_____ and _____.

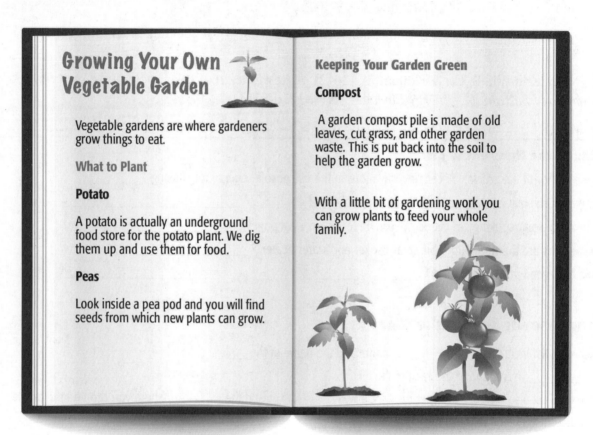

Growing Your Own Vegetable Garden

Vegetable gardens are where gardeners grow things to eat.

What to Plant

Potato

A potato is actually an underground food store for the potato plant. We dig them up and use them for food.

Peas

Look inside a pea pod and you will find seeds from which new plants can grow.

Keeping Your Garden Green

Compost

A garden compost pile is made of old leaves, cut grass, and other garden waste. This is put back into the soil to help the garden grow.

With a little bit of gardening work you can grow plants to feed your whole family.

3. Extend Knowledge: Make Meaning

1. The chapter includes _____ and_____.
2. Titles, headings, and subheadings let us know the _____ that we will read about in each section.
3. Headings are related to the _____.
4. Subheadings are related to the _____ they are listed under.

5. The _____ summarizes what the chapter or text has said about a topic.

chapter title headings heading conclusion subheadings main idea

We learned that strong readers use the _____, _____, _____, and
_____ to understand the topics that are presented in the text.

Print Concepts Lesson 8 Practice Page
Illustrations and Photographs

1. Prior Knowledge and Home Language Connections

My home language is _____.

How do you say, "illustrations" or "photographs" in your home language? _____

2. Recognize Informational Text Features: Illustrations and Photographs
In this informational textbook,

What does the illustration show? _____

What does the photograph show? _____

How do the illustration and photograph help you understand what you are reading in the text?

_____

Late Stone Age People

Toward the end of the Stone Age, two groups of larger-brained humans appeared. Both groups had more-developed cultures than earlier people, but only one group would survive.

Neanderthals

A group known as Neanderthals appeared in Europe and parts of Asia about 200,000 years ago. Their name comes from the Neander Valley in present-day Germany, where their fossil remains were first found.

Modern Humans

About 100,000 years ago, the last new group of humans appeared. The scientific name of this group is Homo sapiens, which means "wise people." Homo sapiens were the first modern humans – or people like you.

3. Extend Knowledge: Make Meaning

1. _____ help the reader better understand the ideas in the text.
2. Photographs and illustrations help readers link the ideas in the text with _____ and ideas that they may be familiar with.
3. _____ are a text feature to help the reader understand the concepts and ideas in the text.
4. Photographs and illustrations show concepts and _____ without using words.
5. Photographs and illustrations work with the titles, _____, and subheadings to help teach the _____ and ideas in the text.

Photographs ideas Illustrations headings information concepts

We learned that strong readers use _____ and _____ to understand the topics that are presented in the text.

Print Concepts Lesson 9 Practice Page
Diagrams

1. Prior Knowledge and Home Language Connections

My home language is _____.

How do you say, **diagrams** in your home language? _____

2. Recognize Informational Text Features: Diagrams
In this informational textbook,

What is the diagram showing?

_____

What information is in the left-hand circle?

_____

What information is in the right-hand circle?

_____

How does the diagram help you understand what you are reading in the text?

_____

Modern humans were like Neanderthals in some ways. Both groups made tools, used fire and hunted animals. Both were intelligent. But modern humans were taller and more athletic. And they had a powerful new tool – complex language.

With language, modern humans could better communicate their ideas. This ability gave them a great advantage in the struggle for survival.

For thousands of years, Neanderthals and modern humans live near one another, but about 30,000 years ago the Neanderthals eventually disappeared.

Humans of the Late Stone Age

This information shwos how Neanderthals and modern humans were different.

Neanderthals
- Appeared about 200,000 years ago
- Simple language skills
- Short, stocky bodies
- Disappeared about 30,000 years ago

- Used stone tools
- Hunters
- Used fire

Modern Humans
- Appeared about 100,000 years ago
- Complex language skills
- Taller, more atheltic bodies
- Survived after disappearance of Neanderthals

This information shows the ways in which Neanderthals and modern humans were the same.

3. Extend Knowledge: Make Meaning

1. Diagrams help you understand the _____ in each chapter, heading, and subheading.
2. Diagrams will _____ you some of the ideas and concepts that are found in the text.
3. Chapter titles, headings, and subheadings are _____ to the diagrams.
4. Diagrams may help you _____ what you may already _____ about the idea or concept to what you are reading in the text.

related   connect   ideas and concepts   know   show

We learned that strong readers use _____ to understand the ideas and concepts that are presented in the text.

Print Concepts Lesson 10 Practice Page
Charts and Tables

1. Prior Knowledge and Home Language Connections

My home language is _____.

How do you say, **charts** or **tables** in your home language? _____

2. Recognize Informational Text Features: Charts and Tables

In this informational textbook,

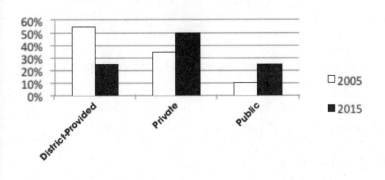

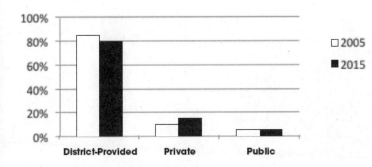

What are the tables showing? _____

What information is being shown in the black columns?

_____

What information is being shown in the white columns?

_____

How does the table help you understand what you are reading in the text? _____

_____

Changing Transportation Trends

Over the past ten years, how students are transported to school has changed.

Urban Transportation Trends

In urban areas, the trend is that more families are using public transportation to transport their children to and from school each day.

Rural Transportation Trends

In rural areas, where there is no public transportation available, the change in transportation patterns has been less significant.

3. Extend Knowledge: Make Meaning

1. Chapter titles, headings, and subheadings are _____ to the charts and tables.
2. Charts and tables may help you _____ what you may already _____ about the idea or concept to what you are reading in the text.
3. Charts and tables will _____ you some of the ideas and concepts that are found in the text.
4. Charts and tables help you understand the _____ in each chapter, heading, and subheading.

related   connect   ideas and concepts   know   show

We learned that strong readers use _____ and _____ to understand the ideas and concepts that are presented in the text.

Print Concepts Lesson 11 Practice Page
Maps, Keys, and Legends

1. Prior Knowledge and Home Language Connections

My home language is _____.

How do you say, **map**, **key**, or **legend** in your home language? _____

2. Recognize Informational Text Features: Maps, Keys, and Legends
In this informational textbook,

What is this map showing? _____

What does ★ represent? _____

What does ● represent? _____

What does ^ ^ ^ represent? _____

What direction is Los Angeles from Oakland? _____

If you were reading about the different regions in California, how would this map and key help you understand what you are reading in the text? _____

[

3. Extend Knowledge: Make Meaning

1. Chapter titles, headings, and subheadings are _____ to the maps and keys or legends.
2. Maps and keys or legends help you understand the _____ in each chapter, heading, and subheading.
3. Maps and keys or legends may help you _____ what you may already _____ about the idea or concept to what you are reading in the text.
4. Maps and keys or legends will _____ you some of the ideas and concepts that are found in the text.

related connect ideas and concepts know show

We learned that strong readers use _____ and _____ or _____ to understand the ideas and concepts that are presented in the text.

Print Concepts Lesson 12 Practice Page

Informational Text Features: Content Emphasis

1. Prior Knowledge and Home Language Connections

My home language is _____.

How do you say, **captions** in your home language? _____

Life Cycle of Painted Lady Butterfly

Black to purple with yellow-green stripes and long spines

The caterpillar attaches itself upside-down to a twig or leaf and forms a hard outer shell.

Pale green egg with 12-14 longitudinal ridges

Larva = Caterpillar
The caterpillar eats and growsa tremendous amount.

Egg
The size of a pinhead

The adult female lays an egg that was fertilized by the male.

Pupa = Chrysalis
Inside the pupa, the caterpillar changes into a butterfly.

A fully-grown adult butterfly emerges from the chrysalis.

Adult = Butterfly
Adults live for only a short time. They cannot eat; they only drink through their straw-like spiral proboscis. They will fly, mate, and reproduce.

2. Recognize Informational Text Features: Content Emphasis

In this informational textbook,

What is this diagram showing? _____

_____

What is a pupa or chrysalis? _____

_____

What happens inside the pupa or chrysalis? _____

_____

What is a larva? _____

_____

What color is the larva? _____

_____

What is an adult called? _____

_____

3. Extend Knowledge: Make Meaning

1. Captions, footnotes, margin notes, and text boxes may help you _____ what you may already _____ about the idea or concept to what you are reading in the text.
2. Captions, footnotes, margin notes, text boxes, and different types of font help you understand the _____ in each chapter, heading, and subheading.
3. Chapter titles, headings, and subheadings are _____ to the captions, footnotes, margin notes, and text boxes.
4. Captions, footnotes, margin notes, text boxes, and different types of font will _____ you some of the ideas and concepts that are found in the text.

related   connect   ideas and concepts   know   show

We learned that strong readers use _____, _____, _____, _____, and _____ to understand the ideas and concepts that are presented in the text.

Phonological Awareness

Lesson Objectives

- Recognize onset and rime words families

Metacognitive Strategy

Selective Auditory Attention

Academic Language

Pair, first, last, part, onset, rime

Materials

- Phonological Awareness Lesson 1 Practice Page

Pre-Assess

Student's ability to determine individual sounds in words.
Student's ability to identify the initial sound in a word.
Student's ability to identify words in the same word family.

Transfer Notes:

The concept of onset and rime does not transfer to Spanish, Vietnamese, Hmong, Tagalog, Korean, Cantonese, Mandarin, Farsi, or Arabic.

1 Recognize Onsets and Rimes

Introduce the Lesson

Say: *Today we will learn what a word family is, and how knowing a word family can help you learn many words. We will also learn how to identify the onset and rime that form the words in a word family. We will recognize onset and rime word families and read text that includes these words. Knowing these patterns will help you recognize approximately 500 of the most common high frequency words in English.*

Phonemic Awareness

Write the letter **c** and **lap** on the board.

Say: *This is the word, "**clap**."*

Say: *Listen to the word **clap**. What is the first letter in the word? /**c**/*

Say: *Listen to the word **clap** again. What are the last sounds that you hear? /**lap**/*

Say: *If I take away the letter **c**, what word do you hear?* **lap**

Say: *The **c** is the onset, and **lap** is the **rime**. The **lap** word family has many different words, each with a different onset, but the same rime, **lap**.*

Word	=	Onset	+	Rime
clap	=	c	+	lap

Repeat using /**t**/ and **-ake** then /**fl**/ and **-ash** onset and rime.

Elicit Prior Knowledge

Display and/or distribute the Practice Page and complete section 1 with students.

Ask: *Are there letters or symbols in your home language that combine to make a pattern that can be applied to create and read a group of words?*

Model: Onset and Rimes

Refer to section 2 of Practice Page 1 with students.

Say: *We will now look at some words and their onsets and rimes.*

Word	=	Onset	+	Rime	Word	=	Onset	+	Rime
clap	=	c	+	-lap	brain	=	br	+	-ain
flap	=	f	+	-lap	chain	=	ch	+	-ain
slap	=	s	+	-lap	grain	=	gr	+	-ain
bale	=	b	+	-ale	meat	=	m	+	-eat
scale	=	sc	+	-ale	heat	=	h	+	-eat
whale	=	wh	+	-ale	treat	=	tr	+	-eat

Practice: Recognize Onsets and Rimes

Read aloud section 3 of the Practice Page in a fluent voice emphasizing intonation and pronunciation of words. Invite students to echo read or chime on cue. Discuss content of text by asking text dependent questions to ensure comprehension. Ask students to recognize and call out cognates.

Ask: *What words do you see that are a part of one a word family with different onsets but the same rimes? Underline the words. Work with your partner to identify the words with different onsets but the same rimes.*

Practice: Recognize Words with Onsets and Rimes in Context

Complete section 3 of Practice Page 1 with students.

Say: *We will now categorize the words that you found in the text, above, with different onsets but the same rimes. Look at the list of rimes below, and write the word under the rime that you found in the word.*

-ain	-eat	-ay	-ice
train	beat	way	nice
grain	heat	day	price
-est	-it	-ink	-uck
best	sit	think	luck
rest	knit	drink	stuck

Extend Language Knowledge: Using Words in Context

Complete section 4 of Practice Page 1 with students.

Say: *We will now look at the words made from onsets and rimes that we have studied and use them in context. Read and complete each sentence with the word from the word bank that makes most sense. Take turns reading the completed sentences to your partner.*

1. The limping dog was **lame.**
2. We heard a **quack** and found a duck and chicken!
3. The **mail** will still be delivered through snow, sleet, and **hail.**
4. He tripped over the **chain.**
5. She wanted to **bake** a **cake.**
6. During the earthquake, the ground began to **shake.**

Spelling/Writing

Say: *Now we can practice writing compound words. I will pronounce each word and you will write it down.*

Pronounce one word at a time, stretching each sound.

Sample words: **pay, play, game, same, bail, jail**

Sample sentence: You have to **pay** to **play** the **game** the **same.** I think it is the same **price** as the **drink**.

Say: *Check your spelling with your partner. Verify the correct spelling and re-write as needed.*

Reflect and Review

Ask: *What did you learn today? Discuss with your partner.*

Provide sentence frames: One thing I learned was _____ . It reminds me of
_____ .It will help me with _____ .

Word Bank

Word	=	Onset	+	Rime
clap	=	c	+	lap
flap	=	f	+	ap
slap	=	s	+	lap
bale	=	b	+	ale
scale	=	sc	+	ale
whale	=	wh	+	ale
brain	=	br	+	ain
chain	=	ch	+	ain
grain	=	gr	+	ain
meat	=	m	+	eat
heat	=	h	+	eat
treat	=	tr	+	eat

Rime Bank

Rime	Rime	Rime	Rime	Rime	Rime
-ack	-an	-aw	-ick	-ing	-op
-all	-ank	-ay	-ide	-ink	-one
-ain	-ap	-eat	-ight	-ip	-or
-ake	-ash	-ell	-ill	-it	-uck
-ale	-at	-est	-in	-ock	-ug
-ame	-ate	-ice	-ine	-oke	-ump
					-unk

✔ **Formative Assessment**	
If the student completes each task correctly, precede to the next skill in the sequence.	
Did the student…?	**Intervention**
Identify the beginning sound or letter in words?	Provide several examples of word groups with the same beginning sound with word cards, then ask student sto identify one of the examples that does not stat with the same sound or letter.
Discern rime when onset is deleted from a spoken word?	Use picture cards and Elkonin boxes and have students practice removing the first toke starting with simple words.

2 Recognize Rhyming Words

Lesson Objectives

- Identify which part of a word is important to rhyming
- Recognize rhyming words

Metacognitive Strategy

Selective Auditory Attention

Academic Language

Pair, first, last, part, rhyme, rhyming

Materials

- Phonological Awareness Lesson 2 Practice Page

Pre-Assess

Student's ability to determine which part of a word is important to rhyming.
Given two rhyming words, notice if student can identify which part is the rhyming part.

Transfer notes:

The concept of rhyming words or symbols transfers in Spanish, Vietnamese, Hmong, Tagalog, Korean, Cantonese, Mandarin, Farsi, and Arabic.

Introduce the Lesson

Say: *Today we will learn what a rhyming word is. We will also learn how to identify the part of the word that is important to rhyming. We will recognize rhyming words and read text that includes these words.*

Phonemic Awareness

Write the words **cat** and **mat** on the board.

Say: *This **pair** of words rhyme. Let's all say the two words together: **cat** and **mat**. Notice how the end of each word sounds very similar?*

Say: *The words **cat** and **mat** rhyme because they have the same ending sound. Rhymes are very common in songs and poems, and make listening to the songs and poems more fun and interesting.*

Say: *What is the part of the word that rhymes in **cat** and **mat**? (-at)*

Write the words **bat, fat, hat, pat, rat, sat,** and **vat.**

Say: *What are some other words that rhyme with **cat** and **mat**? Let's all say the words together (As you are pointing to the words the **cat, mat, bat, fat, hat, pat, rat, sat,** and **vat**)*

Say: *(Referring to the word on the board for **cat, mat, bat, fat, hat, pat, rat, sat,** and **vat**) What is the part of the word that rhymes? (-at) Say it together with me: -at.*

Elicit Prior Knowledge

Display and/or distribute Practice Page 2 and complete section 1 with students.

Ask: *Are there words or symbols in your home language that rhyme like we are learning today? Can you think of a words or symbols in your home language that rhyme?*

Model: Rhyming Words

Refer to section 2 of Practice Page 2 with students.

Say: *We will now look at some rhyming words and the part of the word that is important to the rhyme.*

Rhyming words	Rhyming part
cat, mat	-at
dog, log	-og
might, light	-ight

Practice: Recognize Rhyming Words

Read aloud section 3 of Practice Page 2 in a fluent voice emphasizing intonation and pronunciation of rhyming words. Invite students to echo read or chime on cue. Discuss content of text by asking text dependent questions to ensure comprehension.Ask students to recognize and call out cognates, if any.

Ask: *What words do you see that rhyme in the poems? Underline the words. Work with your partner to identify the rhyming words.*

Practice: Recognize Rhyming Words in Context

Complete section 4 of the Practice Page with students.

Say: *We will now list the rhyming words that you found in the poems, above. After you write each set of rhyming words in the table, identify the rhyming part, as we did earlier.*

Rhyming words	Rhyming part
light, bright, tonight, might	-ight
dock, clock	-ock

Extend Language Knowledge: Make Meaning

Complete section 4 of Practice Page 2 with students.

Say: *Read the clues and choose the word from the word bank that best answers the clue. Take turns reading the clues and their answers with your partner.*

1. The opposite of left; the opposite of day (**right night**)
2. The heavy feline (**fat cat**)
3. The damp animal (**wet pet**)
4. A male after being out in the sun (**tan man**)
5. A flash of white (**bright light**)
6. Just tall enough (**right height**)

Spelling/Writing

Say: *Now we can practice writing rhyming words. I will pronounce each word and you will write it down.*

Pronounce one word at a time, stretching each sound.

Sample words: **clan, flan, cat, hat, flat, ran, van, fight, night**

Sample sentence: The **clan** sat down to eat the **flan** when the **cat** landed on the **hat** and made it **flat**, and then **ran** to the **van** where it got into a **fight** that very **night**.

Say: *Check your spelling with your partner. Verify the correct spelling and re-write as needed.*

Reflect and Review

Ask: *What did you learn today? Discuss with your partner.*

Provide sentence frames: One thing I learned was _____. It reminds me of _____.It will help me with _____.

Word Bank

Rhyming words	Rhyming part
chair, fair, hair, lair, pair	-air
bat, brat, cat, fat, flat, hat, mat, pat, rat, sat, slat, vat	-at
can, clan, fan, flan, man, pan, plan, ran, tan, van	-an
bet, get, jet, let, met, net, pet, set, vet, wet	-et
bit, fit, hit, kit, lit, pit, sit	-it
bright, fight, height, light, might, night, right	-ight
bog, cog, dog, fog, hog, jog, log, nog	-og
born, corn, horn, torn, worn	-orn
burn, churn, turn	-urn

✔Formative Assessment

If the student completes each task correctly, precede to the next skill in the sequence.

Did the student...?	Intervention
Recognize the pair of rhyming words?	Say the rhyming words aloud slowly. Have the students repeat each word slowly, emphasizing the part that sounds the same in each word.
Identify the part of the word that rhymed?	Tell the student the part of the pair of rhyming words that makes the words rhyme. Then use the picture cards to have the student discern the rhyming part correctly.

Lesson Objectives

- Recognize compound words
- Identify root words in compound words

Metacognitive Strategy

Selective Auditory Attention

Academic Language

Pair, first, last, part, root words, compound word

Materials

- Phonological Awareness Lesson 3 Practice Page

Pre-Assess

Student's ability to determine the root words in a compound word. Given a compound word, notice if student can break it correctly into its parts.

Transfer Notes:

The concept of compound words, or in idiographic systems, compound symbols, transfers in Spanish, Vietnamese, Hmong, Tagalog, Korean, Cantonese, Mandarin, Farsi, and Arabic.

3 Recognize Compound Words

Introduce the Lesson

Say: *Today we will learn what a compound word is and how it helps us use fewer words to say what we want to say. We will also learn how to divide* **compound words** *into the* **root words** *that form the compound word. We will recognize compound words and read text that includes these words.*

Phonemic Awareness

Write **hair brush** on the board.

Say: *This pair of words come together or combine to make a new word. This word is the compound word* **hairbrush.** *Let's all say the word together:* **hairbrush.**

Say: *The word,* **hairbrush,** *is a compound word. A compound word is a word made up of two or more root words. A compound word lets you use fewer words to say what you want to say. Instead of saying, "the brush that I use for brushing my hair," you can say,* **hairbrush.** *It lets you say what you want to say using one word instead of nine words.*

Say: *What is the first part, or root word, of the compound word* **hairbrush?** *(hair) What is the last part, or root word?* **(brush)**

Write the words **notebook** on the board.

Say: *(Pointing to the word* **notebook***) What is the first part or root word of this compound word?* **(note;** *point to* **note** *in the word) Say it together with me:* **note.** *What is the second part, or root word?* **(book;** *point to* **book** *in the word) Say it together with me:* **book.**

Say: *Now let's put them together to form the compound word, again. Say it together with me:* **notebook.** *Instead of saying, "the book in which you can write notes," you can say,* **notebook.**

Elicit Prior Knowledge

Display and/or distribute Practice Page 3 and complete section 1 with students.

Ask: *Are there words or symbols in your home language that combine to make a compound word or symbol like we are learning today? Can you think of a compound word or symbol in your home language?*

Model: Compound Words

Refer to section 2 of Practice Page 3 with students.

Say: *We will now look at some compound words and their root words.*

Echo read list of compound words and their root words.

Compound word	=	Root word	+	Root word
raindrop	=	rain	+	drop
playground	=	play	+	ground
waterfall	=	water	+	fall

Practice: Recognize Compound Words

Read aloud section 3 of Practice Page 3 in a fluent voice emphasizing intonation and pronunciation of compound words. Invite students to echo read or chime on cue. Discuss content of text by asking text dependent questions to ensure comprehension. Ask students to recognize and call out cognates.

Ask: *What words do you see that are compound words? Underline the words. Work with your partner to identify the compound words.*

Practice: Recognize Compound Words in Context

Complete section 4 of Practice Page 3 with students.

Say: *We will now list the compound words that you found in the text, above. After you write each compound word in the table, break it into its two root words, as we did earlier.*

Compound word	=	Root word	+	Root word
baseball	=	base	+	ball
downtown	=	down	+	town
thunderstorm	=	thunder	+	storm
afternoon	=	after	+	noon
peanuts	=	pea	+	nuts
hotdogs	=	hot	+	dogs
fireworks	=	fire	+	works
flashlight	=	flash	+	light

Extend Language Knowledge: Using Words in Context

Complete section 4 of Practice Page 3 with students.

Say: *We will now look at the compound words that we have studied and use them in context. Read and complete each sentence with the word from the word bank that makes most sense. Take turns reading the completed sentences to your partner.*

1. My **grandmother** likes **baseball.**
2. After an **earthquake,** the **railroad** tracks must be checked to be sure they're safe.
3. Always cross the street in the **crosswalk!**
4. I rode my **skateboard downtown** yesterday **afternoon.**
5. I take my **toothbrush** and **toothpaste** with me when I go away for the night.
6. My brother is a **daredevil** on a **motorcycle.**

Spelling/Writing

Say: *Now we can practice writing compound words. I will pronounce each word and you will write it down.*

Pronounce one word at a time, stretching each sound.

Say: Check your spelling with your partner. Verify the correct spelling and re-write as needed.

Reflect and Review

Ask: *What did you learn today? Discuss with your partner.*

Provide sentence frames: One thing I learned was _____. It reminds me of _____. It will help me with _____.

Home Connection

Say: The advantages of knowing two languages are many. You will be able to communicate and help your family and community if you keep your home language and learn English. Compound words help make what you are saying more understandable using fewer words. Share some of the compound words you learned today with a family member.

Word Bank

Compound word	=	Root word	+	Root word
fireworks	=	fire	+	works
baseball	=	base	+	ball
grandmother	=	grand	+	mother
crosswalk	=	cross	+	walk
railroad	=	rail	+	road
earthquake	=	earth	+	quake
skateboard	=	skate	+	board
whiteboard	=	white	+	board
chalkboard	=	chalk	+	board
thunderstorm	=	thunder	+	storm
afternoon	=	after	+	noon
motorcycle	=	motor	+	cycle
toothbrush	=	tooth	+	brush
downtown	=	down	+	town
fingerprint	=	finger	+	print
password	=	pass	+	word
hotdog	=	hot	+	dog

✔ Formative Assessment

If the student completes each task correctly, precede to the next skill in the sequence.

Did the student...?	Intervention
Recognize the correct order of the parts of a compound word?	Say the compound words aloud slowly. Have the students repeat each word slowly with the parts in the correct order.
Break down a compound word into its correct parts?	Tell the student the name of a compound word pictured on a card. Then use the picture cards to help the student discern the parts correctly.

Phonological Awareness Lesson 1 Practice Page

Recognizing Onsets and Rimes

1. Prior Knowledge and Home Language Connections

My home language is _____.

Today's onset and rimes compared to my home language:

Are there letters or symbols in your home language that combine to make a pattern that can be applied to create and read a group of words?

Word/Symbol	=	Onset (letters or symbols)	+	Rime (word or symbol family)
	=		+	

2. Recognize Onset and Rimes

Word	=	Onset	+	Rime	Word	=	Onset	+	Rime
clap	=	c	+	-lap	brain	=	br	+	-ain
flap	=	f	+	-lap	chain	=	ch	+	-ain
slap	=	s	+	-lap	grain	=	gr	+	-ain
bale	=	b	+	-ale	meat	=	m	+	-eat
scale	=	sc	+	-ale	heat	=	h	+	-eat
whale	=	wh	+	-ale	treat	=	tr	+	-eat

3. Shared Reading Text

Have you ever ridden on a train? It is exciting to travel through the fields of grain on the countryside and through cities on your way to your destination! You can beat the heat as the train makes its way throughout the day. It is a nice way to travel for the price, and the best part is you get to rest or sit and knit as the train keeps on rolling. If you are hungry or think you want a drink, you can go to the dining car, just like in a restaurant! With a little bit of luck you won't get stuck behind a freight train, and will arrive on time, ready to enjoy your visit at your destination!

4. Recognize Onset and Rimes in Context

-ain	-eat	-ay	-ice

-est	-it	-ink	-uck

5. Extend Language Knowledge: Using Words in Context

1. The limping dog was _____
2. We heard a _____ and found a duck and chicken!
3. The _____ will still be delivered through snow, sleet, and _____
4. He tripped over the _____
5. She wanted to _____ a _____
6. During the earthquake, the ground began to _____.

chain mail bake shake lame hail cake quack

One thing I learned was _____. It reminds me of _____. It will help me with _____.

Phonological Awareness Lesson 2 Practice Page

Recognize Rhyming Words

1. Prior Knowledge and Home Language Connections

My home language is _____.

Today's lesson compared to my home language:

Are there words in your home language that rhyme like we learned today? Can you think of two words that rhyme? What do each of them mean?

Rhyming Words	Meaning

2. Recognize Rhyming Words

Rhyming words	Rhyming part
cat, mat	-at
dog, log	-og
might, light	-ight

3. Shared Reading Text

Star light, star bright,
first star I see tonight,
I wish I may, I wish I might,
Have the wish I wish tonight.
Hickory, dickory, dock.
The mouse ran up the clock.
The clock struck one,
The mouse ran down,
Hickory, dickory, dock.

4. Recognize Rhyming Words

Rhyming words	Rhyming part

5. Extend Language Knowledge: Make Meaning

1. The opposite of left; the opposite of day _____ _____
2. The heavy feline_____ _____
3. The damp animal_____ _____
4. A male after being out in the sun_____ _____
5. A flash of white_____ _____
6. Just tall enough_____ _____

right height   wet pet   right night   bright light   fat cat   tan man

Something I learned today was _____. This knowledge helps me _____. I like _____.

Phonological Awareness Lesson 3 Practice Page
Recognize Compound Words

1. Prior Knowledge and Home Language Connections

My home language is _____.

Today's letters compared to my home language:

Are there words or symbols in your home language that combine to make a compound word or symbol like we are learning today? Can you think of a compound word or symbol in your home language?

Compound word/symbols	=	Root word	+	Root word
	=		+	drop

2. Recognize Compound Words

Compound word	=	Root word	+	Root word
raindrop	=	rain	+	drop
playground	=	play	+	ground
waterfall	=	water	+	fall

3. Shared Reading Text

Have you been to a baseball game downtown? It is a lot of fun! You will be able to see the two teams do their best to win the game. You can cheer for your favorite team, and will probably get a chance to sing, "Take Me Out to the Ball Game," during the seventh-inning stretch! Be sure to take warm clothes and an umbrella to keep you dry if there is a thunderstorm in the forecast. If you are able to attend an afternoon game, you may be there late enough to enjoy some peanuts and hotdogs for dinner. An extra special treat would be to see the fireworks at the end of the game, but be sure to bring a flashlight to help you find your way back home!

4. Recognize Compound Words in Context

Compound word	=	Root word	+	Root word
	=		+	
	=		+	
	=		+	
	=		+	
	=		+	
	=		+	
	=		+	
	=		+	

5. Extend Language Knowledge: Using Words in Context

1. My _____ likes _____.
2. After an _____, the _____ tracks must be checked to be sure they're safe.
3. Always cross the street in the _____!
4. I rode my _____ _____ yesterday _____.
5. I take my _____ and _____ with me when I go away for the night.
6. My brother is a _____ on a _____.

crosswalk toothbrush daredevil grandmother downtown earthquake afternoon baseball railroad motorcycle toothpaste skateboard

One thing I learned was _____. It reminds me of _____. It will help me with _____.

Phonics

1 Continuous Sounding Consonants l, m, and n

Lesson Objectives

- Identify and name the letters **l**, **m**, and **n**.
- Produce the sound of letters **l**, **m**, and **n**.
- Relate the sound **/l/**, **/m/**, and **/n/** to each corresponding letter.
- Recognize sounds **/l/**, **/m/**, and **/n/** in words orally and in writing.
- Recognize letters in initial, medial and final position within words.
- Read and write common high frequency words.

Metacognitive Strategy

Selective auditory attention

Academic Language

letter name, letter sound, initial sound, medial sound, final sound.

Materials

- Frieze Cards l, m, n
- Phonics Lesson 1 Practice Page

Pre-Assess

- Recognition of sounds represented by the blends **sc-**, **sk-**, **sn-**, **sp-**, **st-**, **sw-**.
- Identification of letters used to represent the souds **/sc/**, **/sk/**, **/sn/**, **/sp/**, **/st/**, **/sw/**

Transfer notes:

The sound **/l/** is used, or approximated in most languages. In Spanish, a double **ll** makes the sound **/y/**. Teach that in English **ll** makes the **/l/** sound.

Introduce the Lesson

Say: *Today we will identify letter names and sounds. We will recognize these letters in the beginning, middle and end of words and read text that includes these letters.*

Sound-Spelling Correspondence

Say: *The letters we will be studying today represent continuous sounds. These sounds can be pronounced continuously and are easy to blend with other sounds.*

Display the **Ll** Frieze Card.

Say: *This is capital **L**. This is lowercase **l**. Listen to this sound /l/. Say it with me: /lll/. Now say it on your own: /l/. We write the sound /l/ with the letter l. Watch me write letter l. Now you write the letter l.*

Ask: *What is the name of the letter? **l** What sound does the letter make? /l/*

Repeat with letters **m** and **n**, and evaluate the students' ability to name each letter, identify the sound it makes, and write it.

Elicit Prior Knowledge

Display and/or distribute the Lesson 1 Practice Page and complete section 1 with students. Elicit students' prior knowledge and acknowledge primary language background.

Ask: *Which of these sounds are the same or different in your home language? Which of these letters are the same or different in your home language? Can you think of a word that has any of these sounds or letters in your home language?*

Model: Recognize Letter Position in Words

Create and fill-in a chart for each letter, one letter at a time.

Say: *The letter _____ can be found at the beginning, middle or end of a word.*

Letter	Initial (Beginning)	Medial (Middle)	Final (Ending)
l	list	color	equal
m	man	name	team
n	new	find	win

Practice: Identify Continuous Sounding Consonants

Read aloud section 2 of the Lesson 1 Practice Page in a fluent voice emphasizing intonation and pronunciation of words and targeted sounds. Invite students to echo read. Discuss content of text by asking text dependent questions to ensure comprehension. Ask students to recognize and call out cognates.

Practice: Recognize Letter Position in Continuous Sounding Consonants Words

Complete section 3 of the Lesson 1 Practice Page with students.

Say: *We will now look at words that include the letters we have studied either at the beginning, middle, or at end of a word.*

Say: *Next, we are going to practice pronunciation by breaking up the words into syllables. We will clap out the syllables as we say each word then annotate syllables with a slash. When done annotating, read each word aloud to your partner.*

Extend Language Knowledge

Practice: Categorize Words with Continuous Sounding Consonants

Complete section 4 of the Lesson 1 Practice Page with students.

Say: *Now you are going to classify words based on where the consonants **l, m,** and **n** are positioned in those words. Read each word aloud to your partner, decide where to place it. Write the word in the column that corresponds to its position.*

Provide examples. Remind students that a double **ll** in English makes the **/l/** sound.

Letter	Initial	Medial	Final
l	love	violin	ball
m	might	family	swim
n	noise	honor	clown

Spelling/Writing

Say: *Now we can practice writing the sounds we hear in each word. I will pronounce each word and you will write it down.*

Pronounce one word at a time, stretching each sound.

Sample words: **list**, **color**, **equal**, **man**, **name**, **team**, **new**, **find**, **win**.

Sample sentence: Find the list of the new team names and colors.

Say: *Check your spelling with your partner. Verify the correct spelling and re-write as needed.*

Reflect and Review

Ask: *What did you learn today? Discuss with your partner.*

Provide sentence frames: Today I learned that _____. This is important because _____. I now know _____.

Word Bank

Letter	Initial	Medial	Final
l	list	alarm	ball
	lock	salad	mail
	love	wallet	bowl
	letter	dollar	spell
	laugh	violin	pencil
m	mad	family	gym
	make	lemon	home
	mask	woman	name
	match	tomato	swim
	might	number	scream
n	nap	peanut	brain
	next	banana	clean
	near	honor	clown
	noise	manner	green
	night	another	phone

✓Formative Assessment

If the student completes each task correctly, precede to the next skill in the sequence.

Did the student...?	Intervention
Pronounce letter in isolation? Pronounce letter in words?	Use mirrors to show movement of mouth, tongue, and teeth as the sound is produced. Use hand over mouth to explore movement of air as the sound is produced.
Do they recognize meaning of words in context?	Explain meaning of words before and after reading the text.
Write letters correctly?	Use mirrors to show movement of mouth, tongue, and teeth as the sound is produced. Use hand over mouth to explore movement of air as the sound is produced.
Spell targeted sounds correctly?	Use simple (CVC) words, practice sound segmentation and blending, use interactive and guided writing.

2 Continuous Sounding Consonants f, r, s

Metacognitive Strategy

Selective auditory attention

Academic Language

letter name, letter sound, initial sound, medial sound, final sound

Materials

- Frieze Cards: Ff, Rr, Ss
- Phonics Lesson 2 Practice Page

Pre-Assess

- Recognition of sounds represented by the letters **f**, **r**, **s**
- Identification of letters used to represent the sounds **/f/**, **/r/**, **/s/**

Transfer notes

In English a double consonant at the end of a word has same sound as the single consonant.

The sound **/f/** does not transfer in Korean or Tagalog.

The sound **/r/** does not transfer in Korean, Cantonese, Mandarin, Farsi or Arabic.

Introduce the Lesson

Say: *Today we will identify the names of three letters and the sounds they make. We will recognize these letters in the beginning, middle and end of words and read text that includes words with these letters.*

Phonemic Awareness and Sound-Spelling Correspondence

Show the **Ff** frieze card.

Say: *This is a capital or uppercase F. This is lowercase f. Listen to this sound /f/. This letter makes a continuous or ongoing sound. Say it with me: /ffff/. Now you say it.*

Say: *The letter f makes the /f/ sound. Watch me write the letter f. Now you write it.*

Ask: *What is the name of the letter? (f) What sound does the letter f make? (/f/)*

Repeat with letters **r** and **s**, and assess students' ability to recognize the name and sound of these letters, and to write them.

Elicit Prior Knowledge

Display the Lesson 2 Practice Page. Prompt students to think about their primary language as you work together to complete section 1.

Ask: *Is the /f/ sound the same in your home language or different? Is the /f/ sound represented by the letter f in your home language? If not what, letter makes the /f/ sound? What is a word in your home language that has the /f/ sound?*

Allow time for students to complete the **f** row on the table. Then repeat the same questions for the letters **r** and **s**.

Model: Recognize Letter Position in Words

Create this chart on the board, emphasizing the target letter sounds as you write and pronounce each sample word.

Say: *The letter f and the /f/ sound can be at the beginning, middle or end of a word.*

Say: *You can hear the /f/ sound at the beginning of the word fun; in the middle of the word after; and at the end of the word surf.*

Repeat with the letters **r** and **s**.

Letter	Initial (Beginning)	Medial (Middle)	Final (Ending)
f	fun	after	surf
r	run	park	ever
s	snake	insect	miss

Practice: Continuous Sounding Consonants

Read aloud section 2 of the Lesson 2 Practice Page in a fluent voice, emphasizing intonation and pronunciation of words and targeted sounds. Invite students to echo read or chime on cue. Ensure comprehension by asking text dependent questions. Have students identify cognates.

Practice: Recognize Letter Position in Words

Display the Word Bank and complete section 3 of the Lesson 2 Practice Page with students.

Say: *Now let's look at words with letters and letter sounds that we have been learning about. The letters are at the beginning, middle or end of each word.*

Have students echo read all or some of the words on the list from left to right emphasizing the targeted letter sound. Allow time for them to fill in the chart.

Extend Language Knowledge

Practice: Use Words in Context

Complete section 4 of the Lesson 2 Practice Page with students.

Say: *Let's think about words with the letters we have been discussing today: **f**, **r**, and **s**. Complete each sentence using words from the word bank on the Practice Page.*

1. Pigs, cows, and horses live on a **farm**.
2. When the sun **sets**, it gets **dark** outside.
3. I like to go down the **slide** at the **park**.
4. Bananas are mushy when they are too **ripe**.
5. Our **class** stayed in for recess because of the **rain** .
6. I do my homework **after** school.

Writing

Say: *Practice writing the sounds you hear as I say each word. Then write the word. I will also use the word in a sentence.*

Pronounce one word at a time from the Word List below, stretching each sound. Use the word in a sentence, and repeat it again after the sentence. For example, say the word **fun**. Then say: *Playing games is lots of fun.* Repeat the word **fun** after the sentence.

Help students as needed to form letters or recognize letters that form these words.

Sample words: **fun, run, son, after, park, outside, surf, ever, bus**

Have students confirm their spelling with a partner, making corrections as needed.

Reflect and Review

Ask: *What did you learn today?*

Have students work with their partners to complete the sentence frames at the end of the Lesson 2 Practice Page, assisting as needed.

Home Connection

Say: *Your family members are very interested in you learning English. They enjoy it when you share what you do at school with them. You may want to share the lesson we did today with a family member. Tell him or her about the letter sounds you learned today, how they are the same or different than the sounds and letters (or symbols) in your home language, and show them the meaning of words you learned today.*

Word Bank

Location	Initial (Beginning)	Medial (Middle)	Final (Ending)
f	face farm feet food five fish	sofa left infant playful barefoot goldfish	safe roof hoof chef loaf leaf
r	rat radio ring rain read rocket	bird horse arm fork shirt park	jar tear pear chair doctor flower
s	sit sick seat said soap sock	listen eraser insect whistle beside popsicle	yes bus rots lips sets miss

✓ Formative Assessment

If the student completes each task correctly, proceed to the next skill in the sequence.

Did the student...?	Intervention
Pronounce letter in isolation Pronounce letter in words	Use a mirror to show movement of mouth, tongue, and teeth as the sound is produced. Use hand over mouth to explore movement of air as the sound is produced.
Do they recognize meaning of words in context	Explain meaning of words before and after reading the text.
Write letters correctly	Provide additional handwriting practice
Spell targeted sounds correctly	Use simple (CVC) words, practice sound segmentation and blending, use interactive and guided writing.

3 Continuous Sounding Consonants v, w, y, z

Lesson Objectives

Identify and name the letters **v**, **w**, **y** and **z**.
Produce the sound of letters **v**, **w**, **y** and **z**.
Relate the sound /v/, /w/, /y/ and /z/ to each corresponding letter.
Recognize sounds /v/, /w/, /y/ and /z/ in words orally and in writing.
Recognize letters **w**, **y** and **z** in initial, medial and final position within words.
Read and write common high frequency words.

Metacognitive Strategy

Selective auditory attention

Academic Language

letter name, letter sound, initial sound, medial sound, final sound

Materials

- Sound Spelling Cards v, w, y, z
- Phonics Lesson 3 Practice Page

Pre-Assess

Student's ability to recognize the sound represented by the targeted letters of the alphabet and to identify the letter used to represent the corresponding sound.

Transfer Notes:

In English a double consonant at the end of a word has same sound as the single consonant.

The sound /v/ does not transfer in Korean, Cantonese, Mandarin, Farsi or Arabic.

The sound /w/ does not transfer in Vietnamese, Hmong, Mandarin or Farsi

The sound /y/ does not transfer in Vietnamese or Mandarin

The sound /z/ does not transfer in Spanish, Korean, Mandarin or Cantonese

Introduce the Lesson

Say: *Today we will identify the names of four letters and the sounds they make. We will recognize these letters in the beginning, middle and end of words and read text that includes words with these letters.*

Phonemic Awareness and Sound-Spelling Correspondence

Show the **Vv** frieze card.

Say: *This is a capital or uppercase **V**. This is lowercase **v**.*

Say: *Listen to this sound /v/. This letter makes a continuous or ongoing sound. Say it with me: /vvvv/. Now say it on your own: /v/. The letter **v** makes the /v/.sound. Watch me write the letter **v**. Now you write the letter **v**.*

Ask: *What is the name of the letter?(**v**) What sound does the letter **f** make? (/v/)*

Repeat with letters **w**, **y**, and **z,** and assess students' ability to recognize the name and sound of these letters, and to write them.

Elicit Prior Knowledge

Display the Lesson 3 Practice Page. Prompt students to think about their primary language as you work together to complete section 1.

Ask: *Is the /v/ sound the same in your home language or different? Is the /v/ sound represented by the letter **v** in your home language? If not what, letter makes the /v/ sound? What is a word in your home language that has the /v/sound?*

*Allow time for students to complete the **v** row on the table. Then repeat the same questions for the letters **w**, **y**, and **z**.*

Model: Recognize Letter Position in Words

Create this chart on the board, emphasizing the target letter sounds as you write and pronounce each sample word.

Say: *The letter **v** and the /v/sound can be at the beginning, middle, or end of a word. You can hear the /v/ sound at the beginning of the word **very** and in the middle of **ever**.*

Repeat with the letters **w**, **y**, and **z**.

Letter	Initial (Beginning)	Medial (Middle)	Final (Ending)
v	very	ever	(very rare ending)
w	went	tower	cow
y	young	layer	baby
z	zebra	lazy	quiz

Practice: Continuous Sounding Consonants

Read aloud section 2 of the Lesson 3 Practice Page in a fluent voice, emphasizing intonation and pronunciation of words and targeted sounds. Invite students to echo read or chime on cue. Ensure comprehension by asking text dependent questions. Have students identify cognates.

Practice: Recognize Letter Position in Words

Display the Word Bank and complete section 3 of the Lesson 3 Practice Page with students.

Say: *Now let's look at words with letters and letter sounds that we have been learning about. The letters are at the beginning, middle or end of each word.*

Have students echo read all or some of the words on the list from left to right emphasizing the targeted letter sound. Allow time for them to fill in the chart.

Extend Language Knowledge

Practice: Use Words in Context

Complete section 4 of the Lesson 3 practice page with students.

Say: *Let's think about words with the letters we have been discussing today: v, w, y, and z. Complete each sentence using words from the word bank on the Practice Page.*

- There are many different countries in the **world**.
- **Zebras** have black and white stripes.
- Have you **ever** seen a shooting star?
- We **went** to the store after school.
- I got a 100% on the math **quiz**.
- Cakes have a **layer** of frosting.
- A **cow** lives on a farm.

Writing

Say: *Practice writing the sounds you hear as I say each word. Then write the word. I will also use the word in a sentence.*

Pronounce one word at a time from the Word List below, stretching each sound. Use the word in a sentence, and repeat it again after the sentence. For example, say the word **baby**. Then say: *The baby is sleeping in her crib.* Repeat the word **baby** after the sentence.

Help students as needed to form letters or recognize letters that form these words.

Sample words: **went, zoo, visit, new, baby, zebras, workers, walk, lazy,**

Have students confirm their spelling with a partner, making corrections as needed.

Reflect and Review

Ask: *What did you learn today? Discuss with your partner.*

Have students work with their partners to complete the sentence frames at the end of the Lesson 2 Practice Page, assisting as needed.

Home Connection

Say: *Your family members are very interested in you learning English. They enjoy it when you share what you do at school with them. You may want to share the lesson we did today with a family member. Tell him or her about the letter sounds you learned today, how they are the same or different than the sounds and letters (or symbols) in your home language, and show them the meaning of words you learned today.*

Word Bank

Location	Initial (Beginning)	Medial (Middle)	Final (Ending)
v	vest vine vase visor voice video	seven shaving travel driver cover advice	[Very few words in English end in consonant v]
w	wait want walk watch world wings	walkway awkward unaware microwave reward	brew grew stew elbow tomorrow wheelbarrow
y	yard yell youth yolk year yummy	kayak lawyer flyer loyal royal New Year	day any grey fly laundry poetry
z	zebra zero zipper zone zoom zapped	puzzle wizard lizard razor dozen freezer	whiz frizz waltz topaz quartz showbiz

✓Formative Assessment

If the student completes each task correctly, proceed to the next skill in the sequence.

Did the student...?	Intervention
Pronounce letter in isolation Pronounce letter in words	Use a mirror to show movement of mouth, tongue, and teeth as the sound is produced. Use hand over mouth to explore movement of air as the sound is produced.
Do they recognize meaning of words in context	Explain meaning of words before and after reading the text.
Write letters correctly	Provide additional handwriting practice
Spell targeted sounds correctly	Use simple (CVC) words, practice sound segmentation and blending, use interactive and guided writing.
Did the student...?	Intervention
Pronounce letter in isolation Pronounce letter in words	Use a mirror to show movement of mouth, tongue, and teeth as the sound is produced. Use hand over mouth to explore movement of air as the sound is produced.
Do they recognize meaning of words in context	Explain meaning of words before and after reading the text.

4 Stop Sound Consonants b, t, g

Introduce the Lesson

Say: *Today we will identify the names of three letters and the sounds they make. We will recognize these letters in the beginning, middle and end of words and read text that includes words with these letters.*

Phonemic Awareness and Sound-Spelling Correspondence

Show the **Bb** Frieze card.

Say: *This is capital or upper case **B**. This is lowercase **b**.*

Say: *Listen to this sound /**b**/. Say it with me: /**b**/. Now say it on your own: /**b**/.*

Say: *We represent the sound /**b**/ with the letter **b**. Watch me write letter **b**. Now you write the letter **b**.* **Ask:** *What is the name of the letter? (**b**) What sound does the letter make? (/**b**/)*

Repeat with letters **t** and **g** (using the hard **g** sound, as in **goat**), and assess students' ability to recognize the name and sound of these letters, and to write them.

Elicit Prior Knowledge

Display the Lesson 4 Practice Page. Prompt students to think about their primary language as you work together to complete section 1.

Ask: *Is the /**b**/ sound the same in your home language or different? Is the /**b**/ sound represented by the letter **b**? If not, what letter makes the /**b**/ sound? What is a word in your home language that has the /**b**/ sound?*

Allow time for students to complete the **b** row on the table. Then repeat the same questions for the letters **t** and **g**.

Model: Recognize Letter Position in Words

Create this chart on the board, emphasizing the target letter sounds as you write and pronounce each sample word.

Say: *The letter **b** and the /**b**/ sound can be at the beginning, middle or end of a word.*

Say: *You can hear the /**b**/ sound at the beginning of the word **big**; in the middle of the word **maybe**; and at the end of the word **run**. Repeat with the letters **t** and **g**.*

Letter	Initial (Beginning)	Medial (Middle)	Final (Ending)
b	big	maybe	rub
t	ten	water	ant
g	get	forget	wag

Practice: Continuous Sounding Consonants

Read aloud section 2 of the Lesson 4 Practice Page in a fluent voice, emphasizing intonation and pronunciation of words and targeted sounds. Invite students to echo read or chime on cue. Ensure comprehension by asking text dependent questions. Have students identify cognates.

Practice: Recognize Letter Position in Words

Display the Word Bank and complete section 3 of the Lesson 4 Practice Page with students.

Say: *Now let's look at words with letters and letter sounds that we have been learning about. The letters are either at the beginning, middle or end of a word. Echo read all or some of the list from left to right emphasizing the targeted letter.*

Extend Language Knowledge

Practice: Use Words in Context

Complete section 4 of the Lesson 4 Practice Page with students.

Say: *Let's think about words with the letters we have been discussing today: **b**, **t**, and **g**. Complete each sentence using words from the word bank on the Practice Page.*

1. The **big** house had lots of rooms.
2. My favorite **sport** is **baseball**.
3. I **giggle** when you say something funny.
4. You should drink lots of **water** on hot days.
5. Worms **wiggle** in the dirt.
6. The **better team** will win the **game** today.

Writing

Say: *Practice writing the sounds you hear as I say each word. Then write the word. I will also use the word in a sentence.*

Pronounce one word at a time from the Word List below, stretching each sound. Use the word in a sentence, and repeat it again after the sentence. For example, say the word **good**. Then say: *Molly is a good friend.* Repeat the word **good** after the sentence.

Help students as needed to form letters or recognize letters that form these words.

Sample words: **list, bear, gum, tiger, better, coat, robot, knob**

Have students confirm their spelling with a partner, making corrections as needed.

Reflect and Review

Ask: *What did you learn today?*

Have students work with their partners to complete the sentence frames at the end of the Lesson 4 Practice Page, assisting as needed.

Home Connection

Say: *Your family members are very interested in you learning English. They enjoy it when you share what you do at school with them. You may want to share the lesson we did today with a family member. Tell him or her about the letter sounds you learned today, how they are the same or different than the sounds and letters (or symbols) in your home language, and show them the meaning of words you learned today*

Word Bank

Location	Initial (Beginning)	Medial (Middle)	Final (Ending)
b	both	robot	job
	bath	bobcat	crab
	butter	habit	club
	bear	robin	scrub
	bean	cowboy	swab
	bone	remember	grab
t	two	liter	eat
	toad	water	boat
	tooth	motel	feet
	talk	biting	fruit
	taste	potato	light
	touch	guitar	float
g	good	tiger	bug
	gift	yoga	rag
	goat	again	pig
	gallon	dragon	fog
	garage	magnet	slug
	gorilla	alligator	flag

✔ Formative Assessment

If the student completes each task correctly, proceed to the next skill in the sequence.

Did the student…?	Intervention
Pronounce letter in isolation Pronounce letter in words	Use a mirror to show movement of mouth, tongue, and teeth as the sound is produced. Use hand over mouth to explore movement of air as the sound is produced.
Recognize meaning of words in context	Explain meaning of words before and after reading the text.
Write letters correctly	Provide additional handwriting practice
Spell targeted sounds correctly	Use simple (CVC) words, practice sound segmentation and blending, use interactive and guided writing.

Lesson Objectives

- Identify and name the letters **p, h,** and **j**.
- Produce the sound of letters p, h, and j.
- Relate the sound **/p/, /h/,** and /j/ to each corresponding letter.
- Recognize sounds **/p/, /h/,** and **/j/** in words orally and in writing.
- Recognize letters **p, h,** and **j** in initial, medial and final position within words.
- Read and write common high frequency words.

Metacognitive Strategy

Selective auditory attention

Academic Language

letter name, letter sound, initial sound, medial sound, final sound.

Materials

- Frieze Cards: Pp, Hh, Jj
- Phonics Lesson 5 Practice Page

Pre-Assess

- Recognition of sounds represented by the letters **p, h,** and **j**
- Identification of letters used to represent the sounds **/p/, /h/,** and **/j/**

Transfer Notes:

The sound **/h/** transfers to Spanish but it is represented by the letter **j**. The letter **h** is silent.

The sound **/h/** does not transfer to Mandarin. The sound **/p/** doesn't transfer to Arabic.

The sound **/g/** approximates a similar sound in Hmong and Korean and does not transfer to Mandarin, Farsi, or Arabic.

5 Stop Sound Consonants p, h, j

Introduce the Lesson

Say: *Today we will identify the names of three letters and the sounds they make. We will recognize these letters in the beginning, middle and end of words and read text that includes words with these letters*

Phonemic Awareness and Sound-Spelling Correspondence

Show the **Pp** Frieze card to review the sound. *Say: This is capital or uppercase **P**. This is lowercase **p**.*

Say: *Listen to this sound /**p**/. This letter makes a stop sound. Your lips block the air so that airflow stops when you pronounce the sound. Say it with me: /**p**/. Now say it on your own, paying attention to your lips: /**p**/.*

Say: *The letter **p** makes the /**p**/ sound. Watch me write the letter **p**. Now you write the letter **p**.*

Ask: *What is the name of the letter? (**p**) What sound does the letter make? (/**p**/)*

Repeat with letters **h** and **j**, and assess students' ability to recognize the name and sound of these letters, and to write them. Point out that for some stop sounds the tongue, rather than the lips, stops the air flow.

Elicit Prior Knowledge

Display the Lesson 5 Practice Page. Prompt students to think about their primary language as you work together to complete section 1.

Ask: *Is the /**p**/ sound the same in your home language or different? Is the /**p**/ sound represented by the letter **p** in your home language? If not what, letter makes the /**p**/ sound? What is a word in your home language that has the /**p**/ sound?*

Allow time for students to complete the **p** row on the table. Then repeat the same questions for the letters **h** and **j**.

Model: Recognize Letter Position in Words

Create this chart on the board, emphasizing the target letter sounds as you write and pronounce each sample word.

Say: *The letter **p** and the /**p**/ sound can be at the beginning, middle or end of a word.*

Say: *You can hear the /**p**/ sound at the beginning of the word **park**; in the middle of the word **super**; and at the end of the word **sip**.*

Repeat with the letters **h** and **j**.

Letter	Initial (Beginning)	Medial (Middle)	Final (Ending)
p	park	super	sip
h	hot	behind	(none found)
j	jump	enjoy	(none found)

Practice: Stop Sound Consonants

Read aloud section 2 of the Lesson 5 Practice Page in a fluent voice, emphasizing intonation and pronunciation of words and targeted sounds. Invite students to echo read or chime on cue. Ensure comprehension by asking text dependent questions. Have students identify cognates.

Ask: *What words do you see that include the letters* **p, h,** *or* **j?** *Underline the words. Work with a partner to identify the words.*

Practice: Recognize Letter Position

Display the Word Bank and complete section 3 of the Lesson 5 Practice Page with students.

Say: *Now let's look at words with letters and letter sounds that we have been learning about. The letters are at the beginning, middle or end of each word. Echo read all or some of the list from left to right emphasizing the targeted letter sound.*

Extend Language Knowledge
Use Words in Context

Complete section 4 of the Lesson 5 Practice Page with students.

Say: *Let's think about words with the letters we have been discussing today:* **p, h,** *and* **j.** *Complete each sentence using words from the word bank on the Practice Page.*

1. I like **pizza** with extra cheese.
2. Some **kids** like to **jump** rope.
3. We were **happy** about winning the soccer game.
4. I **enjoy** playing basketball.
5. My brother likes to **help** me with my homework.
6. I hide **behind** the big tree when I play **hide** and seek.

Writing

Say: *Practice writing the sounds you hear as I say each word. Then write the word. I will also use the word in a sentence.*

Pronounce one word at a time from the Word List below, stretching each sound. Use the word in a sentence, and repeat it again after the sentence. For example, say the word **hot**. Then say: *The fire is hot!* Repeat the word **hot** after the sentence.

Help students as needed to form letters or recognize letters that form these words.

Sample words: **enjoy, park, hop, skip, jump, hot, help, keep**

Have students confirm their spelling with a partner, making corrections as needed.

Reflect and Review

Ask: *What did you learn today? Discuss with your partner.*

Have students work with their partners to complete the sentence frames at the end of the Lesson 5 Practice Page, assisting as needed.

Word Bank

Location	Initial (Beginning)	Medial (Middle)	Final (Ending)
p	party pencil penny point pizza parade	copy open camper super napkin depend	hoop ship trip sweep ketchup asleep
h	hall hand heart health height house	uphill reheat beehive rehearsal fishhook forehead	
j	joy just jeans joke journal jungle	major object project subject reject hijack	(none found)

✓ Formative Assessment

If the student completes each task correctly, precede to the next skill in the sequence.

Did the student...?	Intervention
Pronounce letter in isolation Pronounce letter in words	Use a mirror to show movement of mouth, tongue, and teeth as the sound is produced. Use hand over mouth to explore movement of air as the sound is produced.
Do they recognize meaning of words in context	Explain meaning of words before and after reading the text.
Write letters correctly	Provide additional handwriting practice
Spell targeted sounds correctly	Use simple (CVC) words, practice sound segmentation and blending, use interactive and guided writing.

6 Stop Sound Consonants k, q, x

Introduce the Lesson

Say: *Today we will identify the names of three letters and the sounds they make. We will recognize these letters in the beginning, middle and end of words and read text that includes words with these letters.*

Phonemic Awareness and Sound-Spelling Correspondence

Show the **Kk** Frieze card to review the sound.

Say: *This is capital or uppercase K. This is lowercase k.*

Say: *Listen to this sound /k/. This letter makes a stop sound. Your tongue blocks the air so that airflow stops when you pronounce the sound. Say it with me: /k/. Now say it on your own, paying attention to your tongue: /k/.*

Say: *The letter k makes the /k/ sound. Watch me write the letter k. Now you write the letter k.*

Ask: *What is the name of the letter? (k) What sound does the letter make? (/k/)*

Repeat with letters **q** and **x**, and assess students' ability to recognize the name and sound of these letters, and to write them.

Elicit Prior Knowledge

Display the Lesson 6 Practice Page. Prompt students to think about their primary language as you work together to complete section 1.

Ask: *Is the /k/ sound the same in your home language or different? Is the /k/ sound represented by the letter k in your home language? If not what, letter makes the /k/ sound? What is a word in your home language that has the /k/ sound?*

Allow time for students to complete the **k** row on the table. Then repeat the same questions for the letters **q** and **x**.

Model: Recognize Letter Position in Words

Create this chart on the board, emphasizing the target letter sounds as you write and pronounce each sample word.

Say: *The letter k and the /k/ sound can be at the beginning, middle or end of a word.*

Say: *You can hear the /k/ sound at the beginning of the word key; in the middle of the word making; and at the end of the word hawk.*

Repeat with the letters **q** and **x**. Note: There are not words that end with the /q/ sound.

Letter	Initial (Beginning)	Medial (Middle)	Final (Ending)
k	key	making	hawk
q	quote	require	(none found)
x	excite	taxes	wax

Practice: Identify Stop Sound Consonants

Lesson Objectives

Identify and name the letters **k, q,** and **x.**
Produce the sound of letters **k, q,** and **x.**
Relate the sound **/k/, /q/,** and **/x/** to each corresponding letter.
Recognize sounds **/k/, /q/,** and **/x/** in words orally and in writing.
Recognize letters **k, q,** and **x** in initial, medial and final position within words.
Read and write common high frequency words.

Metacognitive Strategy

Selective auditory attention

Academic Language

letter name, letter sound, initial sound, medial sound, final sound

Materials

Frieze Cards: **Kk, Qq, Xx**
Phonics Lesson 6 Practice page

Pre-Assess

- ability to recognize sounds represented by the letters **k, q,** and **x**
- ability to identify the letter used to represent the sounds **/k/, /q/,** and **/x/**

Transfer Notes:

The sound /k/ transfers to Spanish, Mandarin, Korean, Vietnamese, Arabic, and Farsi.

The sound /q/ does not transfer to Mandarin, Arabic, Farsi, or Hmong.

The sound /x/ does not transfer to Mandarin, Vietnamese, Arabic, Farsi, or Hmong.

Read aloud section 2 of the Lesson 6 Practice Page, using intonation and emphasizing targeted letter sounds. Ensure comprehension by asking text dependent questions. Have students identify cognates.

Practice: Recognize Letter Position in Words with Stop Sound Consonants

Display the Word Bank and complete section 3 of the Lesson 6 Practice Page with students.

Say: *Now let's look at words with letters and letter sounds that we have been learning about. The letters are at the beginning, middle or end of each word. Echo read all or some of the list from left to right emphasizing the targeted letter sound.*

Extend Language Knowledge

Practice: Use Words in Context

Complete section 4 of the Lesson 6 Practice Page with students.

Say: *Let's think about words with the letters we have been discussing today:* **k, q,** *and* **x.** *Complete each sentence using words from the word bank on the Practice Page.*

1. I **keep** my money in a safe place.
2. The **king** and **queen** live in a castle.
3. The **x-ray** machine **required** a skilled worker to operate.
4. My **book** is due at the library today.
5. There is a **fox** living in the woods near my house.
6. I **lock** the door with a **key** so no one can get inside.

Writing

Say: *Practice writing the sounds you hear as I say each word. Then write the word. I will also use the word in a sentence.*

Pronounce one word at a time from the Word List below, stretching each sound. Use the word in a sentence, and repeat it again after the sentence. For example, say the word **wax**. Then say: *Candles are made of wax.* Repeat the word **wax** after the sentence.

Help students as needed to form letters or recognize letters that form these words.

Sample words: **key, making, king, queen, taxes, keeping, hawk, taking, wax**

Have students confirm their spelling with a partner, making corrections as needed.

Reflect and Review

Ask: *What did you learn today? Discuss with your partner.*

Have students work with their partners to complete the sentence frames at the end of the Lesson 6 Practice Page, assisting as needed.

Word Bank

Location	Initial (Beginning)	Medial (Middle)	Final (Ending)
k	key kid kite kind kitten kayak	baking biking napkin taking looking breakfast	look hook book cheek sneak hawk
q	quit question quart quarter queasy quack quick	request equal equator inquire liquid earthquake	(none found)
x	x-ray excite expert excellent exit	axe taxi axis next oxen flexible	fix fox box mix wax

✓ Formative Assessment

If the student completes each task correctly, proceed to the next skill in the sequence.

Did the student…?	Intervention
Pronounce letter in isolation Pronounce letter in words	Use a mirror to show movement of mouth, tongue, and teeth as the sound is produced. Use hand over mouth to explore movement of air as the sound is produced.
Recognize meaning of words in context	Explain meaning of words before and after reading the text.
Write letters correctly	Provide additional handwriting practice
Spell targeted sounds correctly	Use simple (CVC) words, practice sound segmentation and blending, use interactive and guided writing.

7 Initial Consonant L-Blends bl-, cl-, fl-, gl-, pl-, sl-

Metacognitive Strategy

Selective auditory attention

Academic Language

consonant, consonant blend, initial, blended sound

Materials

Frieze Cards: bl, cl, fl, gl, pl, sl
Phonics Lesson 7 Practice Page

Pre-Assess

- Recognition of sounds represented by the blends **bl-, cl-, fl-, gl-, pl-,** and **sl-.**
- Identification of letters used to represent the sounds **/bl/, /cl/, /fl/, /gl/, /pl/, /sl/**

Transfer Notes:

Blends are important for English learners because of the many consonant blends in English words. Some words have more than one consonant blend and can be harder to hear and pronounce.

Introduce the Lesson

Say: *Today we will identify initial consonant l-blends. We will recognize the consonants that combine with the letter **l** at the beginning of words and read text that includes initial consonant l-blends.*

Phonemic Awareness and Sound-Spelling Correspondence

Say: *Some consonant blends are made up of two consonants. Each letter sound is heard when pronounced, but the sounds blend together. We are going to study words that begin with an l-blend.*

Say: *Listen to the sound /b/. Listen to the sound /l/. Now blend the two sounds with me: /**bl**/. Now blend them on your own: /**bl**/.*

Say: *We write consonant blend /**bl**/ with the letters **b** and **l**.*

Elicit Prior Knowledge

Display the Lesson 7 Practice Page. Prompt students to think about their primary language as you work together to complete section 1.

Ask: *What are some examples in your home language of two letters or symbols that combine to make a new sound?*

Say: *Think of a word in your home language that blends these letters or symbols together.*

Model: Recognize Initial Consonant L-Blends

Direct students' attention to section 2 of the Lesson 7 Practice Page.

Say: *Let's look at words that begin with these consonant l-blends.*

Have students echo read the words for each consonant blend, emphasizing targeted blend sounds.

bl	cl	fl	gl	pl	sl
black	class	flag	glove	play	slip
blade	clap	flower	glad	please	slope

Practice: Initial Consonant L-Blends

Read aloud section 3 of the Lesson 7 Practice Page in a fluent voice, emphasizing intonation and pronunciation of words and targeted sounds. Invite students to echo read or chime on cue. Ensure comprehension by asking text dependent questions. Have students identify cognates.

Practice: Recognize Initial Consonants L-Blends

Display the Word Bank and complete section 4 of the Lesson 7 Practice Page with students.

Say: *Now let's look at words that have an initial consonant l-blend.*

Have students echo read the words on the list for each initial consonant blend, emphasizing the targeted blend. Allow time for students to fill in the chart.

Extend Language Knowledge

Practice: Make Meaning

Complete section 5 of the Lesson 7 Practice Page with students.

Say: *Let's read each clue together. Then work with a partner to find an answer from the word bank. Write the answer on the line.*

1. A color (blue)
2. Opposite of quickly (slowly)
3. A compound word (blackbird)
4. You can see them in the sky (clouds)
5. What birds can do (fly)
6. Some windows are made out of this material (glass)

Writing

Say: *Practice writing the initial consonant blend you hear in each word I read aloud.*

Pronounce one word at a time from the Word List below, stretching each sound. Use the word in a sentence, and repeat it again after the sentence. For example, say the word **flag**. Then say: *The flag waves in the wind.* Repeat the word **flag** after the sentence.

Help students as needed to form letters or recognize letters that form these words.

Sample words: **flag, play, clap, glad, blood, slip, slope**

Reflect and Review

Ask: *What did you learn today?*

Have students work with their partners to complete the sentence frames at the end of the Lesson 7 Practice Page, assisting as needed.

Word Bank

bl-	cl-	fl-
blade	clad	flap
blast	clap	flame
bland	claim	flight
blanch	clamp	flail
blanket	clash	flake
blaring	clarinet	flabbergast
gl-	**pl-**	**sl-**
glad	place	slab
glare	plain	slam
gland	placate	slack
glamour	plaque	slide
glacier	planet	slight
glance	plaintiff	slander

✔Formative Assessment

If the student completes each task correctly, proceed to the next skill in the sequence.

Did the student...?	Intervention
Pronounce letter in isolation Pronounce letter in words	Use a mirror to show movement of mouth, tongue, and teeth as the sound is produced. Use hand over mouth to explore movement of air as the sound is produced.
Recognize meaning of words in context	Explain meaning of words before and after reading the text.
Write letters correctly	Provide additional handwriting practice
Spell targeted sounds correctly	Use simple (CCVC) words, practice sound segmentation and blending, use interactive and guided writing.

8 Initial Consonant R-Blends br-, cr-, dr-, fr-, gr-, pr-, tr-

Metacognitive Strategy

Selective auditory attention

Academic Language

consonant, consonant blend, initial, blended sound

Materials

- Frieze Cards:br, cr, dr, fr, gr, pr, tr
- Phonics Lesson 8 Practice Page

Pre-Assess

- Recognition of sounds represented by the blends **br-, cr-, dr-, fr-, gr-, pr-,** and tr-.
- Identification of letters used to represent the sounds **/br/, /cr/, /dr/, /fr/,/gr/, /pr/, /tr/**

Transfer Notes:

Blends are important for English learners because of the many consonant blends in English words. Some words have more than one consonant blend and can be harder to hear and pronounce.

Introduce the Lesson

Say: *Today we will identify initial consonant r-blends. We will recognize the consonants that combine with the letter r at the beginning of words and read text that includes initial consonant r-blends.*

Phonemic Awareness and Sound-Spelling Correspondence

Say: *Some consonant blends are made up of two consonants. Each letter sound is heard when pronounced, but the sounds blend together. We are going to study words that begin with a r-blend.*

Say: *Listen to the sound /b/. Listen to the sound /r/. Now blend the two sounds with me: /br/. Now blend them on your own: /br/.*

Say: *We write consonant blend /br/ with the letters b and r.*

. Repeat with initial consonant r-blends **br-, cr-, dr-, fr-, gr-, pr-, and tr-,** and assess students' ability to recognize, name, and pronounce each letter and blend.

Elicit Prior Knowledge

Display the Lesson 8 Practice Page. Prompt students to think about their primary language as you work together to complete section 1.

Ask: *What are some examples in your home language of two letters or symbols that combine to make a new sound?*

Say: *Think of a word in your home language that blends these letters or symbols together.*

Model: Recognize Initial Consonant R-Blends

Direct students' attention to section 2 of the Lesson 8 Practice Page.

Say: *Let's look at words that begin with these consonant r-blends.*

Have students echo read the words for each consonant blend, emphasizing targeted blend sounds.

br-	cr-	dr-	fr-	gr-	pr-	tr-
brand	crab	drag	frame	green	price	trace
brow	crowd	drop	frog	grass	prank	truck

Practice: Initial Consonant R-Blends

Read aloud section 3 of the Lesson 8 Practice Page in a fluent voice, emphasizing intonation and pronunciation of words and targeted sounds. Invite students to echo read or chime on cue. Ensure comprehension by asking text dependent questions. Have students identify cognates.

Practice: Recognize Initial Consonants R-Blends

Display the Word Bank and complete section 4 of the Lesson 8 Practice Page with students.

Say: *Now let's look at words that have an initial consonant r-blend.*

Have students echo read the words on the list for each initial consonant blend, emphasizing the targeted blend. Allow time for students to fill in the chart.

Extend Language Knowledge

Practice: Make Meaning

Complete section 5 of the Lesson 8 Practice Page with students.

Say: *Let's read each clue together. Then work with a partner to find an answer from the word bank. Write the answer on the line.*

1. Children color with it (crayon)
2. It grows in a yard (grass)
3. The color of dirt (brown)
4. A salty snack (pretzel)
5. Water goes down it (drain)
6. Opposite of back (front)
7. A path in the woods (trail)

Writing

Say: *Practice writing the initial consonant blend you hear in each word I read aloud.*

Pronounce one word at a time from the Word List below, stretching each sound. Use the word in a sentence, and repeat it again after the sentence. For example, say the word **drink**. Then say: *I drink water when I'm thirsty.* Repeat the word **drink** after the sentence.

Help students as needed to form letters or recognize letters that form these words.

Sample words: **bridge, crash, front, frame, trace, drink**

Have students confirm their spelling with a partner, making corrections as needed.

Reflect and Review

Ask: *What did you learn today?*

Have students work with their partners to complete the sentence frames at the end of the Lesson 8 Practice Page, assisting as needed.

Word Bank

br-	cr-	dr-	tr-
braid	crab	drab	trace
bridge	craft	drop	track
broken	crane	drove	trunk
brake	crack	drama	traction
bright	crash	dragon	tradition
brawn	cranium	drawing	tremendous

fr-	gr-	pr-	
front	grab	proud	
frame	grade	predict	
frantic	grand	practice	
fright	ground	prairie	
fraction	granite	prayer	
fragment	grammar	precaution	

✓ Formative Assessment

If the student completes each task correctly, proceed to the next skill in the sequence.

Did the student...?	Intervention
Pronounce letter in isolation Pronounce letter in words	Use a mirror to show movement of mouth, tongue, and teeth as the sound is produced. Use hand over mouth to explore movement of air as the sound is produced.
Recognize meaning of words in context	Explain meaning of words before and after reading the text.
Write letters correctly	Provide additional handwriting practice
Spell targeted sounds correctly	Use simple (CCVC) words, practice sound segmentation and blending, use interactive and guided writing.

9 Initial Consonant S-Blends sc-, sk-, sn-, sp-, st-, sw-

- Identify and name the initial consonant S-blends **sc-, sk-, sn-, sp-, st-, and sw-**.
- Produce the sound of initial consonant S-blends **sc-, sk-, sn-, sp-, st-, and sw-**.
- Relate the sounds **/sc/, /sk/, /sn/, /sp/, /st/,** and **/sw/** to each corresponding consonant blend.
- Recognize the initial consonant S-blend sounds **/sc/, /sk/, /sn/, /sp/, /st/,** and **/sw/** in words.
- Read common high frequency words.

Metacognitive Strategy

Selective auditory attention

Academic Language

consonant, consonant blend, initial, blended sound

Materials

- Frieze Cards: sc, sk, sn, sp, st, sw
- Phonics Lesson 9 Practice Page

Pre-Assess

- Recognition of sounds represented by the blends **sc-, sk-, sn-, sp-, st-, sw-**.
- Identification of letters used to represent the sounds **/sc/, /sk/, /sn/, /sp/,/st/, /sw/**

Transfer Notes:

Blends are important to English Learners because there are so many consonant blends in English words. Some words have more than one consonant blend and can be harder to hear and pronounce.

Introduce the Lesson

Say: *Today we will identify initial consonant **S-blends.** We will recognize the consonants that combine with the letter **S** at the beginning of words, and we will read text that includes initial consonant **s-blends.***

Phonemic Awareness and Sound-Spelling Correspondence

Say: *Some consonant blends are made up of two consonants. Each letter sound is heard when pronounced, but the sounds blend together. We are going to study words that begin with an **s-blend.***

Say: *Listen to the sound **/s/**. Listen to the sound **/c/** (the hard **c /k/** sound). Now blend the two sounds with me: **/sc/**. Now blend them on your own: **/sc/**.*

Say: *We write the consonant blend **/sc/** with the letters **s** and **c**.*

Repeat with initial consonant **s-blends sc-, sk-, sn-, sp-, st-**, and **sw-** and assess students' ability to recognize, name, and pronounce each letter and blend.

Elicit Prior Knowledge

Display the Lesson 9 Practice Page. Prompt students to think about their primary language as you work together to complete section 1.

Ask: *What are some examples in your home language of two letters or symbols that combine to make a new sound?*

Say: *Think of a word in your home language that blends these letters or symbols together.*

Model: Recognize Initial Consonant S-Blends

Direct students' attention to section 2 of the Lesson 9 Practice Page.

Say: *Let's look at words that begin with these consonant **s-blends.***

Have students echo read the words for each consonant blend, emphasizing targeted blend sounds.

sc-	sk-	sn-	sp-	st-	sw-
score	skirt	snail	special	storm	swing
scale	skull	snow	sport	sting	swat

Practice: Initial Consonant S-Blends

Read aloud section 3 of the Lesson 9 Practice Page in a fluent voice, emphasizing intonation and pronunciation of words and targeted sounds. Invite students to echo read or chime on cue. Ensure comprehension by asking text dependent questions. Have students identify cognates.

Practice: Recognize Initial Consonants S-Blends

Display the Word Bank and complete section 4 of the Lesson 9 Practice Page with students.

Say: *Now let's look at words that have an initial consonant s-blend.*

Have students echo read the words on the list for each initial consonant blend, emphasizing the targeted blend. Allow time for students to fill in the chart.

Extend Language Knowledge

Practice: Use Words in Context

Complete section 5 of the Lesson 9 Practice Page with students.

Say: *Let's think about words with the initial consonant blends we have been discussing today: sc-, sk-, sn-, sp-, st-, and sw-. Complete each sentence using words from the word bank on the Practice Page.*

1. The water ran **swiftly** in the river.
2. A weigh the apples on a **scale**.
3. I wear **sneakers** to gym class.
4. We can **skate** when the pond is frozen.
5. My favorite **snack** is pretzels.
6. The little boy uses the **stool** to reach the high shelf.
7. I use a **spoon** to stir the batter.
8. He likes to **swim** in the ocean.

Writing

Say: *Practice writing the sounds you hear as I say each word. Then write the word. I will also use the word in a sentence.*

Pronounce one word at a time from the Word List below, stretching each sound. Use the word in a sentence, and repeat it again after the sentence. For example, say the word **swarm**. Then say: *The bees swarm around the flower.* Repeat the word **swarm** after the sentence.

Help students as needed to form letters or recognize letters that form these words.

Sample words: **swarm, scooter, skunk, sneak, stop, sport**

Have students confirm their spelling with a partner, making corrections as needed.

Reflect and Review

Ask: *What did you learn today?*

Have students work with their partners to complete the sentence frames at the end of the Lesson 9 Practice Page, assisting as needed.

Word Bank

sc-	sk-	sn-
scale	ski	snore
scary	skate	snack
score	skunk	snip
scoop	sketch	sneer
scar	sky	snail
scallop	skeleton	snowball
sp-	**st-**	**sw-**
sport	stay	swim
space	stool	swap
speech	sticker	sweet
spill	stamp	swell
special	steer	swallow
spacecraft	stomach	swan

✔ Formative Assessment

If the student completes each task correctly, proceed to the next skill in the sequence.

Did the student...?	Intervention
Pronounce letter in isolation Pronounce letter in words	Use a mirror to show movement of mouth, tongue, and teeth as the sound is produced. Use hand over mouth to explore movement of air as the sound is produced.
Recognize meaning of words in context	Explain meaning of words before and after reading the text.
Write letters correctly	Provide additional handwriting practice
Spell targeted sounds correctly	Use simple (CCVC) words, practice sound segmentation and blending, use interactive and guided writing.

10 Letter Initial Consonant Blends
scr-, spl-, spr-, squ-, str-

Lesson Objectives

- Identify and name the 3-letter initial consonant blends **scr-, spl-, spr-, squ-,** and **str-**
- Produce the sound of 3-letter initial consonant blends **scr-, spl-, spr-, squ-,** and **str-.**
- Relate the sounds **/scr/, /spl/, /spr/, /squ/,** and **/str/** to each corresponding consonant blend.
- Recognize the 3-letter initial consonant blends **scr, scr-, spl-, spr-, squ-,** and **str-** in words.
- Read common high frequency words.

Metacognitive Strategy

Selective auditory attention

Academic Language

consonant, consonant blend, initial, blended sound

Materials

- Frieze Cards: scr, spl, spr, squ, str
- Phonics Lesson 10 Practice Page

Pre-Assess

- Recognition of sounds represented by the blends **scr-, spl-, spr-, squ-,** and **str-**
- Identification of letters used to represent the sounds **/scr/, /spl/, /spr/, /squ/, /str/**

Transfer Notes:

Blends are important to English Learners because there are so many consonant blends in English words. Some words have more than one consonant blend and can be harder to hear and pronounce.

Introduce the Lesson

Say: *Today we will identify 3-letter initial consonant blends that begin with the letter S and read text that include the 3-letter initial consonant blends.*

Phonemic Awareness and Sound-Spelling Correspondence

Say: *A consonant blend is made up of two or more consonants. Each consonant sound is heard when pronounced, but the sounds blend together. We are going to study words that begin with 3-letter consonant blends.*

Say: *Listen to the sound /s/. Say it with me: /s/. Now say it on your own: /s/*

Repeat with the sounds /c/ and /r/.

Say: *Listen to the sound that /s/, /c/, and /r/ make when they blend together: /scr/. Blend the three sounds with me: /scr/. Now blend them on your own: /scr/.*

Say: *We write the consonant blend scr with the letters s, c, and r.*

Repeat with the other 3-letter initial consonant blends **scr-, spl-, spr-, squ-,** and **str-** and assess students' ability to recognize, name, and pronounce each letter and blend.

Elicit Prior Knowledge

Display the Lesson 10 Practice Page. Prompt students to think about their primary language as you work together to complete section 1.

Ask: *What are some examples in your home language of words made up of these sounds, letters, or symbols blended together?*

Model: Recognize 3-Letter Initial Consonant Blends

Direct students' attention to section 2 of the Lesson 10 Practice Page.

Say: *Let's look at words that begin with these initial 3-letter consonant blends.*

Have students echo read the words for each consonant blend, emphasizing targeted blend sounds.

scr-	spl-	spr-	squ-	str-
scrub	splash	spring	squad	strict
screen	split	sprain	square	strain

Practice: 3-Letter Initial Consonant Blends

Read aloud section 3 of the Lesson 10 Practice Page in a fluent voice, emphasizing intonation and pronunciation of words and targeted sounds. Invite students to echo read or chime on cue. Ensure comprehension by asking text dependent questions. Have students identify cognates.

Practice: Recognize 3-Letter Initial Consonant Blends

Display the Word Bank and complete section 4 of the Lesson 10 Practice Page with students.

Say: *Now let's look at words that begin with a 3-letter consonant blend.*

Have students echo read the words on the list for each initial consonant blend, emphasizing the targeted blend. Allow time for students to fill in the chart.

Extend Language Knowledge

Practice: Use Words in Context

Complete section 5 of the Lesson 10 practice page with students.

Say: *Let's think about words that begin with the 3-letter consonant blends we have been discussing today: scr-, spl-, spr-, squ-, str-. Complete each sentence using words from the word bank on the Practice Page.*

1. Children like to **scribble** on paper with crayons.
2. If you're not careful you can get a **splinter** from touching something wooden.
3. Every morning, I **spread** butter on my toast.
4. The pigs **squeal** with delight as they roll in the mud.
5. A **square** is a shape with four equal sides.
6. A ruler can help you make a **straight** line.
7. When you have an itch, you **scratch** it to feel better.

Writing

Say: *Practice writing the sounds you hear as I say each word. Then write the word. I will also use the word in a sentence.*

Pronounce one word at a time from the Word List below, stretching each sound. Use the word in a sentence, and repeat it again after the sentence. For example, say the word **scream**. Then say: *We scrub the dishes until they are clean.* Repeat the word **scrub** after the sentence.

Help students as needed to form letters or recognize letters that form these words.

Sample words: **scrub, splash, strict, sprinkle, squash**

Have students confirm their spelling with a partner, making corrections as needed.

Reflect and Review

Ask: *What did you learn today?*

Have students work with their partners to complete the sentence frames at the end of the Lesson 10 Practice Page, assisting as needed.

Word Bank

scr-	spl-	spr-
scram	split	sprig
scream	splay	spring
scratch	splice	sprain
scrappy	splurge	sprawl
scribble	splinter	spread
scrawny	splatter	sprinkle

squ-	str-	
squad	stress	
squat	strict	
squash	strain	
squeal	straddle	
square	strange	
squash	strategy	

✓Formative Assessment

If the student completes each task correctly, proceed to the next skill in the sequence.

Did the student...?	Intervention
Pronounce letter in isolation Pronounce letter in words	Use mirrors to show movement of mouth, tongue, and teeth as the sound is produced. Use hand over mouth to explore movement of air as the sound is produced.
Recognize meaning of words in context	Explain meaning of words before and after reading the text.
Write letters correctly	Provide additional handwriting practice
Spell targeted sounds correctly	Use simple (CCVC) words, practice sound segmentation and blending, use interactive and guided writing.

11 Ending Consonant Blends -ct, -ft

Lesson Objectives

- Identify and name the ending consonant blends **-ct** and **-ft.**
- Produce the sound of ending consonant blends **-ct** and **-ft.**
- Relate the sounds **/ct/** and **/ft/** to each corresponding consonant blend.
- Recognize the ending consonant blends **-ct** and **–ft** in words.
- Read common high frequency words.

Metacognitive Strategy

Selective auditory attention

Academic Language

consonant, consonant blend, initial, blended sound

Materials

- Frieze Cards: -ct, -ft
- Phonics Lesson 11 Practice Page

Pre-Assess

- Recognition of sounds represented by the blends **-ct, -ft**
- Identification of letters used to represent the sounds **/ct/, /ft/**

Transfer Notes:

Blends are important to English Learners because there are so many consonant blends in English words. Some words have more than one consonant blend and can be harder to hear and pronounce.

Introduce the Lesson

Say: *Today we will identify consonants that combine at the end of words. We will recognize these consonant blends in words and read text that includes these ending consonant blends.*

Phonemic Awareness and Sound-Spelling Correspondence

Say: *A consonant blend is made up of two or more consonants. Each consonant sound is heard when pronounced, but the sounds blend together. We are going to study consonants at the end of words.*

Say: *Listen to the sound /c/. Say it with me: /c/. Now say it on your own: /c/*

Repeat with the sound /**t**/.

Say: *Listen to the sound that /c/ and /t/ make when they are blended together: /ct/. Now blend the two sounds with me: /ct/.*

Say: *We write consonant blend /ct/ is with the letters **c** and **t**.*

Repeat with ending consonant blend **-ft** and assess students' ability to recognize, name, and pronounce each letter and blend.

Elicit Prior Knowledge

Display the Lesson 11 Practice Page. Prompt students to think about their primary language as you work together to complete section 1.

Ask: *What are some examples in your home language of words with these letters or symbols that blend to make a new sound?*

Model: Recognize Ending Consonant Blends

Direct students' attention to section 2 of the Lesson 11 Practice Page.

Say: *Let's look at words that end with these consonant blends.*

Have students echo read the words for each ending consonant blend, emphasizing targeted blend sounds.

-ct	-ft
act	raft
fact	left

Practice: Identify Ending Consonant Blends

Read aloud section 3 of the Lesson 11 Practice Page in a fluent voice, emphasizing intonation and pronunciation of words and targeted sounds. Invite students to echo read or chime on cue. Ensure comprehension by asking text dependent questions. Have students identify cognates.

Practice: Recognize Ending Consonant Blends in Context

Display the Word Bank and complete section 4 of the Lesson 10 Practice Page with students.

Say: *Now let's look at words that end with the consonant blends that we have studied.*

Have students echo read the words on the list for each ending consonant blend, emphasizing the targeted blend. Allow time for students to fill in the chart.

Say: *Next, we are going to practice pronunciation by breaking up the words into syllables. We will clap out the syllables as we say each word then annotate syllables with a slash. When done annotating, read each word aloud to your partner.*

Extend Language Knowledge: Use words in context

Complete section 5 of the Lesson 11 Practice Page with students.

Say: *Let's read each clue together. Then work with a partner to find an answer from the word bank. Write the answer on the line.*

1. Opposite of right (left)
2. A boat may do this (drift)
3. Something that is true (fact)
4. To move from one thing to another (shift)
5. A rough copy (draft)
6. Something you give to someone (gift)
7. You have to give this to get this (respect)
8. It floats (raft)

Writing

Say: *Practice writing the sounds you hear as I say each word. Then write the word. I will also use the word in a sentence.*

Pronounce one word at a time from the Word List below, stretching each sound. Use the word in a sentence, and repeat it again after the sentence. For example, say the word **exact**. Then say: *You must be exact when measuring the size of something.* Repeat the word **exact** after the sentence.

Help students as needed to form letters or recognize letters that form these words.

Sample words: **fact, act, craft, draft, object, exact**

Have students confirm their spelling with a partner, making corrections as needed.

Reflect and Review

Ask: *What did you learn today?*

Have students work with their partners to complete the sentence frames at the end of the Lesson 11 Practice Page, assisting as needed.

Word Bank

-ct	-ft
fact	craft
direct	drift
expect	shift
object	draft
project	gift
respect	raft

✓Formative Assessment

If the student completes each task correctly, precede to the next skill in the sequence.

Did the student…?	Intervention
Pronounce letter in isolation Pronounce letter in words	Use a mirror to show movement of mouth, tongue, and teeth as the sound is produced. Use hand over mouth to explore movement of air as the sound is produced.
Do they recognize meaning of words in context	Explain meaning of words before and after reading the text.
Write letters correctly	Provide additional handwriting practice
Spell targeted sounds correctly	Use simple (CVCC) words, practice sound segmentation and blending, use interactive and guided writing.

12 Ending Consonant Blends -ld, -lf, -lk, -lt, -lp

- Identify and name the ending consonant blends **-ld, -lf, -lk, -lt**, and -lp.
- Produce the sound of ending consonant blends **-ld, -lf, -lk, -lt**, and **-lp.**
- Relate the sounds **/ld/, /lf/, /lk/, /lt/,** and **/lp/** to each corresponding consonant blend.
- Recognize the ending consonant blends **-ld, -lf, -lk, -lt,** and **-lp**in words.
- Read common high frequency words.

Metacognitive Strategy

Selective auditory attention

Academic Language

consonant, consonant blend, initial, blended sound

Materials

- Frieze Cards: -ld, -lf, -lk, -lt, -lp
- Phonics Lesson 12 Practice Page

Pre-Assess

- Recognition of sounds represented by the blends **-ld, -lf, -lk, -lt, -lp**
- Identification of letters used to represent the sounds **/ld/, /lf/, /lk/, /lt/, /lp/**

Introduce the Lesson

Say: *Today we will identify consonants that combine at the end of words. We will recognize these consonant blends in words and read text that includes these ending consonant blends.*

Phonemic Awareness and Sound-Spelling Correspondence

Say: *A consonant blend is made up of two or more consonants. Each consonant sound is heard when pronounced, but the sounds blend together. We will study consonant blends that appear at the end of words.*

Say: *Listen to the sound /l/. Say it with me: /l/. Now say it on your own: /l/*

Repeat with the sound /**d**/.

Say: *Listen to the sound that /l/ and /d/ make when they blend together: /**ld/**. Now blend the two sounds with me: /**ld/**.*

Say: *We write the consonant blend /**ld/** with the letters **l** and **d**.*

Repeat with ending consonant blends **-lf, -lk, -lt,** and **–lp** and assess students' ability to recognize, name, and pronounce each letter and blend.

Elicit Prior Knowledge

Display the Lesson 12 Practice Page. Prompt students to think about their primary language as you work together to complete section 1.

Ask: *What are some examples in your home language of words with these letters or symbols that blend to make a new sound?*

Model: Recognize Ending Consonant Blends

Direct students' attention to section 2 of the Lesson 12 Practice Page.

Say: *Let's look at words that end with these consonant blends.*

Have students echo read the words for each ending consonant blend, emphasizing targeted blend sounds.

-ld	-lf	-lk	-lt	-lp
old	elf	milk	salt	gulp
told	gulf	silk	belt	yelp

Practice: Ending Consonant Blends

Read aloud section 3 of the Lesson 12 Practice Page in a fluent voice, emphasizing intonation and pronunciation of words and targeted sounds. Invite students to echo read or chime on cue. Ensure comprehension by asking text dependent questions. Have students identify cognates.

Practice: Recognize Ending Consonant Blends

Display the Word Bank and complete section 4 of the Lesson 10 Practice Page with students.

Say: *Now let's look at words that end with the consonant blends that we have studied.*

Have students echo read the words on the list for each ending consonant blend, emphasizing the targeted blend. Allow time for students to fill in the chart.

Extend Language Knowledge

Practice: Use Words in Context

Complete section 5 of the Lesson 12 practice page with students.

Say: *Let's think about words that end with the consonant blends we have been discussing today: -ld, -lf, -lk, -lt, -lp. Complete each sentence using words from the word bank on the Practice Page. Take turns reading the completed sentences to a partner.*

1. The **child** is learning to read.
2. The blouse is made of a **silk**.
3. The ice cream will **melt** in the sun.
4. I need **help** answering the question.
5. We like **salt** on our popcorn.
6. I wear a sweater when it is **cold**.
7. She looks at **herself** in the mirror.
8. The big men **lift** heavy weights at the gym.

Writing

Say: *Practice writing the sounds you hear as I say each word. Then write the word. I will also use the word in a sentence.*

Pronounce one word at a time from the Word List below, stretching each sound. Use the word in a sentence, and repeat it again after the sentence. For example, say the word **hold**. Then say: *We must hold hands when we cross the street.* Repeat the word **hold** after the sentence.

Help students as needed to form letters or recognize letters that form these words.

Sample words: **belt, fold, help, adult, hold, wild, wolf**

Have students confirm their spelling with a partner, making corrections as needed.

Reflect and Review

Ask: *What did you learn today?*

Have students work with their partners to complete the sentence frames at the end of the Lesson 12 Practice Page, assisting as needed.

Word Bank

-ld	-lf	-lk
cold	elf	milk
fold	golf	silk
gold	gulf	bulk
held	self	skulk
hold	wolf	elk
wild	shelf	

-lt	-lp	
adult	gulp	
belt	help	
melt	yelp	
result	pulp	
salt	scalp	
difficult	whelp	

✔Formative Assessment

If the student completes each task correctly, proceed to the next skill in the sequence.

Did the student…?	Intervention
Pronounce letter in isolation Pronounce letter in words	Use a mirror to show movement of mouth, tongue, and teeth as the sound is produced. Use hand over mouth to explore movement of air as the sound is produced.
Recognize meaning of words in context	Explain meaning of words before and after reading the text.
Write letters correctly	Provide additional handwriting practice
Spell targeted sounds correctly	Use simple (CVCC) words, practice sound segmentation and blending, use interactive and guided writing.

PHONICS

13 Ending Consonant Blends -mp, -pt

Lesson Objectives

- Identify and name the ending consonant blends **-mp** and **-pt.**
- Produce the sound of ending consonant blends **-mp** and **-pt.**
- Relate the sounds **/mp/** and **/pt/** to each corresponding consonant blend.
- Recognize the ending consonant blends **-mp** and **-pt** in words.
- Read common high frequency words.

Metacognitive Strategy

Selective auditory attention

Academic Language

consonant, consonant blend, initial, blended sound

Materials

- Frieze Cards: -mp, -pt
- Phonics Lesson 13 Practice Page

Pre-Assess

- Recognition of sounds represented by the blends **-mp, -pt**
- Identification of letters used to represent the sounds **/mp/, /pt/**

Introduce the Lesson

Say: *Today we will identify consonants that combine at the end of words. We will recognize these consonant blends in words and read text that includes these ending consonant blends.*

Phonemic Awareness and Sound-Spelling Correspondence

Say: *consonant blend is made up of two or more consonants. Each consonant sound is heard when pronounced, but the sounds blend together. We will study consonant blends that appear at the end of words.*

Say: *Listen to the sound /m/. Say it with me: /m/. Now say it on your own: /m/.*

Repeat with the sound /**p**/.

Say: *Listen to the sound that /m/ and /p/ make when they blend together: /mp/. Now blend the two sounds with me: /mp/.*

Say: *We write consonant blend -mp with the letters m and p.*

Repeat with ending consonant blend **-pt** and assess students' ability to recognize, name, and pronounce each letter and blend.

Elicit Prior Knowledge

Display the Lesson 13 Practice Page. Prompt students to think about their primary language as you work together to complete section 1.

Ask: *What are some examples in your home language of words with these letters or symbols that blend to make a new sound?*

Model: Recognize Ending Consonant Blends

Direct students' attention to section 2 of the Lesson 13 Practice Page.

Say: *Let's look at words that end with these consonant blends.*

Have students echo read the words for each ending consonant blend, emphasizing targeted blend sounds.

-mp	-pt
pump	adopt
swamp	except

Practice: Identify Ending Consonant Blends

Read aloud section 3 of the Lesson 13 Practice Page in a fluent voice, emphasizing intonation and pronunciation of words and targeted sounds. Invite students to echo read or chime on cue. Ensure comprehension by asking text dependent questions. Have students identify cognates.

Practice: Recognize Ending Consonant Blends

Display the Word Bank and complete section 4 of the Lesson 13 Practice Page with students.

Say: *Now let's look at words that end with the consonant blends that we have studied.*

Have students echo read the words on the list for each ending consonant blend, emphasizing the targeted blend.

Extend Language Knowledge

Practice: Make Meaning

Complete section 5 of the Lesson 13 Practice Page with students.

Say: *Let's read each clue together. Then work with a partner to find an answer from the word bank. Write the answer on the line.*

1. Moist (damp)
2. A place for junk (dump)
3. To have moved slowly (crept)
4. You sleep in tents (camp)
5. You do this on a trampoline (jump)
6. To try (attempt)
7. What you did last night (slept)
8. You put this on an envelope to mail it (stamp)

Writing

Say: *Practice writing the sounds you hear as I say each word. Then write the word. I will also use the word in a sentence.*

Pronounce one word at a time from the Word List below, stretching each sound. Use the word in a sentence, and repeat it again after the sentence. For example, say the word **lamp**. Then say: *Turn on the lamp so I can read.* Repeat the word **lamp** after the sentence.

Help students as needed to form letters or recognize letters that form these words.

Sample words: **slept, camp, accept, damp, jump, lamp**

Have students confirm their spelling with a partner, making corrections as needed.

Reflect and Review

Ask: *What did you learn today?*

Have students work with their partners to complete the sentence frames at the end of the Lesson 13 Practice Page, assisting as needed.

Word Bank

-mp	-pt
camp	accept
damp	attempt
dump	crept
jump	kept
lamp	slept
stamp	except

✔ Formative Assessment

If the student completes each task correctly, proceed to the next skill in the sequence.

Did the student...?	Intervention
Pronounce letter in isolation Pronounce letter in words	Use a mirror to show movement of mouth, tongue, and teeth as the sound is produced. Use hand over mouth to explore movement of air as the sound is produced.
Recognize meaning of words in context	Explain meaning of words before and after reading the text.
Write letters correctly	Provide additional handwriting practice
Spell targeted sounds correctly	Use simple (CVCC) words, practice sound segmentation and blending, use interactive and guided writing.

Lesson Objectives

- Identify and name the ending consonant blends **-nd, -nk,** and **-nt.**
- Produce the sound of ending consonant blends **-nd, -nk,** and **-nt.**
- Relate the sounds **/nd/, /nk/,** and **/nt/** to each corresponding consonant blend.
- Recognize the ending consonant blends **-nd, -nk,** and **-nt** in words.
- Read common high frequency words.

Metacognitive Strategy

Selective auditory attention

Academic Language

consonant, consonant blend, initial, blended sound

Materials

Frieze Card: -nd, -nk, -nt
Blackline Master Phonics 14

Pre-Assess

- Recognition of sounds represented by the blends **-nd, -nk, -nt**
- Identification of letters used to represent the sounds **/nd/, /nk/, /nt/**

14 Ending Consonant Blends -nd, -nk, -nt

Introduce the Lesson

Say: *Today we will identify consonants that combine at the end of words. We will recognize these consonant blends in words and read text that includes these ending consonant blends.*

Phonemic Awareness and Sound-Spelling Correspondence

Say: *A consonant blend is made up of two or more consonants. Each consonant sound is heard when pronounced, but the sounds blend together. We will study consonant blends that appear at the end of words.*

Say: *Listen to the sound /n/. Say it with me: /n/. Now say it on your own: /n/.*

Repeat with the sound /**d**/.

Say: *Listen to the sound that /n/ and /d/ make when they blend together: /nd/. Now blend the two sounds with me: /nd/.*

Say: *We write the consonant blend /nd/ with the letters **n** and **d.***

Repeat with ending consonant blends **–nk** and **–nt** and assess students' ability to recognize, name, and pronounce each letter and blend.

Elicit Prior Knowledge

Display the Lesson 14 Practice Page. Prompt students to think about their primary language as you work together to complete section 1.

Ask: *What are some examples in your home language of words with these letters or symbols that blend to make a new sound?*

Model: Recognize Ending Consonant Blends

Direct students' attention to section 2 of the Lesson 14 Practice Page.

Say: *Let's look at words that end with these consonant blends.*

Have students echo read the words for each ending consonant blend, emphasizing targeted blend sounds.

-nd	-nk	-nt
find	bank	plant
land	sink	spent

Practice: Identify Ending Consonant Blends

Read aloud section 3 of the Lesson 14 Practice Page in a fluent voice, emphasizing intonation and pronunciation of words and targeted sounds. Invite students to echo read or chime on cue. Ensure comprehension by asking text dependent questions. Have students identify cognates.

Practice: Recognize Ending Consonant Blends in Context

Display the Word Bank and complete section 4 of the Lesson 14 Practice Page with students.

Say: *Now let's look at words that end with the consonant blends that we have studied.*

Have students echo read the words on the list for each ending consonant blend, emphasizing the targeted blend. Allow time for students to fill in the chart.

Extend Language Knowledge

Practice: Make Meaning

Complete section 5 of the Lesson 14 practice page with students.

Say: *Let's think about words that end with the consonant blends we have been discussing today: **-nd, -nk, -nt**. Complete each sentence using words from the word bank on the Practice Page. Take turns reading the completed sentences to a partner.*

1. You can get a **drink** from the **sink** if you are thirsty.
2. The flute **and** the trumpet are part of a **band**.
3. Let's **thank** the **kind** man for his help.
4. We **plant** crops in the **land**.
5. Red and white **blend** to make **pink**.
6. It is **important** to vote for the **president**.
7. The **student** **went** to class.
8. You need a **parent** to open a **bank** account if you're a child.

Writing

Say: *Practice writing the sounds you hear as I say each word. Then write the word. I will also use the word in a sentence.*

Pronounce one word at a time from the Word List below, stretching each sound. Use the word in a sentence, and repeat it again after the sentence. For example, say the word *bank*. Then say: *I keep my money at the bank.* Repeat the word *bank* after the sentence.

Help students as needed to form letters or recognize letters that form these words.

Sample words: **president, bank, drink, and, band, thank, kind**

Have students confirm their spelling with a partner, making corrections as needed.

Reflect and Review

Ask: *What did you learn today?*

Have students work with their partners to complete the sentence frames at the end of the Lesson 14 Practice Page, assisting as needed.

Word Bank

-nd	-nk	-nt
blend	bank	different
hand	pink	important
fund	sink	parent
kind	skunk	student
land	honk	want
stand	think	mint

✓Formative Assessment

If the student completes each task correctly, proceed to the next skill in the sequence.
If not, refer to suggested Intervention 2.

Did the student…?	Intervention
Pronounce letter in isolation Pronounce letter in words	Use a mirror to show movement of mouth, tongue, and teeth as the sound is produced. Use hand over mouth to explore movement of air as the sound is produced.
Recognize meaning of words in context	Explain meaning of words before and after reading the text.
Write letters correctly	Provide additional handwriting practice
Spell targeted sounds correctly	Use simple (CVCC) words, practice sound segmentation and blending, use interactive and guided writing.

15 Ending Consonant Blends -sk, -sp, -st

Lesson Objectives

- Identify and name the ending consonant blends **-sk, -sp,** and **-st.**
- Produce the sound of ending consonant blends **-sk, -sp,** and **-st.**
- Relate the sounds **/sk/, /sp/,** and **/st/** to each corresponding consonant blend.
- Recognize the ending consonant blends **-sk, -sp,** and **-st** in words.
- Read common high frequency words.

Metacognitive Strategy

Selective auditory attention

Academic Language

consonant, consonant blend, initial, blended sound

Materials

- Frieze Cards: -sk, -sp, -st
- Phonics Lesson 15 Practice Page

Pre-Assess

- Recognition of sounds represented by the blends **-sk, -sp, -st**
- Identification of letters used to represent the sounds **/sk/, /sp/, /st/**

Introduce the Lesson

Say: *Today we will identify consonants that combine at the end of words. We will recognize these consonant blends in words and read text that includes these ending consonant blends.*

Phonemic Awareness and Sound-Spelling Correspondence

Say: *A consonant blend is made up of two or more consonants. Each consonant sound is heard when pronounced, but the sounds blend together. We will study consonant blends that appear at the end of words.*

Say: *Listen to the sound /s/. Say it with me: /s/. Now say it on your own: /s/.*

Repeat with the sound **/k/.**

Say: *Listen to the sound that /s/ and /k/ make when they blend together: /sk/. Now blend the two sounds with me: /sk/.*

Say: *We write consonant blend /sk/ with the letters s and k.*

Repeat with ending consonant blends **-sp** and **-st** and assess students' ability to recognize, name, and pronounce each letter and blend.

Elicit Prior Knowledge

Display the Lesson 15 Practice Page. Prompt students to think about their primary language as you work together to complete section 1.

Ask: *What are some examples in your home language of words with these letters or symbols that blend to make a new sound?*

Model: Recognize Ending Consonant Blends

Direct students' attention to section 2 of the Lesson 15 Practice Page.

Say: *Let's look at words that end with these consonant blends.*

Have students echo read the words for each ending consonant blend, emphasizing targeted blend sounds.

-sk	-sp	-st
mask	crisp	must
desk	wasp	rest

Practice: Identify Ending Consonant Blends

Read aloud section 3 of the Lesson 15 Practice Page in a fluent voice, emphasizing intonation and pronunciation of words and targeted sounds. Invite students to echo read or chime on cue. Ensure comprehension by asking text dependent questions. Have students identify cognates.

Practice: Recognize Ending Consonant Blends in Context

Display the Word Bank and complete section 4 of the Lesson 15 Practice Page with students.

Say: *Now let's look at words that end with the consonant blends that we have studied.*

Have students echo read the words on the list for each ending consonant blend, emphasizing the targeted blend. Allow time for students to fill in the chart.

Extend Language Knowledge

Practice: Make Meaning

Complete section 5 of the Lesson 15 Practice Page with students.

Say: *Let's read each clue together. Then work with a partner to find an answer from the word bank. Write the answer on the line.*

1. Opposite of slow (fast)
2. Where you sit at school (desk)
3. Opposite of first (last)
4. The outer covering of an ear of corn (husk)
5. To hold on to (grasp)
6. What you do when you sleep (rest)
7. A flying insect that stings (wasp)
8. Another word for right after sunset (dusk)

Writing

Say: *Practice writing the sounds you hear as I say each word. Then write the word. I will also use the word in a sentence.*

Pronounce one word at a time from the Word List below, stretching each sound. Use the word in a sentence, and repeat it again after the sentence. For example, say the word **bank**. Then say: *I keep my money at the bank*. Repeat the word **bank** after the sentence.

Help students as needed to form letters or recognize letters that form these words.

Sample words: **best, mask, wasp, ask, dusk, lost, rest**

Have students confirm their spelling with a partner, making corrections as needed.

Reflect and Review

Ask: *What did you learn today?*

Have students work with their partners to complete the sentence frames at the end of the Lesson 15 Practice Page, assisting as needed.

Word Bank

-sk	-sp	-st
desk	clasp	best
disk	cusp	fast
dusk	gasp	just
husk	grasp	last
risk	lisp	must
task	wisp	trust

✔Formative Assessment

If the student completes each task correctly, proceed to the next skill in the sequence.

Did the student...?	Intervention
Pronounce letter in isolation Pronounce letter in words	Use a mirror to show movement of mouth, tongue, and teeth as the sound is produced. Use hand over mouth to explore movement of air as the sound is produced.
Recognize meaning of words in context	Explain meaning of words before and after reading the text.
Write letters correctly	Provide additional handwriting practice
Spell targeted sounds correctly	Use simple (CVCC) words, practice sound segmentation and blending, use interactive and guided writing.

16 Initial Consonant Digraph wh-

Introduce the Lesson

Say: *Today we will identify a consonant digraph that combines two letters at the beginning of words. We will also read text that includes this consonant digraph.*

Phonemic Awareness and Sound-Spelling Correspondence

Say: *A consonant digraph is made up of two consonants. The two letters together create one sound that is different than the sound each individual consonant makes.*

Say: *Listen to the sound /w/. Say it with me: /w/. Now say it on your own: /w/.*

Repeat with the sound /h/.

Say: *Listen to the new sound that /w/ and /h/ make when they are combined: /wh/. Now say the new sound with me: /wh/.*

Say: *We write the consonant digraph wh- with the letters w and h.*

Elicit Prior Knowledge

Display the Lesson 16 Practice Page. Prompt students to think about their primary language as you work together to complete section 1.

Ask: *What are some examples in your home language of words with these letters or symbols that blend to make a new sound?*

Model: Recognize Initial Consonant Digraphs

Direct students' attention to section 2 of the Lesson 16 Practice Page.

Say: *Let's look at words that begin with this consonant digraph.*

Have students echo read the list, emphasizing the digraph in each word.

wh-
what
where
whale
wheat

Practice: Identify Initial Consonant Digraphs

Read aloud section 3 of the Lesson 16 Practice Page in a fluent voice, emphasizing intonation and pronunciation of words and targeted sounds. Invite students to echo read or chime on cue. Ensure comprehension by asking text dependent questions. Have students identify cognates.

Lesson Objectives

- Identify and name the initial consonant digraph **wh-.**
- Produce the sound of the initial consonant digraph **wh-.**
- Relate the sound /**wh**/ to the corresponding initial consonant digraph.
- Recognize the initial consonant digraph **wh-** in words.
- Read common high frequency words.

Metacognitive Strategy

Selective auditory attention

Academic Language

consonant, consonant digraph, initial

Materials

- Frieze Card: wh-
- Phonics Lesson 16 Practice Page

Pre-Assess

- Recognition of sounds represented by the blend **wh-**
- Identification of letters used to represent the sound /**wh**/

Transfer Notes:

English learners need explicit instruction in articulation of diagraphs, and the understanding that letters in a diagraph combine to produce a new sound, different than what we associate with what the individual letters represent.

Practice: Recognize Initial Consonant Digraphs in Context

Display the Word Bank and complete section 4 of the Lesson 16 Practice Page with students.

Say: *We will now look at words that include the initial consonant diagraph that we have studied.*

Have students echo read the words on the list for each ending consonant blend, emphasizing the targeted blend. Allow time for students to fill in the chart.

Extend Language Knowledge

Practice: Make Meaning

Complete section 5 of the Lesson 16 practice page with students.

Say: *Let's think about words that begin with the consonant digraph we have been studying today: wh-. Complete each sentence using words from the word bank on the Practice Page. Take turns reading the completed sentences to a partner.*

1. **Where** are my keys?
2. A **whale** is a big ocean animal.
3. Children sometimes **whine** when they don't get what they want.
4. Please **whisper** in the library
5. The bread was made from **wheat** flour.
6. The kitten has long **whiskers** on it face.

Writing

Practice writing the sounds you hear as I say each word. Then write the word. I will also use the word in a sentence.

Pronounce one word at a time from the Word List below, stretching each sound. Use the word in a sentence, and repeat it again after the sentence. For example, say the word **when**. Then say: *When are you going to the play?* Repeat the word **when** after the sentence.

Help students as needed to form letters or recognize letters that form these words.

Sample words: **when, while, whale, whipped, wheel, whim**

Have students confirm their spelling with a partner, making corrections as needed.

Reflect and Review

Ask: *What did you learn today? Discuss with your partner.*

Have students work with their partners to complete the sentence frames at the end of the Lesson 16 Practice Page, assisting as needed.

Word Bank

wh-			
what	whet	whimper	whisper
wheat	whether	whimsical	whistle
wheel	which	whine	white
wheeze	whiff	whip	whittle
when	while	whirl	whiz
where	whim	whisk	who
		whisker	why

✔Formative Assessment

If the student completes each task correctly, proceed to the next skill in the sequence.

Did the student...?	Intervention
Pronounce letter in isolation Pronounce letter in words	Use a mirror to show movement of mouth, tongue, and teeth as the sound is produced. Use hand over mouth to explore movement of air as the sound is produced.
Recognize meaning of words in context	Explain meaning of words before and after reading the text.
Write letters correctly	Provide additional handwriting practice
Spell targeted sounds correctly	Use simple (CCVC) words, practice sound segmentation and blending, use interactive and guided writing.

17 Initial, Medial, and Final Consonant Digraphs sh, ch

Lesson Objectives

- Identify and name the consonant digraphs **sh** and **ch**.
- Produce the sound of the consonant digraphs **sh** and **ch**.
- Relate the sounds **/sh/** and **/ch/** to the corresponding consonant digraphs.
- Recognize the consonant digraphs **sh** and **ch** in words.
- Read common high frequency words.

Metacognitive Strategy

Selective auditory attention

Academic Language

consonant, consonant digraph, initial, medial, final

Materials

- Frieze Cards: sh, ch
- Phonics Lesson 17 Practice Page

Pre-Assess

- Recognition of sounds represented by the digraphs **sh**, **ch**
- Identification of letters used to represent the sound **/sh/**, **/ch/**

Transfer Notes:

English learners need explicit instruction in articulation of digraphs, and the understanding that letters in a digraph combine to produce a new sound, different than what we associate with what the individual letters represent.

Introduce the Lesson

Say: *Today we will identify initial (beginning), medial (middle), and final (ending) consonant digraphs. We will also read text that includes these consonant digraphs.*

Phonemic Awareness and Sound-Spelling Correspondence

Say: *A consonant digraph is made up of two consonants. The two letters together create one sound that is different than the sound each individual consonant makes. We will study consonant digraphs that appear at the beginning, middle, and end of words.*

Say: *Listen to the sound /s/. Say it with me: /s/. Now say it on your own: /s/.*

Repeat with the sound /h/.

Say: *Listen to the new sound that /s/ and /h/ make when they are combined: /sh/. Now say the new sound with me: /sh/.*

Say: *We write consonant digraph sh with the letters s and h.*

Repeat with consonant digraph **ch**.

Elicit Prior Knowledge

Display the Lesson 17 Practice Page. Prompt students to think about their primary language as you work together to complete section 1.

Ask: *What are some examples in your home language of words with these letters or symbols that blend to make a new sound?*

Model: Recognize Consonant Digraphs

Direct students' attention to section 2 of the Lesson 17 Practice Page.

Say: *Let's look at words that have these consonant digraphs.*

Have students echo read the list, emphasizing the digraph in each word.

	Initial (Beginning)	Medial (Middle)	Final (Ending)
sh	short	wishes	dish
ch	cheat	inches	which

Practice: Identify Consonant Digraphs

Read aloud section 3 of the Lesson 17 Practice Page in a fluent voice, emphasizing intonation and pronunciation of words and targeted sounds. Invite students to echo read or chime on cue. Ensure comprehension by asking text dependent questions. Have students identify cognates.

Practice: Recognize Consonant Digraphs in Context

Display the Word Bank and complete section 4 of the Lesson 17 Practice Page with students.

Say: *We will now look at words that include consonant digraphs that we have studied.*

Have students echo read the words on the list for each digraph, emphasizing the targeted blend. Allow time for students to fill in the chart.

Extend Language Knowledge

Practice: Make Meaning

Complete section 5 of the Lesson 17 Practice Page with students.

Say: *Let's read each clue together. Then work with a partner to find an answer from the word bank. Write the answer on the line.*

1. Opposite of tall (short)
2. The meal you eat at noon (lunch)
3. It has scales and lives in water (fish)
4. What happens when you jump in water (splash)
5. To talk with someone (chat)
6. Where the ocean meets land (beach)

Writing

Say: *Practice writing the sounds you hear as I say each word. Then write the word. I will also use the word in a sentence.*

Pronounce one word at a time from the Word List below, stretching each sound. Use the word in a sentence, and repeat it again after the sentence. For example, say the word **cheese**. Then say: *I enjoy ham and cheese sandwiches.* Repeat the word **cheese** after the sentence.

Help students as needed to form letters or recognize letters that form these words.

Sample words: **child, chewed, cheese, sandwich, lunchbox, wash, wash, brush, seashore, fish.**

Have students confirm their spelling with a partner, making corrections as needed.

Reflect and Review

Ask: *What did you learn today?*

Have students work with their partners to complete the sentence frames at the end of the Lesson 15 Practice Page, assisting as needed.

Word Bank

	Initial (Beginning)	Medial (Middle)	Final (Ending)
sh	she	bushes	brush
	shot	dishes	leash
	shape	fishing	flash
	shelf	cushion	fresh
	should	sunshine	crash
	shout	mushroom	polish
ch	chair	kitchen	ranch
	chart	matches	bench
	cheese	peaches	coach
	chest	pitcher	pitch
	chop	bleachers	watch
	change	touchdown	stretch

✔ Formative Assessment

If the student completes each task correctly, proceed to the next skill in the sequence.

Did the student...?	Intervention
Pronounce letter in isolation Pronounce letter in words	Use a mirror to show movement of mouth, tongue, and teeth as the sound is produced. Use hand over mouth to explore movement of air as the sound is produced.
Recognize meaning of words in context	Explain meaning of words before and after reading the text.
Write letters correctly	Provide additional handwriting practice
Spell targeted sounds correctly	Use simple (CCVC) words, practice sound segmentation and blending, use interactive and guided writing.

Lesson Objectives

- Identify and name the consonant digraph **th.**
- Produce the sound of the consonant digraph **th.**
- Relate the sounds /**th**/ to the corresponding consonant digraph.
- Recognize the consonant digraph **th** in words.
- Read common high frequency words.

Metacognitive Strategy

Selective auditory attention

Academic Language

consonant, consonant digraph, initial, medial, final

Materials

- Frieze Card: th
- Phonics Lesson 18 Practice Page

Pre-Assess

- Recognition of sounds represented by the digraphs **th**
- Identification of letters used to represent the sound /**th**/

Transfer Notes:

English learners need explicit instruction in articulation of digraphs, and the understanding that letters in a digraph combine to produce a new sound, different than what we associate with what the individual letters represent.

18 Initial, Medial, and Final Consonant Digraph th

Introduce the Lesson

Say: *Today we will recognize two consonants that combine at the beginning, middle, or end of words. We will also read text that includes this consonant digraph.*

Phonemic Awareness and Sound-Spelling Correspondence

Say: *A consonant digraph is made up of two consonants. The two letters together create one sound that is different than the sound each individual consonant makes. We will study a consonant digraph that appears at the beginning, middle, and end of words.*

Say: *Listen to the sound /t/. Say it with me: /t/. Now say it on your own: /t/.*

Repeat with the sound /h/.

Say: *Listen to the new sound that /t/ and /h/ make when they are combined together: /th/. Now say the new sound with me: /th/.*

Say: *We write the consonant digraph th is with the letters t and h.*

Elicit Prior Knowledge

Display the Lesson 18 Practice Page. Prompt students to think about their primary language as you work together to complete section 1.

Ask: *What are some examples in your home language of words with these letters or symbols that blend to make a new sound?*

Model: Recognize Consonant Digraphs

Direct students' attention to section 2 of the Lesson 18 Practice Page.

Say: *Let's look at words that have this consonant digraph.*

Have students echo read the list, emphasizing the digraph in each word.

	Initial (Beginning)	Medial (Middle)	Final (Ending)
th	this thing	mother panther	bath math

Practice: Identify Consonant Digraphs

Read aloud section 3 of the Lesson 18 Practice Page in a fluent voice, emphasizing intonation and pronunciation of words and targeted sounds. Invite students to echo read or chime on cue. Ensure comprehension by asking text dependent questions. Have students identify cognates.

Practice: Recognize Consonant Digraphs in Context

Display the Word Bank and complete section 4 of the Lesson 18 Practice Page with students.

Say: *We will now look at words that include the consonant digraph* **th**.

Have students echo read the words on the list for each digraph, emphasizing the targeted blend. Allow time for students to fill in the chart.

Extend Language Knowledge

Practice: Use Words in Context

Complete section 5 of the Lesson 18 practice page with students.

Say: *Let's think about words that include the consonant digraph* **th**. *Complete each sentence using words from the word bank on the Practice Page. Take turns reading the completed sentences to a partner.*

1. The **thunder** was very loud during the storm.
2. We ate lots of cake at the **birthday** party.
3. A **moth** flew through a window and into **the** house.
4. The **athlete** wore running **clothes** for the race.
5. I gave my dog a **bath** in the **bathtub**.
6. My **mother** the **father** are the greatest parents.
7. I have lots of **teeth** in my **mouth**!

Writing

Practice writing the sounds you hear as I say each word. Then write the word. I will also use the word in a sentence.

Pronounce one word at a time from the Word List below, stretching each sound. Use the word in a sentence, and repeat it again after the sentence. For example, say the word **Thursday**. Then say: *Thursday is the day after Wednesday.* Repeat the word **Thursday** after the sentence.

Help students as needed to form letters or recognize letters that form these words.

Sample words: **the**, **three**, **athletes**, **birthday**, **Thursday**, **their**

Have students confirm their spelling with a partner, making corrections as needed.

Reflect and Review

Ask: *What did you learn today? Discuss with your partner.*

Have students work with their partners to complete the sentence frames at the end of the Lesson 18 Practice Page, assisting as needed.

Word Bank

	Initial (Beginning)	Medial (Middle)	Final (Ending)
th	think	bathtub	cloth
	thing	athlete	moth
	three	birthday	math
	thick	feather	tooth
	third	clothing	path
	that	other	month
	than		breath
	they		bath
	their		earth
	them		mouth
	these		truth
	this		teeth
	those		south

✓Formative Assessment

If the student completes each task correctly, proceed to the next skill in the sequence.

Did the student…?	Intervention
Pronounce letter in isolation Pronounce letter in words	Use a mirror to show movement of mouth, tongue, and teeth as the sound is produced. Use hand over mouth to explore movement of air as the sound is produced.
Recognize meaning of words in context	Explain meaning of words before and after reading the text.
Write letters correctly	Provide additional handwriting practice
Spell targeted sounds correctly	Use simple (CCVC, CVCC) words, practice sound segmentation and blending, use interactive and guided writing.

19 Initial, Medial, and Final Consonant Digraph ph

Introduce the Lesson

Say: *Today we will recognize two consonants that combine at the beginning, middle, or end of words. We will also read text that includes this consonant digraph.*

Phonemic Awareness and Sound-Spelling Correspondence

Say: *A consonant digraph is made up of two consonants. The two letters together create one sound that is different than the sound each individual consonant makes. We will study a consonant digraph that appears at the beginning, middle, and end of words.*

Say: *Listen to the sound /p/. Say it with me: /p/. Now say it on your own: /p/.*

Repeat with the sound /h/.

Say: *Listen to the new sound that /p/ and /h/ make when they are combined together: /ph/. Now say the new sound with me: /ph/.*

Say: *We write consonant digraph **ph** with the letters **p** and **h**.*

Elicit Prior Knowledge

Display the Lesson 19 Practice Page. Prompt students to think about their primary language as you work together to complete section 1.

Ask: *What are some examples in your home language of words with these letters or symbols that blend to make a new sound?*

Model: Recognize Consonant Digraphs

Direct students' attention to section 2 of the Lesson 19 Practice Page.

Say: *Let's look at words that have this consonant digraph.*

Have students echo read the list, emphasizing the digraph in each word.

	Initial (Beginning)	Medial (Middle)	Final (Ending)
ph	phone photo	orphan elephant	autograph graph

Practice: Identify Consonant Digraphs

Read aloud section 3 of the Lesson 19 Practice Page in a fluent voice, emphasizing intonation and pronunciation of words and targeted sounds. Invite students to echo read or chime on cue. Ensure comprehension by asking text dependent questions. Have students identify cognates.

Lesson Objectives

- Identify and name the consonant digraph **ph.**
- Produce the sound of the consonant digraph **ph.**
- Relate the sound /**ph**/ to the corresponding consonant digraph.
- Recognize the consonant digraph **ph** in words.
- Read common high frequency words.

Metacognitive Strategy

Selective auditory attention

Academic Language

consonant, consonant digraph, initial, medial, final

Materials

Frieze Card: ph
Phonics Lesson 19 Practice Page

Pre-Assess

- Recognition of sounds represented by the digraphs **ph**
- Identification of letters used to represent the sound /**ph**/

Transfer Notes:

English learners need explicit instruction in articulation of digraphs, and the understanding that letters in a digraph combine to produce a new sound different than what we associate with what the individual letters represent.

Practice: Recognize Consonant Digraphs in Context

Display the Word Bank and complete section 4 of the Lesson 19 Practice Page with students.

Say: *We will now look at words that include the consonant digraph **ph**.*

Have students echo read the words on the list for each digraph, emphasizing the targeted blend. Allow time for students to fill in the chart.

Extend Language Knowledge

Practice: Make Meaning

Complete section 5 of the Lesson 19 Practice Page with students.

Say: *Let's read each clue together. Then work with a partner to find an answer from the word bank. Write the answer on the line.*

1. You take it with a camera (photograph)
2. The son of your brother or sister (nephew)
3. In English, there are 26 letters in this (alphabet)
4. Singers use this so we can hear them (microphone)
5. Your signature (autograph)
6. You use it to make calls (telephone)

Writing

Practice writing the sounds you hear as I say each word. Then write the word. I will also use the word in a sentence.

Pronounce one word at a time from the Word List below, stretching each sound. Use the word in a sentence, and repeat it again after the sentence. For example, say the word **elephant**. Then say: *The elephant has a long trunk.* Repeat the word **elephant** after the sentence.

Help students as needed to form letters or recognize letters that form these words.

Sample words: **elephant**, **graph**, **orphan**, **telephone**, **autograph**

Have students confirm their spelling with a partner, making corrections as needed.

Reflect and Review

Ask: *What did you learn today? Discuss with your partner.*

Have students work with their partners to complete the sentence frames at the end of the Lesson 19 Practice Page, assisting as needed.

Word Bank

	Initial (Beginning)	Medial (Middle)	Final (Ending)
ph	phrase	gopher	graph
	phone	hyphen	morph
	phonics	orphan	digraph
	phantom	alphabet	triumph
	photo	dolphin	autograph
	pharmacy	emphasis	photograph
	phony	microphone	telegraph

✓Formative Assessment

If the student completes each task correctly, proceed to the next skill in the sequence.

Did the student...?	Intervention
Pronounce letter in isolation Pronounce letter in words	Use a mirror to show movement of mouth, tongue, and teeth as the sound is produced. Use hand over mouth to explore movement of air as the sound is produced.
Recognize meaning of words in context	Explain meaning of words before and after reading the text.
Write letters correctly	Provide additional handwriting practice
Spell targeted sounds correctly	Use simple (CCVC, CVCC) words, practice sound segmentation and blending, use interactive and guided writing.

20 Initial, Medial, and Final Consonant Digraph gh

Metacognitive Strategy

Selective auditory attention

Academic Language

consonant, consonant digraph, initial, medial, final

Materials

- Frieze Card: gh
- Phonics Lesson 20 Practice Page

Pre-Assess

- Recognition of sounds represented by the digraphs **gh**
- Identification of letters used to represent the sound /**gh**/

Transfer Notes:

English learners need explicit instruction in articulation of digraphs, and the understanding that letters in a digraph combine to produce a new sound, different than what we associate with what the individual letters represent.

Introduce the Lesson

Say: *Today we will recognize two consonants that combine at the beginning, middle, or end of words. We will also read text that includes this consonant digraph.*

Phonemic Awareness and Sound-Spelling Correspondence

Say: *A consonant digraph is made up of two consonants. The two letters together create one sound that is different than the sound each individual consonant makes. We will study a consonant digraph that appears at the beginning, middle, and end of words.*

Say: *Listen to the sound /**g**/. Say it with me: /**g**/. Now say it on your own: /**g**/.*

Repeat with the sound /h/

Say: *Listen to the new sound that /**g**/ and /**h**/ make when they are combined together: /**gh**/. Now say the new sound with me: /**gh**/. The letters **gh** sometimes makes the /**f**/ sound or can be silent.*

Say: *We write consonant digraph **gh** with the letters **g** and **h**.*

Elicit Prior Knowledge

Display the Lesson 20 Practice Page. Prompt students to think about their primary language as you work together to complete section 1.

Ask: *What are some examples in your home language of words with these letters or symbols that blend to make a new sound?*

Model: Recognize Consonant Digraphs

Direct students' attention to section 2 of the Lesson 20 Practice Page.

Say: *Let's look at words that have this consonant digraph.*

Have students echo read the list, emphasizing the digraph in each word.

	Initial (Beginning)	Medial (Middle)	Final (Ending)
gh	ghost (/gh/)	afghan (/gh/) laughing (/gh/ like /f/) right (silent /gh/)	laugh (/gh/ like /f/) though (silent /gh/)

Practice: Recognize Consonant Digraphs

Read aloud section 3 of the Lesson 20 Practice Page in a fluent voice, emphasizing intonation and pronunciation of words and targeted sounds. Invite students to echo read or chime on cue. Ensure comprehension by asking text dependent questions. Have students identify cognates.

Practice: Recognize Consonant Digraphs in Context

Display the Word Bank and complete section 4 of the Lesson 20 Practice Page with students.

Say: *We will now look at words that include the consonant digraph* **gh.**

Have students echo read the words on the list for each digraph, emphasizing the targeted blend. Allow time for students to fill in the chart.

Extend Language Knowledge

Practice: Use Words in Context

Say: *Let's think about words that include the consonant digraph* **gh.** *Complete each sentence using words from the word bank on the Practice Page. Take turns reading the completed sentences to a partner.*

1. The sandpaper feels **rough** against my skin.
2. I **laugh** when someone tickles me.
3. I would be very scared if I saw a **ghost**.
4. Sometimes we borrow sugar from our next door **neighbor**.
5. We like **doughnuts** with powdered sugar.
6. You should cover your mouth when you **cough**.

Writing

Practice writing the sounds you hear as I say each word. Then write the word. I will also use the word in a sentence.

Pronounce one word at a time from the Word List below, stretching each sound. Use the word in a sentence, and repeat it again after the sentence. For example, say the word **night**. Then say: *The sun goes down at night.* Repeat the word **night** after the sentence.

Help students as needed to form letters or recognize letters that form these words.

Sample words: **ghost, cough, laughter, tough, night, neighbor**

Have students confirm their spelling with a partner, making corrections as needed.

Reflect and Review

Ask: *What did you learn today? Discuss with your partner.*

Have students work with their partners to complete the sentence frames at the end of the Lesson 20 Practice Page, assisting as needed.

Word Bank

	Initial (Beginning)	Medial (Middle)	Final (Ending)
gh	(/gh/)	(/gh/)	(/gh/ like /f/)
	ghost	afghan	enough
	ghetto	(/gh/ like /f/)	rough
	gherkin	rougher	laugh
	ghoul	laughter	tough
	ghastly	toughen	cough
		(silent /gh/)	(silent /gh/)
		right	high
		sight	sigh
		fight	dough
		doughnuts	though
		delight	neighbor

✓Formative Assessment

If the student completes each task correctly, precede to the next skill in the sequence.

Did the student...?	Intervention
Pronounce letter in isolation Pronounce letter in words	Use a mirror to show movement of mouth, tongue, and teeth as the sound is produced. Use hand over mouth to explore movement of air as the sound is produced.
Recognize meaning of words in context	Explain meaning of words before and after reading the text.
Write letters correctly	Provide additional handwriting practice
Spell targeted sounds correctly	Use simple (CCVC, CVCC) words, practice sound segmentation and blending, use interactive and guided writing.

21 Final Consonant Digraph -ng

Lesson Objectives

- Identify and name the final consonant digraph -**ng**.
- Produce the sound of the final consonant digraph -**ng**.
- Relate the sounds /**ng**/ to the corresponding consonant digraph.
- Recognize the consonant digraph -**ng** in words.
- Read common high frequency words.

Metacognitive Strategy

Selective auditory attention

Academic Language

consonant, consonant digraph, final

Materials

- Frieze Card: ng
- Phonics Lesson 21 Practice Page

Pre-Assess

- Recognition of sounds represented by the digraphs **ng**
- Identification of letters used to represent the sound /**ng**/

Transfer Notes:

English learners need explicit instruction in articulation of digraphs, and the understanding that letters in a digraph combine to produce a new sound, different than what we associate with what the individual letters represent.

Introduce the Lesson

Say: *Today we will recognize two consonants that combine at the end of words. We will also read text that includes this consonant digraph.*

Phonemic Awareness and Sound-Spelling Correspondence

Say: *A consonant digraph is made up of two consonants. The two letters together create one sound that is different than the sound each individual consonant makes. We will study a consonant digraph that appears at the end of words.*

Say: *Listen to the sound /**n**/. Say it with me: /**n**/. Now say it on your own: /**n**/.*

Repeat with the sound /**g**/

Say: *Listen to the new sound that /**n**/ and /**g**/ make when they are combined: /**ng**/. Now say the new sound with me: /**ng**/.*

Say: *We write consonant digraph -**ng** with the letters **n** and **g**.*

Elicit Prior Knowledge

Display the Lesson 21 Practice Page. Prompt students to think about their primary language as you work together to complete section 1.

Ask: *What are some examples in your home language of words with these letters or symbols that blend to make a new sound?*

Model: Recognize Final Consonant Digraph -ng

Direct students' attention to section 2 of the Lesson 21 Practice Page.

Say: *Let's look at words that end with consonant digraph -**ng**.*

Have students echo read the list, emphasizing the digraph in each word.

Final (Ending) -ng	
bang	long
swing	strong
king	stung

Practice: Final Consonant Digraph -ng

Read aloud section 3 of the Lesson 21 Practice Page in a fluent voice, emphasizing intonation and pronunciation of words and targeted sounds. Invite students to echo read or chime in on cue. Ensure comprehension by asking text dependent questions. Have students identify cognates.

Practice: Recognize Final Consonant Digraph -ng

Display the Word Bank and complete section 4 of the Lesson 21 Practice Page with students.

Say: *We will now look at words that end with consonant digraph /**ng**/.*

Have students echo read the words on the list, emphasizing the final consonant digraph. Allow time for students to fill in the chart.

Extend Language Knowledge

Practice: Make Meaning

Complete section 5 of the Lesson 21 Practice Page with students.

Say: *Let's read each clue together. Then work with a partner to find an answer from the word bank. Write the answer on the line.*

1. What some birds do(sing)
2. The sound you hear when a drum is hit(bang)
3. The royal head of a government(king)
4. Bats like to do this upside-down(hang)
5. The organ in your body you use to breathe(lung)
6. Opposite of weak(strong)

Writing

Say: *Practice writing the sounds you hear as I say each word. Then write the word. I will also use the word in a sentence.*

Pronounce one word at a time from the Word List below, stretching each sound. Use the word in a sentence, and repeat it again after the sentence. For example, say the word **strong**. Then say: *The strong wind almost blew me off my feet!* Repeat the word **strong** after the sentence.

Help students as needed to form letters or recognize letters that form these words.

Sample words: **stung, strong, sang, song, long**

Have students confirm their spelling with a partner, making corrections as needed.

Reflect and Review

Ask: *What did you learn today? Discuss with your partner.*

Have students work with their partners to complete the sentence frames at the end of the Lesson 21 Practice Page, assisting as needed.

Word Bank

Final (Ending) -ng		
bang	long	song
belong	lung	spring
cling	pang	string
ding	rang	strong
fang	ring	stung
gang	sang	thing
hang	sing	wing
king	slang	oblong

✔Formative Assessment

If the student completes each task correctly, precede to the next skill in the sequence.

Did the student...?	Intervention
Pronounce letter in isolation Pronounce letter in words	Use a mirror to show movement of mouth, tongue, and teeth as the sound is produced. Use hand over mouth to explore movement of air as the sound is produced.
Recognize meaning of words in context	Explain meaning of words before and after reading the text.
Write letters correctly	Provide additional handwriting practice
Spell targeted sounds correctly	Use simple (CCVC, CVCC) words, practice sound segmentation and blending, use interactive and guided writing.

22 Silent Consonant Digraphs dg, gn

Lesson Objectives

- Identify and name the silent consonant digraphs **dge** and **gn.**
- Produce the sound of the silent consonant digraphs **dge** and **gn.**
- Relate the sounds **/j/** and **/n/** to the corresponding consonant digraphs dge and gn.
- Recognize the silent consonant digraphs **dge** and **gn** in words.
- Read common high frequency words.

Metacognitive Strategy

Selective auditory attention

Academic Language

consonant, consonant digraph, initial, medial, final

Materials

- Frieze Card: dge, gn
- Phonics Lesson 22 Practice Page

Pre-Assess

- Recognition of sounds represented by the digraphs **dge, gn**
- Identification of of silent letters that represent the sounds **/j/, /n/**

Transfer Notes:

English learners need explicit instruction in articulation of digraphs, and the understanding that letters in a digraph combine to produce a new sound, different from what we associate with what the individual letters represent. Silent letters are challenging for English learners because they are difficult to discern for sound or spelling. Therefore, the letter patterns in familiar words need to be explicitly taught and memorized.

Introduce the Lesson

Say: *Today we will identify initial, medial, and final silent consonant digraphs. We will recognize these silent consonant digraphs in words and read text that includes these digraphs.*

Phonemic Awareness and Sound-Spelling Correspondence

Say: *A consonant digraph is made up of two consonants that produce one sound. In English, a silent letter is one that appears in a word but is not pronounced. In the digraph* **dge,** *the* **d** *is silent and the* **g** *makes soft g sound.*

Say: *Listen to the sound* **d, g,** *and* **e** *make when combined* **/g/.** *Say it with me:* **/g/.** *Now say it on your own:* **/d/.**

Repeat for the sound /j/.

Say: *Listen to the new sound that /d/ and /g/ make when they are combined: /g/.* **Say:** *We write consonant digraph* **dge** *is with the letters* **d, g, e.** *The letter* **e** *is silent.*

Repeat with consonant digraph **gn.**

Elicit Prior Knowledge

Display the Lesson 22 Practice Page. Prompt students to think about their primary language as you work together to complete section 1.

Ask: *What are some examples in your home language of sounds, letters, or symbols that when combined one letter is silent?*

Model: Recognize Silent Consonant Digraphs dge, gn

Direct students' attention to section 2 of the Lesson 22 Practice Page.

Say: *Let's look at words that have silent consonant digraphs at beginning, middle, or end of a word.*

Medial (middle) dge	Initial (beginning) gn	Medial (middle) gn	Final (ending) gn
bridge	gnu	cologne	sign
nudge	gnome	assignments	assign

Practice: Silent Consonant Digraphs dge, gn

Read aloud section 3 of the Lesson 22 Practice Page in a fluent voice, emphasizing intonation and pronunciation of words and targeted sounds. Invite students to echo read or chime on cue. Ensure comprehension by asking text dependent questions. Have students identify cognates.

Practice: Recognize Silent Consonant Digraphs dge, gn

Display the Word Bank and complete section 4 of the Lesson 22 Practice Page with students.

Say: *We will now look at words with consonant digraphs **dge** and **gn**.*

Have students echo read the words on the list, emphasizing the consonant digraph. Allow time for students to fill in the chart.

Extend Language Knowledge

Practice: Using Words in Context

Complete section 5 of the Lesson 22 practice page with students.

Say: *We will now look at words that include the silent consonant digraphs **dge** and **gn**. Complete each sentence using words from the word bank on the Practice Page. Take turns reading the completed sentences to a partner.*

1. I judged who had made the best **fudge**.
2. The **gnome** was small and cute.
3. Our teacher **assigns** too much homework.
4. The police officer wears a **badge**.
5. A **partridge** is a kind of bird.
6. The **gnats** are buzzing in my ear.

Writing

Practice writing the sounds you hear as I say each word. Then write the word. I will also use the word in a sentence.

Pronounce one word at a time from the Word List below, stretching each sound. Use the word in a sentence, and repeat it again after the sentence. For example, say the word **edge**. Then say: *Don't stand too close to the edge.* Repeat the word **edge** after the sentence.

Help students as needed to form letters or recognize letters that form these words.

Sample words: **ridge, gnome, edge, judge, gnashing, gnarly**

Have students confirm their spelling with a partner, making corrections as needed.

Reflect and Review

Ask: *What did you learn today? Discuss with your partner.*

Have students work with their partners to complete the sentence frames at the end of the Lesson 22 Practice Page, assisting as needed.

Word Bank

Medial (middle) dge		
bridge	grudge	
judge	hedge	
badge	nudge	
dodge	pledged	
fudge	ridge	
budget	smudge	
lodge	trudge	
edge	widget	
Initial (beginning) gn	**Medial (middle) gn**	**Final (ending) gn**
gnome	dignify	sign
gnats	magnet	design
gnu	cologne	align
gnash	dislodged	assign
gnarly	designate	malign
	diagnose	reign
	alignment	foreign
	assignments	sovereign
	magnificent	campaign

✔ Formative Assessment

If the student completes each task correctly, precede to the next skill in the sequence.

Did the student…?	Intervention
Pronounce letter in isolation Pronounce letter in words	Use a mirror to show movement of mouth, tongue, and teeth as the sound is produced. Use hand over mouth to explore movement of air as the sound is produced.
Recognize meaning of words in context	Explain meaning of words before and after reading the text.
Write letters correctly	Provide additional handwriting practice
Spell targeted sounds correctly	Use simple (CCVC, CVCC) words, practice sound segmentation and blending, use interactive and guided writing.

Lesson Objectives

- Identify and name the digraphs **kn-** and **wr-**
- of the initial silent consonant digraphs **kn-** and **wr-**.
- Relate the sounds **/n/** and **/r/** to the corresponding initial consonant digraphs **kn-** and **wr-**.
- Recognize the initial silent consonant digraphs **kn-** and **wr-** in words..
- Read common high frequency words.

Metacognitive Strategy

Selective auditory attention

Academic Language

consonant, consonant digraph, initial, medial, final

Materials

- Frieze Card: dge, gn
- Phonics Lesson 23 Practice Page

Pre-Assess

- Recognition of sounds represented by the initial silent consonant digraphs **kn-** and **wr-**
- Identification of silent consonant digraphs that represent the sounds **/n/** and **/r/**

Transfer Notes:

English learners need explicit instruction in articulation of digraphs, and the understanding that letters in a digraph combine to produce a new sound, different from what we associate with what the individual letters represent. Silent letters are challenging for English learners because they are difficult to discern for sound or spelling. Therefore, the letter patterns in familiar words need to be explicitly taught and memorized.

23 Silent Consonant Digraphs kn-, wr-

Introduce the Lesson

Say: *Today we will identify and recognize initial silent consonant digraphs and read text that includes these digraphs.*

Phonemic Awareness and Sound-Spelling Correspondence

Say: *A consonant digraph is made up of two consonants that produce one sound. In English, a silent letter is one that appears in a word but is not pronounced. In the digraph* **kn-,** *the* **k** *is silent.*

Say: *Listen to the sound that* **k** *and* **n** *make when combined: /n/. Now say the sound with me: /n/.*

Now say it on your own: **/n/**.

Say: *We write consonant digraph* **kn-** *with the letters* **k** *and* **n.**

Repeat with initial silent consonant digraph **wr-.**

Elicit Prior Knowledge

Display the Lesson 23 Practice Page. Prompt students to think about their primary language as you work together to complete section 1.

Ask: *What are some examples in your home language of words with silent letters?*

Model: Recognize Initial Silent Consonant Digraphs kn-, wr-

Direct students' attention to section 2 of the Lesson 23 Practice Page.

Say: *Let's look at words that have initial silent consonant digraphs* **kn-** *and* **wr-.**

Have students echo read the lists, emphasizing the digraph in each word.

	kn-	wr-
Initial (beginning)	knot knock	write wrap

Practice: Initial Silent Consonant Digraphs kn-, wr-

Read aloud section 3 of the Lesson 23 Practice Page in a fluent voice, emphasizing intonation and pronunciation of words and targeted sounds. Invite students to echo read or chime on cue. Ensure comprehension by asking text dependent questions. Have students identify cognates.

Practice: Recognize Initial Silent Consonant Digraphs kn-, wr-

Display the Word Bank and complete section 4 of the Lesson 23 Practice Page with students.

Say: *We will now look at words with initial silent consonant digraphs **kn-** and **wr-**.*

Have students echo read the words on the list, emphasizing the digraph. Allow time for students to fill in the chart.

Extend Language Knowledge

Practice: Make Meaning

Complete section 5 of the Lesson 23 Practice Page with students.

Say: *Let's read each clue together. Then work with a partner to find an answer from the word bank. Write the answer on the line.*

1. What you do to a gift before you give it (wrap)
2. What you turn to open a door (knob)
3. What you do to a door to see if anyone is home (knock)
4. Where your hand is connected to your arm (wrist)
5. In medieval times, he often wore a suit of armor (knight)
6. You use this to cut food (knife)

Writing

Say: *Practice writing the sounds you hear as I say each word. Then write the word. I will also use the word in a sentence.*

Pronounce one word at a time from the Word List below, stretching each sound. Use the word in a sentence, and repeat it again after the sentence. For example, say the word **knee**. Then say: *Your knee is part of your leg.* Repeat the word **knee** after the sentence.

Help students as needed to form letters or recognize letters that form these words.

Sample words: **wrinkle, knit, knock, knee, write**

Have students confirm their spelling with a partner, making corrections as needed.

Reflect and Review

Ask: *What did you learn today? Discuss with your partner.*

Have students work with their partners to complete the sentence frames at the end of the Lesson 23 Practice Page, assisting as needed.

Word Bank

kn-	wr-
knit	wry
knot	wrap
knob	wrath
knee	wreck
know	wrist
knew	write
kneel	wrong
knock	wrote
knife	wring
known	wrung
knuckle	wrench
knight	wrestle
knowledge	wrinkles

✓Formative Assessment

If the student completes each task correctly, precede to the next skill in the sequence. If not, refer to suggested Intervention 2.

Did the student…?	Intervention
Pronounce letter in isolation Pronounce letter in words	Use a mirror to show movement of mouth, tongue, and teeth as the sound is produced. Use hand over mouth to explore movement of air as the sound is produced.
Recognize meaning of words in context	Explain meaning of words before and after reading the text.
Write letters correctly	Provide additional handwriting practice
Spell targeted sounds correctly	Use simple (CCVC, CVCC) words, practice sound segmentation and blending, use interactive and guided writing.

24 Final Silent Consonant Digraphs -ld, -lf, -lk

Introduce the Lesson

Say: *Today we will identify and recognize final silent consonant digraphs and read text that includes these digraphs.*

Phonemic Awareness and Sound-Spelling Correspondence

Say: *A consonant digraph is made up of two consonants that produce one sound. In English, a silent letter is one that appears in a word but is not pronounced. In the digraph -ld, the l is silent.*

Say: *Listen to the sound that l and d make when combined: /d/. Now say the sound with me: /d/.*

Now say it on your own: /d/.

Say: *We write consonant digraph -ld with the letters l and d.*

Repeat with final silent consonant digraphs **-lf** and **-lk.**

Elicit Prior Knowledge

Display the Lesson 24 Practice Page. Prompt students to think about their primary language as you work together to complete section 1.

Ask: *What are some examples in your home language of words with silent letters?*

Model: Recognize Final Silent Consonant Digraphs -ld, -lf, -lk

Direct students' attention to section 2 of the Lesson 24 Practice Page.

Say: *Let's look at words that have final silent consonant digraphs -ld, -lf, -lk.*

Have students echo read the lists, emphasizing the digraph in each word.

	-ld	-lf	-lk
Final (ending)	could should	calf half	walk yolk

Practice: Final Silent Consonant Digraphs -ld, -lf, -lk

Read aloud section 3 of the Lesson 24 Practice Page in a fluent voice, emphasizing intonation and pronunciation of words and targeted sounds. Invite students to echo read or chime on cue. Ensure comprehension by asking text dependent questions. Have students identify cognates.

Lesson Objectives

- Identify and name the final silent consonant digraphs **-ld, -lf,** and **-lk.**
- Produce the sound of the final silent consonant digraphs **-ld, -lf,** and **-lk.**
- Relate the sounds **/d/, /f/,** and **/k/** to the corresponding final silent consonant digraphs.
- Recognize the final silent consonant digraphs **-ld, -lf,** and **-lk** in words.
- Read common high frequency words.

Metacognitive Strategy

Selective auditory attention

Academic Language

consonant, consonant digraph, initial, medial, final

Materials

- Frieze Card: ld, lf, lk
- Phonics Lesson 24 Practice Page

Pre-Assess

- Recognition of sounds represented by the final silent consonant digraphs **-ld, -lf,** and **-lk**
- Identification of silent consonant digraphs that represent the sounds **/d/, /f/** and **/k/**

Transfer Notes:

English learners need explicit instruction in articulation of digraphs, and the understanding that letters in a digraph combine to produce a new sound, different from what we associate with what the individual letters represent. Silent letters are challenging for English learners because they are difficult to discern for sound or spelling. Therefore, the letter patterns in familiar words need to be explicitly taught and memorized.

Practice: Recognize Final Silent Consonant Digraphs -ld, -lf, -lk

Display the Word Bank and complete section 4 of the Lesson 24 Practice Page with students.

Say: *We will now look at words with final silent consonant digraphs -ld, -lf, and –lk.*

Have students echo read the words on the list, emphasizing the digraph. Allow time for students to fill in the chart.

Extend Language Knowledge

Practice: Using Words in Context

Complete section 5 of the Lesson 22 Practice Page with students.

Say: *We will now look at words that include the final silent consonant digraphs -ld, -lf, and -lk. Complete each sentence using words from the word bank on the Practice Page. Take turns reading the completed sentences to a partner.*

1. I **would** like to **talk** with you.
2. You **should** get at least 8 hours of sleep each night.
3. I'll split my cookie in **half** to share with you.
4. I **could** ride my bike or **walk** to school.
5. The teacher writes on the board with **chalk**.
6. A **calf** is a baby cow.

Writing

Say: *Practice writing the sounds you hear as I say each word. Then write the word. I will also use the word in a sentence.*

Pronounce one word at a time from the Word List below, stretching each sound. Use the word in a sentence, and repeat it again after the sentence. For example, say the word **talk**. Then say: *Don't talk with food in your mouth.* Repeat the word **talk** after the sentence.

Help students as needed to form letters or recognize letters that form these words.

Sample words: **half, folk, calf, half, talk, would**

Have students confirm their spelling with a partner, making corrections as needed.

Reflect and Review

Ask: *What did you learn today? Discuss with your partner.*

Have students work with their partners to complete the sentence frames at the end of the Lesson 24 Practice Page, assisting as needed.

Word Bank

-ld	-lf	-lk
could	half	walk
would	calf	talk
should		folk
		balk
		stalk
		chalk

✔Formative Assessment

If the student completes each task correctly, precede to the next skill in the sequence.

Did the student…?	Intervention
Pronounce letter in isolation Pronounce letter in words	Use a mirror to show movement of mouth, tongue, and teeth as the sound is produced. Use hand over mouth to explore movement of air as the sound is produced.
Recognize meaning of words in context	Explain meaning of words before and after reading the text.
Write letters correctly	Provide additional handwriting practice
Spell targeted sounds correctly	Use simple (CCVC, CVCC) words, practice sound segmentation and blending, use interactive and guided writing.

Lesson Objectives

- Identify and name the medial and final silent consonant digraphs **lm, mb,** and **mn**.
- Produce the sound of the medial and final silent consonant digraphs **lm, mb,** and **mn**.
- Relate the sound **/m/** to the corresponding silent consonant digraphs lm, **mb**, and **mn**.
- Recognize the medial and final silent consonant digraphs **lm, mb,** and **mn** in words.
- Read common high frequency words.

Metacognitive Strategy

Selective auditory attention

Academic Language

consonant, consonant digraph, initial, medial, final

Materials

- Frieze Card: lm, mb, mn
- Phonics Lesson 25 Practice Page

Pre-Assess

- Recognition of sounds represented by the silent consonant digraphs **lm**, **mb**, and **mn**
- Identification of silent consonant digraphs that represent the sound **/m/**

Transfer Notes:

English learners need explicit instruction in articulation of digraphs, and the understanding that letters in a digraph combine to produce a new sound, different from what we associate with what the individual letters represent. Silent letters are challenging for English learners because they are difficult to discern for sound or spelling. Therefore, the letter patterns in familiar words need to be explicitly taught and memorized.

25 Silent Consonant Digraphs -lm, -mb, -mn

Introduce the Lesson

Say: *Today we will identify and recognize medial and final silent consonant digraphs and read text that includes these digraphs.*

Phonemic Awareness and Sound-Spelling Correspondence

Say: *A consonant digraph is made up of two consonants that produce one sound. In English, a silent letter is one that appears in a word but is not pronounced. In the digraph -lm the l is silent.*

Say: *Listen to the sound that l and m make when combined: /m/. Now say the sound with me: /m/. Now say it on your own: /m/.*

Say: *We write consonant digraph lm with the letters l and m.*

Repeat with silent consonant digraphs **mb** and **mn**.

Elicit Prior Knowledge

Display the Lesson 24 Practice Page. Prompt students to think about their primary language as you work together to complete section 1.

Ask: *What are some examples in your home language of words with silent letters?*

Model: Recognize Silent Consonant Digraphs -lm, -mb, -mn

Direct students' attention to section 2 of the Lesson 25 Practice Page.

Say: *Let's look at words that have silent consonant digraphs lm, mb, mn.*

Have students echo read the lists, emphasizing the digraph in each word.

	lm	mb	mn
Medial (middle)	salmon	n/a	n/a
Final (ending)	calm palm	comb lamb	column autumn

Practice: Silent Consonant Digraphs -lm, -mb, -mn

Read aloud section 3 of the Lesson 25 Practice Page in a fluent voice, emphasizing intonation and pronunciation of words and targeted sounds. Invite students to echo read or chime on cue. Ensure comprehension by asking text dependent questions. Have students identify cognates.

Practice: Recognize Silent Consonant Digraphs -lm, -mb, -mn

Complete section 4 of the Lesson 25 practice page with students.

Say: *We will now look at words with silent consonant digraphs **lm**, **mb**, and **mn**.*

Have students echo read the words on the list, emphasizing the digraph. Allow time for students to fill in the chart.

Extend Language Knowledge

Practice: Make Meaning

Complete section 5 of the Lesson 25 Practice Page with students.

Say: *Let's read each clue together. Then work with a partner to find an answer from the word bank. Write the answer on the line.*

- The season before winter (autumn)
- A song sung in a church (hymn)
- Where one is buried (tomb)
- A type of fish (salmon)
- The opposite of worried (calm)
- An arm or a leg (limb)

Writing

Say: *Practice writing the sounds you hear as I say each word. Then write the word. I will also use the word in a sentence.*

Pronounce one word at a time from the Word List below, stretching each sound. Use the word in a sentence, and repeat it again after the sentence. For example, say the word **climb**. Then say: *It will take hours to climb the mountain.* Repeat the word **climb** after the sentence.

Help students as needed to form letters or recognize letters that form these words.

Sample words: **lamb, crumb, thumb, hymn, climb, limb, calm, autumn**

Have students confirm their spelling with a partner, making corrections as needed.

Reflect and Review

Ask: *What did you learn today? Discuss with your partner.*

Have students work with their partners to complete the sentence frames at the end of the Lesson 25 Practice Page, assisting as needed.

Word Bank

	lm	mb	mn
Medial (middle)	salmon	n/a	n/a
Final (ending)	calm palm balm	bomb comb crumb dumb lamb numb climb limb thumb tomb	autumn column condemn hymn solemn

✔Formative Assessment

If the student completes each task correctly, precede to the next skill in the sequence.

Did the student...?	Intervention
Pronounce letter in isolation Pronounce letter in words	Use a mirror to show movement of mouth, tongue, and teeth as the sound is produced. Use hand over mouth to explore movement of air as the sound is produced.
Recognize meaning of words in context	Explain meaning of words before and after reading the text.
Write letters correctly	Provide additional handwriting practice
Spell targeted sounds correctly	Use simple (CCVC, CVCC) words, practice sound segmentation and blending, use interactive and guided writing.

Lesson Objectives

- Identify and name the initial silent consonant digraph **rh-**.
- Produce the sound of the initial silent consonant digraph **rh-**.
- Relate the sound **/r/** to the corresponding initial silent consonant digraph **rh-**.
- Recognize the initial silent consonant digraph **rh-** in words.
- Read common high frequency words.

Metacognitive Strategy

Selective auditory attention

Academic Language

consonant, consonant digraph, initial

Materials

- Frieze Card: rh
- Phonics Lesson 26 Practice Page

Pre-Assess

- Recognition of sounds represented by the silent consonant digraph **rh-**
- Identification of a silent consonant digraph that represents the sound **/r/**

Transfer Notes:

English learners need explicit instruction in articulation of digraphs, and the understanding that letters in a digraph combine to produce a new sound, different from what we associate with what the individual letters represent. Silent letters are challenging for English learners because they are difficult to discern for sound or spelling. Therefore, the letter patterns in familiar words need to be explicitly taught and memorized.

26 Initial Silent Consonant Digraph rh-

Introduce the Lesson

Say: *Today we will identify and recognize medial and final silent consonant digraphs and read text that includes these digraphs.*

Phonemic Awareness and Sound-Spelling Correspondence

Say: *A consonant digraph is made up of two consonants that produce one sound. In English, a silent letter is one that appears in a word but is not pronounced. In the digraph **rh-**, the **h** is silent.*

Say: *Listen to the sound that **r** and **h** make when combined: /r/. Now say the sound with me: /r/. Now say it on your own: /r/.*

Say: *We write the silent consonant digraph **rh-** with the letters **r** and **h**.*

Elicit Prior Knowledge

Display the Lesson 26 Practice Page. Prompt students to think about their primary language as you work together to complete section 1.

Ask: *What are some examples in your home language of words with silent letters?*

Model: Recognize Initial Consonant Digraph rh-

Direct students' attention to section 2 of the Lesson 26 Practice Page.

Say: Let's look at words that have initial silent consonant digraph **rh-**.

Have students echo read the list, emphasizing the digraph in each word.

	rh-	
Initial (beginning)	rhinoceros rhyme	rhythm rhumba

Practice: Initial Silent Consonant Digraph rh-

Read aloud section 3 of the Lesson 26 Practice Page in a fluent voice, emphasizing intonation and pronunciation of words and targeted sounds. Invite students to echo read or chime on cue. Ensure comprehension by asking text dependent questions. Have students identify cognates.

Practice: Recognize Initial Silent Consonant Digraph rh-

Complete section 4 of the Lesson 26 practice page with students.

Say: *We will now look at words with initial silent consonant digraph **rh-**.*

Have students echo read the words on the list, emphasizing the digraph. Allow time for students to fill in the chart.

Extend Language Knowledge

Practice: Use Words in Context

Complete section 5 of the Lesson 26 practice page with students.

Say: *We will now look at words that include the initial silent consonant digraph **rh-**. Complete each sentence using words from the word bank on the Practice Page. Take turns reading the completed sentences to a partner.*

1. The **rhinoceros** lives in the grasslands.
2. A **rhombus** has four equal sides.
3. The words how and now **rhyme**.
4. I danced to the **rhythm** of the drum.
5. I love my grandmother's **rhubarb** pie.
6. Here tiara was covered in **rhinestones**.

Writing

Say: *Practice writing the sounds you hear as I say each word. Then write the word. I will also use the word in a sentence.*

Pronounce one word at a time from the Word List below, stretching each sound. Use the word in a sentence, and repeat it again after the sentence. For example, say the word **rhinestone**. Then say: *The ring has a rhinestone in it.* Repeat the word **rhinestone** after the sentence.

Help students as needed to form letters or recognize letters that form these words.

Sample words: **rhinoceros, rhythm, rhinestone, rhapsody**

Have students confirm their spelling with a partner, making corrections as needed.

Reflect and Review

Ask: *What did you learn today? Discuss with your partner.*

Have students work with their partners to complete the sentence frames at the end of the Lesson 26 Practice Page, assisting as needed.

Word Bank

rh-	
rhino	rhumba
rhyme	rhythm
rhombi	rhapsody
rhombus	rhetoric
rhinestone	rhinoceros

✔ Formative Assessment

If the student completes each task correctly, precede to the next skill in the sequence.

Did the student...?	Intervention
Pronounce letter in isolation Pronounce letter in words	Use a mirror to show movement of mouth, tongue, and teeth as the sound is produced. Use hand over mouth to explore movement of air as the sound is produced.
Recognize meaning of words in context	Explain meaning of words before and after reading the text.
Write letters correctly	Provide additional handwriting practice
Spell targeted sounds correctly	Use simple (CCVC, CVCC) words, practice sound segmentation and blending, use interactive and guided writing.

Lesson Objectives

- Identify and name the medial and final silent consonant digraph **bt.**
- Produce the sound of the medial and final silent consonant digraph **bt.**
- Relate the sounds **/t/** to the corresponding medial and final silent consonant digraph.
- Recognize the medial and final silent consonant digraph **bt** in words.
- Read common high frequency words.

Metacognitive Strategy

Selective auditory attention

Academic Language

consonant, consonant digraph, initial, medial, final

Materials

- Frieze Card: bt
- Phonics Lesson 27 Practice Page

Pre-Assess

- Recognition of sounds represented by the silent consonant digraph **bt**
- Identification of a silent consonant digraph that represents the sound **/t/**

Transfer Notes:

English learners need explicit instruction in articulation of digraphs, and the understanding that letters in a digraph combine to produce a new sound, different from what we associate with what the individual letters represent. Silent letters are challenging for English learners because they are difficult to discern for sound or spelling. Therefore, the letter patterns in familiar words need to be explicitly taught and memorized.

27 Medial and Final Silent Consonant Digraph bt

Introduce the Lesson

Say: *Today we will identify and recognize medial and final silent consonant digraphs and read text that includes these digraphs.*

Phonemic Awareness and Sound-Spelling Correspondence

Say: *A consonant digraph is made up of two consonants that produce one sound. In English, a silent letter is one that appears in a word but is not pronounced. In the digraph* **bt,** *the* **b** *is silent.*

Say: *Listen to the sound that* **b** *and* **t** *make when combined:* **/t/.** *Now say the sound with me:* **/t/.** *Now say it on your own:* **/t/.**

Say: *We write the silent consonant digraph* **bt** *with the letters* **b** *and* **t.**

Elicit Prior Knowledge

Display the Lesson 27 Practice Page. Prompt students to think about their primary language as you work together to complete section 1.

Ask: *What are some examples in your home language of words with silent letters?*

Model: Recognize Silent Consonant Digraph bt

Direct students' attention to section 2 of the Lesson 27 Practice Page.

Say: *Let's look at words that have initial silent consonant digraph* **bt.**

Have students echo read the list, emphasizing the digraph in each word.

	bt
Medial (middle)	subtle debtor
Final (ending)	debt doubt

Practice: Silent Consonant Digraph bt

Read aloud section 3 of the Lesson 27 Practice Page in a fluent voice, emphasizing intonation and pronunciation of words and targeted sounds. Invite students to echo read or chime on cue. Ensure comprehension by asking text dependent questions. Have students identify cognates.

Practice: Silent Consonant Digraph bt

Complete section 4 of the Lesson 27 Practice Page with students.

Say: *We will now look at words with initial silent consonant digraph* **bt-.**

Have students echo read the words on the list, emphasizing the digraph. Allow time for students to fill in the chart.

Extend Language Knowledge

Practice: Make Meaning

Complete section 5 of the Lesson 27 practice page with students.

Say: *We will now look at words that include the initial silent consonant digraph bt. Complete each sentence using words from the word bank on the Practice Page. Take turns reading the completed sentences to a partner.*

1. The opposite of obvious (subtle)
2. Someone who owes you money (debtor)
3. To not believe something (doubt)
4. When you owe something to someone (debt)
5. When there is likely that something is true (doubtless)
6. When it is unlikely that something is true (doubtful)

Writing

Say: *Practice writing the sounds you hear as I say each word. Then write the word. I will also use the word in a sentence.*

Pronounce one word at a time from the Word List below, stretching each sound. Use the word in a sentence, and repeat it again after the sentence. For example, say the word **doubt**. Then say: *I doubt that you climbed to the top of the mountain.* Repeat the word **doubt** after the sentence.

Help students as needed to form letters or recognize letters that form these words.

Sample words: **subtle, debtor, debt, doubt**

Have students confirm their spelling with a partner, making corrections as needed.

Reflect and Review

Ask: *What did you learn today? Discuss with your partner.*

Have students work with their partners to complete the sentence frames at the end of the Lesson 27 Practice Page, assisting as needed.

Word Bank

	bt
Medial (middle)	subtle debtor doubts subtlety doubtless doubtful
Final (ending)	debt doubt

✔ Formative Assessment

If the student completes each task correctly, precede to the next skill in the sequence.

Did the student...?	Intervention
Pronounce letter in isolation Pronounce letter in words	Use a mirror to show movement of mouth, tongue, and teeth as the sound is produced. Use hand over mouth to explore movement of air as the sound is produced.
Recognize meaning of words in context	Explain meaning of words before and after reading the text.
Write letters correctly	Provide additional handwriting practice
Spell targeted sounds correctly	Use simple (CCVC, CVCC) words, practice sound segmentation and blending, use interactive and guided writing.

Lesson Objectives

- Identify and name the letters **a, e, i, o,** and **u.**
- Produce the short vowel sound of letters a**a, e, i, o,** and **u.**
- Relate the sounds **/a/, /e/, /i/, /o/,** and **/u/** to the corresponding letters **a, e, i, o,** or **u.**
- Recognize medial short vowel sound of**a, e, i, o,** and **u** in words.
- Recognize the CVC letter pattern.
- Read common high frequency words.

Metacognitive Strategy

Selective auditory attention, imagery, auditory representation

Academic Language

letter name, letter sound, vowel, short sound, medial sound, middle

Materials

- Frieze Cards: a, e , i, o, u
- Phonics Lesson 28 Practice Page

Pre-Assess

- Recognition of short vowel sounds represented by the letters **a, e, i, o,** and **u**
- Identification of letters that represents the vowel sounds /ă/, /ĕ/, /ĭ/, /ŏ/, and /ŭ/

Transfer Notes:

English learners need explicit instruction in articulation of digraphs, and the understanding that letters in a digraph combine to produce a new sound, different from what we associate with what the individual letters represent. Silent letters are challenging for English learners because they are difficult to discern for sound or spelling. Therefore, the letter patterns in familiar words need to be explicitly taught and memorized.

28 Medial (CVC) Short Vowels a, e, i, o, u

Introduce the Lesson

Say: *Today we will identify the name and sound of short vowels **a, e, i, o,** and **u.** We will recognize the short vowel sounds the letters produce in words in which the vowel is between two consonants,*

Phonemic Awareness and Sound-Spelling Correspondence

Show the long a frieze card.

Say: *This letter is a vowel. All vowels have a long and a short sound.*

Say: *Listen to the short a sound /a/. Say it with me: /a/. Now say it on your own: /a/.*

Say: *We write /a/ with the letter **a,** and it is usually between two consonants.*

Repeat with **e, i, o** and **u.**

Elicit Prior Knowledge

Display the Lesson 28 Practice Page. Prompt students to think about their primary language as you work together to complete section 1.

Ask: *What are some examples in your home language of words with silent letters?*

Model: Recognize Medial (CVC) Short Vowels

Direct students' attention to section 2 of the Lesson 28 Practice Page.

Say: *Notice that in each word, the vowel is in the middle of the word, between two consonants. The pattern is consonant-vowel-consonant, or a CVC pattern.*

Have students echo read the list, emphasizing the digraph in each word.

	ă	ĕ	ĭ	ŏ	ŭ
	CVC	CVC	CVC	CVC	CVC
Medial (middle)	bat mat	bet met	bit hit	cot hot	cut hut

Practice: Medial Short Vowels

Read aloud section 3 of the Lesson 28 Practice Page in a fluent voice, emphasizing intonation and pronunciation of words and targeted sounds. Invite students to echo read or chime on cue. Ensure comprehension by asking text dependent questions. Have students identify cognates.

Practice: Recognize Medial Short Vowels

Complete section 4 of the Lesson 28 Practice Page with students.

Say: *We will now look at words with a medial short vowel sound that have a CVC pattern.*

Have students echo read the words on the list, emphasizing the digraph. Allow time for students to fill in the chart.

Extend Language Knowledge

Practice: Use Words in Context

Complete section 5 of the Lesson 28 Practice Page with students.

Say: *We will now look at words with medial short vowels. Complete each sentence using words from the word bank on the Practice Page. Take turns reading the completed sentences to your partner.*

- The men took a cab to their job.
- The pen has run out of ink.
- The sick cat went to the vet.
- My mom and dad are the best parents.
- He hit the ball hard with a bat.
- The pig rolled in the mud to get cool on the hot day.

Writing

Say: *Practice writing the sounds you hear as I say each word. Then write the word. I will also use the word in a sentence.*

Pronounce one word at a time from the Word List below, stretching each sound. Use the word in a sentence, and repeat it again after the sentence. For example, say the word **sun**. Then say: *The sun shines brightly at the beach.* Repeat the word **sun** after the sentence.

Help students as needed to form letters or recognize letters that form these words.

Sample words: **man, kid, ran, get, bus, jet, big, hut, sun**

Have students confirm their spelling with a partner, making corrections as needed.

Reflect and Review

Ask: *What did you learn today? Discuss with your partner.*

Have students work with their partners to complete the sentence frames at the end of the Lesson 28 Practice Page, assisting as needed.

Word Bank

	ă	ĕ	ĭ
	CVC	CVC	CVC
Medial (middle)	bad	web	bib
	sad	bed	hid
	rag	fed	big
	ham	led	dig
	can	hen	fin
	man	men	win
	cap	pen	hip
	map	bet	lip
	bat	get	bit
	cat	let	fit
	ŏ	ŭ	
	CVC	CVC	
Medial (middle)	job	rub	
	sob	tub	
	pod	bug	
	rod	hug	
	fog	gum	
	log	sum	
	hop	fun	
	top	sun	
	cot	cup	
	dot	hut	

✔ Formative Assessment

If the student completes each task correctly, precede to the next skill in the sequence. If not, refer to suggested Intervention 2.

Did the student…?	Intervention 2
Pronounce letter in isolation Pronounce letter in words	Use a mirror to show movement of mouth, tongue, and teeth as the sound is produced. Use hand over mouth to explore movement of air as the sound is produced.
Recognize meaning of words in context	Explain meaning of words before and after reading the text. Draw a quick sketch of the word.
Spell targeted sounds correctly	Use simple (CVC) words, practice sound segmentation and blending, use interactive and guided writing.

29 Medial (CVC) Short Vowels (a, e, i, o, u) in Multisyllabic Words

Lesson Objectives

- Identify and name the letters **a, e, i, o,** and **u.**
- Produce the sound of letters **a, e, i, o,** and **u.**
- Relate the sounds **/a/, /e/, /i/, /o/, /u/,** to the corresponding letter **a, e, i, o,** or **u.**
- Recognize medial short vowel sound of **a, e, i, o,** and **u** in multisyllabic words.
- Recognize the CVC letter pattern in multisyllabic words.
- Read common high frequency words.

Metacognitive Strategy

Selective auditory attention, imagery, auditory representation

Academic Language

letter name, letter sound, vowel, short sound, medial sound, middle

Materials

- Frieze Cards: a, e , i, o, u
- Phonics Lesson 29 Practice Page

Pre-Assess

- Recognition of short vowel sounds represented by the letters **a, e, i, o,** and **u**
- Identification of letters that represents the vowel sounds **/ă/, /ĕ/, /ĭ/, /ŏ/,** and **/ŭ/**

Transfer Notes:

English learners need explicit instruction in vowels in English, as most English short vowels do not transfer to Spanish, Vietnamese, Hmong, Tagalog, Korean, Cantonese, Mandarin, Farsi, or Arabic. English has both short and long vowels, which is challenging for English learners because it can be difficult to determine whether the vowel is long or short in a word. Letter patterns need to be emphasized.

Introduce the Lesson

Say: *Today we will identify the name and sound of short vowels **a, e, i, o,** and **u**. We will recognize the short vowel sounds the letters produce in words in which the vowel is between two consonants,*

Phonemic Awareness and Sound-Spelling Correspondence

Show the vowel frieze cards.

Say: *These letters are vowels. Remember vowels have two sounds: a long sound and a short sound. Today we will focus on the short vowel sound of the letters **a, e, i, o,** and **u** when they appear in the middle of multisyllabic words.*

Elicit Prior Knowledge

Display the Lesson 29 Practice Page. Prompt students to think about their primary language as you work together to complete section 1.

Ask: *What are some examples in your home language of words with silent letters?*

Model: Recognize Medial (CVC) Short Vowels in Multisyllabic Words

Create this chart on the board, emphasizing the short vowel sound as you write and pronounce each sample word.

Say: *Notice that in each multisyllabic word, the vowel is in the middle of the word, between two consonants. The pattern is consonant-vowel-consonant, or a CVC pattern.*

	ă	ĕ	ĭ	ŏ	ŭ
	CVC	CVC	CVC	CVC	CVC
Medial (middle)	dragon capital	pencil reject	winter kitten	hotdog confirm	number justify

Practice: Medial Short Vowels in Multisyllabic Words

Read aloud section 3 of the Lesson 29 Practice Page in a fluent voice, emphasizing intonation and pronunciation of words and targeted sounds. Invite students to echo read or chime on cue. Ensure comprehension by asking text dependent questions. Have students identify cognates.

Practice: Recognize Medial (CVC) Short Vowels in Multisyllabic Words

Complete section 4 of the Lesson 29 Practice Page with students.

Say: *We will now look at multisyllabic words with a medial short vowel sound that have a CVC pattern.*

Have students echo read the words on the list, emphasizing the short vowel sound. Allow time for students to fill in the chart.

Extend Language Knowledge

Practice: Use Words in Context

Complete section 5 of the Lesson 29 Practice Page with students.

Say: *Let's read each clue together. Then work with a partner to find an answer from the word bank. Write the answer on the line.*

1. A baby cat (kitten)
2. An instrument in a band (trumpet)
3. Almost the same (similar)
4. Upper case letter (capital)
5. Opposite of accept (reject)
6. A place for sick people (hospital)

Writing

Say: *Practice writing the sounds you hear as I say each word. Then write the word. I will also use the word in a sentence.*

Pronounce one word at a time from the Word List below, stretching each sound. Use the word in a sentence, and repeat it again after the sentence. For example, say the word **little**. Then say: *The little child could not reach the shelf.* Repeat the word **little** after the sentence.

Help students as needed to form letters or recognize letters that form these words.

Sample words: **dragon, standing, kitten, graphic, flipper, little, shimmering**

Have students confirm their spelling with a partner, making corrections as needed.

Reflect and Review

Ask: *What did you learn today? Discuss with your partner.*

Have students work with their partners to complete the sentence frames at the end of the Lesson 29 Practice Page, assisting as needed.

Word Bank

	ă	ĕ	ĭ
	CVC	CVC	CVC
Medial (middle)	factor	pencil	shimmer
	crackers	level	vision
	standing	spelling	flipper
	plastic	inspect	different
	dragon	extend	kitten
	sandbox	reject	window
	capital	excellent	dedicate
	graphic	destiny	similar
	handful	prevent	within
	fantastic	testify	hidden
	pelican	interpretation	behind

	ŏ	ŭ	
	CVC	CVC	
Medial (middle)	hotdog	trumpet	
	broccoli	mushroom	
	monster	number	
	dolphin	sudden	
	hospital	hundred	
	concept	slumber	
	balcony	multiple	
	laptop	justify	
	problem	frustrate	
	consider	furnish	
	complex	lumber	

✓ Formative Assessment

If the student completes each task correctly, precede to the next skill in the sequence.

Did the student...?	Intervention 2
Pronounce letter in isolation Pronounce letter in words	Use a mirror to show movement of mouth, tongue, and teeth as the sound is produced. Use hand over mouth to explore movement of air as the sound is produced.
Recognize meaning of words in context	Explain meaning of words before and after reading the text. Draw a quick sketch of the word.
Spell targeted sounds correctly	Use simple (CVC) words, practice sound segmentation and blending, use interactive and guided writing.

30 (CVCe) Long Vowels a, i, o, u

Metacognitive Strategy

Selective auditory attention, imagery, auditory representation

Academic Language

letter name, letter sound, vowel, long sound, silent e

Materials

- Frieze Cards: a, i, o, u
- Phonics Lesson 30 Practice Page

Pre-Assess

- Recognition of short vowel sounds represented by the letters **a, i, o,** and **u**
- Identification of letters that represents the vowel sounds /ā/, /ī/, /ō/, and /ū/

Transfer Notes:

Except for the long , most English long vowel sounds approximate or transfer to Spanish, Vietnamese, Hmong, Tagalog, Korean, Cantonese, Mandarin, Farsi, and Arabic. English learners need explicit instruction in CVCe letter patterns, as well as in the articulation of long vowel sounds. It is beneficial to emphasize that long vowel sounds in English sound like the vowel's name and to reinforce the meaning of words.

Introduce the Lesson

Say: *Today we will identify the name and sound of long vowels **a, i, o,** and **u.** We will recognize the long vowel sounds in words in which the first vowel is between two consonants and that has a final silent **e.***

Phonemic Awareness and Sound-Spelling Correspondence

Show the a frieze card.

Say: *This letter is a vowel. Remember all vowels have a long and a short sound.*

Say: *Listen to the long a sound: /ā/. Say it with me: /ā/. Now say it on your own: /ā/.*

Say: *We write /ā/ with the letter a. In words with a long a sound, the a appears between two consonants and there is a silent e at the end of the word.*

Repeat with long vowel sounds for **i, o,** and **u.**

Elicit Prior Knowledge

Display the Lesson 30 Practice Page. Prompt students to think about their primary language as you work together to complete section 1.

Say: *Think of a word in your home language that has a sound similar to long vowel sounds we learned today?*

Model: (CVCe) Long Vowels

Create this chart on the board, emphasizing the long vowel sound as you write and pronounce each sample word.

Say: *Let's look at words with long vowels sounds. Notice that in each word, the vowel is in the middle, between two consonants and that there is a silent **e** at the end. The pattern is consonant-vowel-consonant-silent **e**, or a CVCE pattern.*

ā	ī	ō	ū
CVCe	CVCe	CVCe	CVCe
cake	bike	joke	mute

Practice: (CVCe) Long Vowels

Read aloud section 3 of the Lesson 30 Practice Page in a fluent voice, emphasizing intonation and pronunciation of words and targeted sound. Invite students to echo read or chime on cue. Ensure comprehension by asking text dependent questions. Have students identify cognates.

Practice: (CVCe) Long Vowels in Context

Complete section 4 of the Lesson 30 practice page with students.

Say: *We will now look at words with a long vowel sound that have CVCe pattern.*

Have students echo read the words on the list, emphasizing the short vowel sound. Allow time for students to fill in the chart.

Extend Language Knowledge

Practice: Use Words in Context

Complete section 5 of the Lesson 30 practice page with students.

Say: *We will now look at words with long vowel sounds. Complete each sentence using words from the word bank on the Practice Page. Take turns reading the completed sentences to your partner.*

1. The **cake** took two hours to **bake**.
2. I ride the bus **home** after school every day.
3. Kittens are so **cute**!
4. The **huge** bear was asleep in the **cave**.
5. It took a long **time** to **rake** all the leaves in the yard.
6. The man whistles a happy **tune** as he works.

Writing

Say: *Practice writing the sounds you hear as I say each word. Then write the word. I will also use the word in a sentence.*

Pronounce one word at a time from the Word List below, stretching each sound. Use the word in a sentence, and repeat it again after the sentence. For example, say the word **game**. Then say: *The game ended in a tie.* Repeat the word **game** after the sentence.

Help students as needed to form letters or recognize letters that form these words.

Sample words: **wife, nice, made, home, rode, bike, take, game**

Reflect and Review

Ask: *What did you learn today? Discuss with your partner.*

Have students work with their partners to complete the sentence frames at the end of the Lesson 30 Practice Page, assisting as needed.

Word Bank

ā	ī	ō	ū
CVCe	CVCe	CVCe	CVCe
face	dice	robe	tube
cake	ride	joke	huge
male	life	hole	rule
tale	tile	home	tune
same	time	tone	cute
cape	mine	hope	mute
date	wise	note	dude
cave	site	vote	mule
ā	ī	ō	ū
CVCe	CVCe	CVCe	CVCe
face	dice	robe	tube
cake	ride	joke	huge
male	life	hole	rule
tale	tile	home	tune
same	time	tone	cute
cape	mine	hope	mute
date	wise	note	dude
cave	site	vote	mule

✓Formative Assessment

If the student completes each task correctly, precede to the next skill in the sequence.

Did the student...?	Intervention 2
Pronounce letter in isolation Pronounce letter in words	Use a mirror to show movement of mouth, tongue, and teeth as the sound is produced. Use hand over mouth to explore movement of air as the sound is produced.
Recognize meaning of words in context	Explain meaning of words before and after reading the text. Draw a quick sketch of the word.
Spell targeted sounds correctly	Use simple (CVC) words, practice sound segmentation and blending, use interactive and guided writing.

31 Long Vowel a Combinations ai, ay, ea, eigh

Lesson Objectives

- Identify and name the letters **ai, ay, ea,** and **eigh**.
- Produce the sound of letters **ai, ay, ea,** and **eigh**.
- Relate the sound /ā/ to the letter **ai, ay, ea,** and **eigh**.
- Recognize long vowel a sound in words with the letters **ai, ay, ea,** and **eigh**.
- Read common high frequency words.

Metacognitive Strategy

Selective auditory attention, imagery, auditory representation

Academic Language

letter name, letter sound, vowel, long sound, combine

Materials

- Frieze Cards: a
- Phonics Lesson 31 Practice Page

Pre-Assess

- Recognition of long vowel sounds represented by the letters **ai, ay, ea,** and **eigh**
- Identification of letters that represents the vowel sound /ā/

Transfer Notes:

English learners need explicit instruction to recognize and spell vowel digraphs because they must recognize the two letters together, rather than a one-to-one letter-sound correspondence. Reinforce the meaning of words, letter patterns, as well as the articulation of sounds.

Introduce the Lesson

Say: *Today we will identify and recognize the long a vowel sound produced by the letter combinations **ai, ay, ea,** and **eigh** and read text that includes words with these letters.*

Phonemic Awareness and Sound-Spelling Correspondence

Show the a frieze card

Say: *This is vowel **a**. Like all vowels, a has a short sound /a/ and a long sound /ā/ that sounds like its name.*

Say: *Listen to the long **a**. sound the letters **ai** make when they are together in a word. Say it with me: /ā/. Now say it on your own: /ā/.*

Say: *One way we write the long **a** sound is with the letters **ai**.*

Repeat with **ay**, **ea**, and **eigh**, and assess students' ability to recognize, name, and pronounce each letter combination.

Elicit Prior Knowledge

Display the Lesson 31 Practice Page. Prompt students to think about their primary language as you work together to complete section 1.

Ask: *What letters or symbols in your home language combine to make a sound similar to the long vowel sound we are learning today?*

Say: *Think of a word in your home language that includes the long a sound.*

Model: Recognize Long Vowel a Letter Combinations ai, ay, ea, eigh

Direct students' attention to section 2 of the Lesson 31 Practice Page.

Say: *Let's look at words that have letter combinations that make the long **a** sound.*

Have students echo read the words for each letter combination, emphasizing the long **a** sound.

Sound	ā			
Letters	ai	ay	ea	eigh
Words	aim gain	day play	break great	eight sleigh

Practice: Long Vowel a Letter Combinations ai, ay, ea, eigh

Read aloud section 3 of the Lesson 31 Practice Page in a fluent voice, emphasizing intonation and pronunciation of words and targeted sound. Invite students to echo read or chime on cue. Ensure comprehension by asking text dependent questions.

Practice: Recognize Long Vowel a Letter Combinations ai, ay, ea, eigh

Complete section 4 of the Lesson 31 practice page with students.

Say: *We will now look at words with the long vowel a letter combinations we have studied.*

Have students echo read the words on the list, emphasizing the long vowel a sound. Allow time for students to fill in the chart.

Extend Language Knowledge

Practice: Make Meaning

Complete section 5 of the Lesson 31 Practice Page with students.

Say: *Let's read each clue together. Then work with a partner to find an answer from the word bank. Write the answer on the line.*

1. You use it to think (brain)
2. The land (terrain)
3. Opposite of fancy (plain)
4. To not follow an agreed upon path (stray)
5. The product of 2 x 4 (eight)
6. Animal that hibernates in a cave (bear)

Writing

Say: *Practice writing the sounds you hear as I say each word. Then write the word. I will also use the word in a sentence.*

Pronounce one word at a time from the Word List below, stretching each sound. Use the word in a sentence, and repeat it again after the sentence. For example, say the word **hay**. Then say: *The horses eat hay.* Repeat the word **hay** after the sentence.

Help students as needed to form letters or recognize letters that form these words.

Sample words: **plain, chain, great, stain, gray, neighbor, hay, day**

Have students confirm their spelling with a partner, making corrections as needed.

Reflect and Review

Ask: *What did you learn today? Discuss with your partner.*

Have students work with their partners to complete the sentence frames at the end of the Lesson 31 Practice Page, assisting as needed.

Word Bank

ā		
ai	**ay**	**ea**
aim	day	break
brain	hay	breaker
chain	play	great
stain	spray	steak
wait	stray	bear
terrain	clay	swear
plain	stray	pear
gain	gray	wear
train	may	tear

✔Formative Assessment

If the student completes each task correctly, precede to the next skill in the sequence.

Did the student…?	Intervention 2
Pronounce letter in isolation Pronounce letter in words	Use a mirror to show movement of mouth, tongue, and teeth as the sound is produced. Use hand over mouth to explore movement of air as the sound is produced.
Recognize meaning of words in context	Explain meaning of words before and after reading the text. Draw a quick sketch of the word.
Spell targeted sounds correctly	Use simple (CVC) words, practice sound segmentation and blending, use interactive and guided writing.

Lesson Objectives

- Identify and name the letters **ea, ee, ei, ie, ey**, and **y**.
- Produce the sound of letters **ea, ee, ei, ie, ey**, and **y**.
- Relate the sound /ē/ to the letter **ea, ee, ei, ie, ey**, and **y**.
- Recognize long vowel e sound in words with the letters **ea, ee, ei, ie, ey**, and **y**.
- Read common high frequency words.

Metacognitive Strategy

Selective auditory attention, imagery, auditory representation

Academic Language

letter name, letter sound, vowel, long sound, combine

Materials

- Frieze Cards: e
- Phonics Lesson 32 Practice Page

Pre-Assess

- Recognition of long vowel sounds represented by the letters **ea, ee, ei, ie, ey**, and **y**
- Identification of letters that represents the vowel sound /ē/

Transfer Notes:

English learners need explicit instruction to recognize and spell vowel digraphs because they must recognize the two letters together, rather than a one-to-one letter-sound correspondence. Reinforce the meaning of words, letter patterns, as well as the articulation of sounds.

32 Long Vowel e Combinations ea, ee, ei, ie, ey, y

Introduce the Lesson

Say: *Today we will identify and recognize the long e vowel sound produced by the letter combinations ea, ee, ei, ie, ey, and y and read text that includes words with these letters.*

Phonemic Awareness and Sound-Spelling Correspondence

Show the e frieze card.

Say: *This is vowel **e**. Like all vowels, **e** has a short sound /e/ and a long sound /ē/ that sounds like its name.*

Say: *Listen to the long **e** sound the letters **ea** make when they are together in a word. Say it with me: /ē/. Now say it on your own: /ē/.*

Say: *One way we write the long **e** sound is with the letters **ea**.*

Elicit Prior Knowledge

Display the Lesson 32 Practice Page. Prompt students to think about their primary language as you work together to complete section 1.

Ask: *What letters or symbols in your home language combine to make a sound similar to the long vowel sound we are learning today?*

Say: *Think of a word in your home language that includes the long **a** sound.*

Model: Recognize Long Vowel e Letter Combinations ea, ee, ei, ie, ey, y

Direct students' attention to section 2 of the Lesson 32 Practice Page.

Say: *Let's look at words that have letter combinations that make the long **e** sound.*

Have students echo read the words for each letter combination, emphasizing the long **e** sound.

Sound	ē					
Letters	ea	ee	ei	ie	ey	y
Words	weak beach	green three	receive deceit	grief piece	monkey hockey	funny happy

Practice: Long Vowel e Letter Combinations ea, ee, ei, ie, ey, y

Read aloud section 3 of the lesson practice page in a fluent voice, emphasizing intonation and pronunciation of words and the targeted vowel sound. Invite students to echo read or chime on cue. Ensure comprehension by asking text dependent questions. Have students identify cognates.

Practice: Recognize Long Vowel e Letter Combinations ea, ee, ei, ie, ey, y

Complete section 4 of the lesson practice page with students.

Say: *We will now look at words with the long vowel e letter combinations we have studied.*

Have students echo read the words on the list, emphasizing the long vowel **e** sound. Allow time for students to fill in the chart.

Extend Language Knowledge

Practice: Use Words in Context

Complete section 5 of the Lesson 32 Practice Page with students.

Say: *Let's think about words with letter combinations that make the long vowel e sound: ea, ee, ei, ie, ey, and y. Complete each sentence using words from the word bank on the Practice Page. Take turns reading the completed sentences to your partner.*

1. The king and **queen** live in a castle.
2. We were **hungry** and weak after the long uphill hike.
3. The **monkey** reaches for the branch.
4. I **sweep** because I like to **keep** the kitchen **clean**.
5. When you **eat** cookies, the crumbs get everywhere!
6. The **thief** took my money!
7. The **hockey** team won the game.
8. I once had a **dream** that I sailed across the seven **seas**.

Writing

Say: *Practice writing the sounds you hear as I say each word. Then write the word. I will also use the word in a sentence.*

Pronounce one word at a time from the Word List below, stretching each sound. Use the word in a sentence, and repeat it again after the sentence. For example, say the word **study**. Then say: *I study for tests.* Repeat the word **study** after the sentence.

Help students as needed to form letters or recognize letters that form these words.

Sample words: **queen, jeans, beach, hockey, study, mean, green, beetle**

Have students confirm their spelling with a partner, making corrections as needed.

Reflect and Review

Ask: *What did you learn today? Discuss with your partner.*

Have students work with their partners to complete the sentence frames at the end of the Lesson 33 Practice Page, assisting as needed.

Word Bank

ē		
ea	**ee**	**ei**
beach	beep	receive
dream	beetle	deceive
reach	green	ceiling
scream	queen	conceit
weak	sweep	deceit
treat	three	perceive
teach	wheel	either
cheat	meet	
jeans	cheek	
mean	see	
ie	**ey**	**y**
believe	alley	creepy
chief	donkey	funny
field	hockey	happy
friend	honey	hungry
grief	money	puppy
shield	valley	easy
cookie	monkey	lady
niece	volley	study
piece	chimney	windy
thief	turkey	candy

✔Formative Assessment

If the student completes each task correctly, precede to the next skill in the sequence.

Did the student…?	Intervention 2
Pronounce letter in isolation Pronounce letter in words	Use a mirror to show movement of mouth, tongue, and teeth as the sound is produced. Use hand over mouth to explore movement of air as the sound is produced.
Recognize meaning of words in context	Explain meaning of words before and after reading the text. Draw a quick sketch of the word.
Spell targeted sounds correctly	Use simple (CVC) words, practice sound segmentation and blending, use interactive and guided writing.

Lesson Objectives

- Identify and name the letters **ie, igh, ind, ild,** and **y.**
- Produce the sound of letters **ie, igh, ind, ild,** and **y.**
- Relate the sound /ī/ to the letter **ie, igh, ind, ild,** and **y.**
- Recognize long vowel **i** sound in words with the letters **ie, igh, ind, ild,** and **y.**
- Read common high frequency words.

Metacognitive Strategy

Selective auditory attention, imagery, auditory representation

Academic Language

letter name, letter sound, vowel, long sound, combine

Materials

- Frieze Cards: 1
- Phonics Lesson 33 Practice Page

Pre-Assess

- Recognition of long vowel sounds represented by the letters **ie, igh, ind, ild,** and **y**
- Identification of letters that represents the vowel sound /ī/

Transfer Notes:

English learners need explicit instruction to recognize and spell vowel digraphs because they must recognize the two letters together, rather than a one-to-one letter-sound correspondence. Reinforce the meaning of words, letter patterns, as well as the articulation of sounds.

33 Long Vowel i Combinations ie, igh, ind, ild, y

Introduce the Lesson

Say: *Today we will identify and recognize the long i vowel sound produced by the letter combinations ie, igh, ind, ild, and y and read text that includes words with these letters.*

Phonemic Awareness and Sound-Spelling Correspondence

Show the **i** frieze card.

Say: *This is vowel i. Like all vowels, i has a short sound /i/ and a long sound /ī/ that sounds like its name.*

Say: *Listen to the long i sound the letters ie make when they are together in a word. Say it with me: /ī/. Now say it on your own: /ī/.*

Say: *One way we write the long i sound is with the letters ie.*

Repeat with **igh, ind, ild,** and **y,** and assess students' ability to recognize, name, and pronounce each letter combination.

Elicit Prior Knowledge

Display the Lesson 33 Practice Page. Prompt students to think about their primary language as you work together to complete section 1.

Ask: *What letters or symbols in your home language combine to make a sound similar to the long vowel sound we are learning today?*

Say: *Think of a word in your home language that includes the long i sound.*

Model: Recognize Long Vowel **i** Letter Combinations **ie, igh, ind, ild, y**

Direct students' attention to section 2 of the Lesson 33 Practice Page.

Say: *Let's look at words that have letter combinations that make the long i sound.*

Have students echo read the words for each letter combination, emphasizing the long i sound.

Sound	ī				
Letters	ie	igh	ind	ild	y
Words	pie lie	high right	find kind	wild child	by dry

Practice: Long Vowel i Letter Combinations ie, igh, ind, ild, y

Read aloud section 3 of the lesson practice page in a fluent voice, emphasizing intonation and pronunciation of words and the targeted vowel sound. Invite students to echo read or chime on cue. Ensure comprehension by asking text dependent questions. Have students identify cognates.

Practice: Recognize Long Vowel i Letter Combinations ie, igh, ind, ild, y

Complete section 4 of the lesson practice page with students.

Say: *We will now look at words with the long vowel **i** letter combinations we have studied.*

Have students echo read the words on the list, emphasizing the long vowel **i** sound. Allow time for students to fill in the chart.

Extend Language Knowledge

Practice: Make Meaning

Complete section 5 of the Lesson 33 Practice Page with students.

Say: *Let's read each clue together. Then work with a partner to find an answer from the word bank. Write the answer on the line.*

1. It happens during a storm (lightning)
2. A pastry dish made with a shell and filling (pie)
3. Opposite of "in front of" (behind)
4. Sneaky (sly)
5. Opposite of tame (wild)
6. We are all a part of this (humankind)

Writing

Say: *Practice writing the sounds you hear as I say each word. Then write the word. I will also use the word in a sentence.*

Pronounce one word at a time from the Word List below, stretching each sound. Use the word in a sentence, and repeat it again after the sentence. For example, say the word **fly**. Then say: *I like to fly in an airplane.* Repeat the word **fly** after the sentence.

Help students as needed to form letters or recognize letters that form these words.

Sample words: **child, wild, rind tried, fly, sigh**

Have students confirm their spelling with a partner, making corrections as needed.

Reflect and Review

Ask: *What did you learn today? Discuss with your partner.*

Have students work with their partners to complete the sentence frames at the end of the Lesson 33 Practice Page, assisting as needed.

Word Bank

ī		
ie	**igh**	**ind**
die	high	behind
died	right	bind
lie	flight	find
pie	sigh	grind
tie	bright	kind
tied	delight	mind
fried	insight	wind
cried	light	rind
tried	lightning	mastermind
lied	midnight	humankind

ild	**y**	
child	by	
wild	fry	
mild	sky	
childhood	why	
grandchild	sly	
wildcat	guy	
wildfire	dry	
wildlife	try	
	sly	
	cry	

✔Formative Assessment

If the student completes each task correctly, precede to the next skill in the sequence.

Did the student...?	Intervention 2
Pronounce letter in isolation Pronounce letter in words	Use a mirror to show movement of mouth, tongue, and teeth as the sound is produced. Use hand over mouth to explore movement of air as the sound is produced.
Recognize meaning of words in context	Explain meaning of words before and after reading the text. Draw a quick sketch of the word.
Spell targeted sounds correctly	Use simple (CVC) words, practice sound segmentation and blending, use interactive and guided writing.

Lesson Objectives

- Identify and name the letters **oa**, **oe**, and **ow**.
- Produce the sound of letters **oa**, **oe**, and **ow**.
- Relate the sound /ō/ to the letters **oa**, **oe**, and **ow**.
- Recognize long vowel **o** sound in words with the letters **oa**, **oe**, and **ow**.
- Read common high frequency words.

Metacognitive Strategy

Selective auditory attention, imagery, auditory representation

Academic Language

letter name, letter sound, vowel, long sound, combine

Materials

- Frieze Cards: o
- Lesson 34 Practice Page

Pre-Assess

- Recognition of long vowel sounds represented by the letters **oa**, **oe**, and **ow**
- Identification of letters that represents the vowel sound /ō/

Transfer Notes:

English learners need explicit instruction to recognize and spell vowel digraphs because they must recognize the two letters together, rather than a one-to-one letter-sound correspondence. Reinforce the meaning of words, letter patterns, as well as the articulation of sounds.

34 Long Vowel o Combinations oa, oe, ow

Introduce the Lesson

Say: *Today we will identify and recognize the long o vowel sound produced by the letter combinations oa, oe, and ow and read text that includes words with these letters.*

Phonemic Awareness and Sound-Spelling Correspondence

Show the **o** frieze card

Say: *This is vowel o. Like all vowels, o has a short sound /o/ and a long sound /ō/ that sounds like its name.*

Say: *Listen to the long o sound the letters oa make when they are together in a word. Say it with me: /ō/. Now say it on your own: /ō/.*

Say: *One way we write the long o sound is with the letters oa.*

Repeat with **oe** and **ow**, and assess students' ability to recognize, name, and pronounce each letter combination.

Elicit Prior Knowledge

Display the Lesson 34 Practice Page. Prompt students to think about their primary language as you work together to complete section 1.

Ask: *What letters or symbols in your home language combine to make a sound similar to the long vowel sound we are learning today?*

Say: *Think of a word in your home language that includes the long o sound.*

Model: Recognize Long Vowel o Letter Combinations oa, oe, ow

Direct students' attention to section 2 of the Lesson 34 Practice Page.

Say: Let's look at words that have letter combinations that make the long **o** sound.

Have students echo read the words for each letter combination, emphasizing the long **o** sound.

Sound	ō		
Letters	oa	oe	ow
Words	boat load	toe foe	mow grow

Practice: Long Vowel o Letter Combinations oa, oe, ow

Read aloud section 3 of the Lesson 34 Practice Page in a fluent voice, emphasizing intonation and pronunciation of words and the targeted vowel sound. Invite students to echo read or chime on cue. Ensure comprehension by asking text dependent questions. Have students identify cognates.

Practice: Recognize Long Vowel o Letter Combinations in Context

Complete section 4 of the Lesson 34 Practice Page with students.

Say: *We will now look at words with the long vowel **o** letter combinations we have studied.*

Have students echo read the words on the list, emphasizing the long vowel o sound. Allow time for students to fill in the chart.

Extend Language Knowledge

Practice: Use Words in Context

Complete section 5 of the Lesson 34 Practice Page with students.

Say: *Let's think about words with letter combinations that make the long vowel **o** sound: **oa, oe,** and **ow.** Complete each sentence using words from the word bank on the Practice Page. Take turns reading the completed sentences to your partner.*

1. The **boat** sailed along the **coast**.
2. The walked **slowly** across the **road**.
3. The grass **grows** so fast that we have to **mow** it every week.
4. The mother had to **tiptoe** out of the sleeping baby's room.
5. Out on the ocean, the water **flows** and the wind **blows**.
6. The **doe** ate grass in the meadow.

Writing

Say: *Practice writing the sounds you hear as I say each word. Then write the word. I will also use the word in a sentence.*

Pronounce one word at a time from the Word List below, stretching each sound. Use the word in a sentence, and repeat it again after the sentence. For example, say the word **blow**. Then say: *We blow bubbles.* Repeat the word **blow** after the sentence.

Help students as needed to form letters or recognize letters that form these words.

Sample words: **goal, boat, coast, blow, toe, tiptoe, boat**

Have students confirm their spelling with a partner, making corrections as needed.

Reflect and Review

Ask: *What did you learn today? Discuss with your partner.*

Have students work with their partners to complete the sentence frames at the end of the Lesson 34 Practice Page, assisting as needed.

Word Bank

ō		
oa	**oe**	**ow**
boat	doe	bow
coast	foe	blow
goal	hoe	elbow
goat	toe	fellow
load	woe	flow
loan	tiptoe	grow
oats		mow
road		shadow
soak		meadow
toad		yellow

✓ Formative Assessment

If the student completes each task correctly, precede to the next skill in the sequence.

Did the student...?	Intervention 2
Pronounce letter in isolation Pronounce letter in words	Use a mirror to show movement of mouth, tongue, and teeth as the sound is produced. Use hand over mouth to explore movement of air as the sound is produced.
Recognize meaning of words in context	Explain meaning of words before and after reading the text. Draw a quick sketch of the word.
Spell targeted sounds correctly	Use simple (CVC) words, practice sound segmentation and blending, use interactive and guided writing.

35 Long Vowel u Combinations ue, ew

Introduce the Lesson

Say: *Today we will identify and recognize the long **u** vowel sound produced by the letter combinations **ue** and **uw** and read text that includes words with these letters.*

Phonemic Awareness and Sound-Spelling Correspondence

Show the **u** frieze card

Say: *This is vowel **u**. Like all vowels, **u** has a short sound /u/ and a long sound /ū/ that sounds like its name.*

Say: *Listen to the long **u** sound the letters **ue** make when they are together in a word. Say it with me: /ū/. Now say it on your own: /ū/.*

Say: *One way we write the long **u** sound is with the letters **ue**.*

Repeat with **ew**, and assess students' ability to recognize, name, and pronounce each letter combination.

Elicit Prior Knowledge

Display the Lesson 35 Practice Page. Prompt students to think about their primary language as you work together to complete section 1.

Ask: *What letters or symbols in your home language combine to make a sound similar to the long vowel sound we are learning today?*

Say: *Think of a word in your home language that includes the long **u** sound.*

Model: Recognize Long Vowel u Letter Combinations ue, ew

Direct students' attention to section 2 of the Lesson 35 Practice Page.

Say: *Let's look at words that have letter combinations that make the long **u** sound. Have students echo read the words for each letter combination, emphasizing the long **u** sound.*

Sound	ū	
Letters	ue	ew
Words	due true	new blew

Practice: Long Vowel u Letter Combinations ue, ew

Read aloud section 3 of the Lesson 35 Practice Page in a fluent voice, emphasizing intonation and pronunciation of words and the targeted vowel sound. Invite students to echo read or chime on cue. Ensure comprehension by asking text dependent questions. Have students identify cognates.

Practice: Recognize Long Vowel u Letter Combinations ue, ew

Complete section 4 of the Lesson 35 Practice Page with students.

Say: *We will now look at words with the long vowel **u** letter combinations we have studied.*

Have students echo read the words on the list, emphasizing the long vowel **u** sound. Allow time for students to fill in the chart.

Extend Language Knowledge

Practice: Make Meaning

Complete section 5 of the Lesson 35 Practice Page with students.

Say: *Let's read each clue together. Then work with a partner to find an answer from the word bank. Write the answer on the line.*

1. The opposite of old (new)
2. Use this to connect two pieces of metal (screw)
3. To save someone (rescue)
4. Opposite of false (true)
5. Past tense of throw (threw)
6. To disagree (argue)

Writing

Say: *Practice writing the sounds you hear as I say each word. Then write the word. I will also use the word in a sentence.*

Pronounce one word at a time from the Word List below, stretching each sound. Use the word in a sentence, and repeat it again after the sentence. For example, say the word **statue**. Then say: *The statue is made of stone.* Repeat the word **statue** after the sentence.

Help students as needed to form letters or recognize letters that form these words.

Sample words: **blue, flew, statue, due, grew, true**

Have students confirm their spelling with a partner, making corrections as needed.

Reflect and Review

Ask: *What did you learn today? Discuss with your partner.*

Have students work with their partners to complete the sentence frames at the end of the Lesson 35 Practice Page, assisting as needed.

Word Bank

ū	
ue	**ew**
glue	new
clue	dew
due	few
true	blew
blue	crew
cue	flew
argue	grew
rescue	knew
statue	screw
tissue	threw

✓Formative Assessment

If the student completes each task correctly, precede to the next skill in the sequence.

Did the student...?	Intervention 2
Pronounce letter in isolation Pronounce letter in words	Use a mirror to show movement of mouth, tongue, and teeth as the sound is produced. Use hand over mouth to explore movement of air as the sound is produced.
Recognize meaning of words in context	Explain meaning of words before and after reading the text. Draw a quick sketch of the word.
Spell targeted sounds correctly	Use simple (CVC) words, practice sound segmentation and blending, use interactive and guided writing.

36 Vowel Combinations aw, au

Lesson Objectives

- Identify and name the letters **aw** and **au**.
- Produce the sound of letters **aw** and **au**.
- Relate the sound **/aw/** to the letters **aw** and **au**.
- Recognize vowel combinations **aw** and **au** in words.
- Read common high frequency words.

Metacognitive Strategy

Selective auditory attention, imagery, auditory representation

Academic Language

letter name, letter sound, vowel, combination, digraph

Materials

- Phonics Lesson 36 Practice Page

Pre-Assess

- Recognition of the vowel sound represented by the digraphs **aw** and **au**
- Identification of letters that represent the vowel sound **/aw/**

Transfer Notes:

English learners need explicit instruction to recognize and spell vowel digraphs because they must recognize the two letters together, rather than a one-to-one letter-sound correspondence. Reinforce the meaning of words, letter patterns, as well as the articulation of sounds.

Introduce the Lesson

Say: *Today we will recognize and identify the vowel sound /aw/ made by letter pairs, or digraphs, aw and au. We will read texts with words that include these vowel digraphs.*

Sound-Spelling Correspondence

Write aw on the board.

Say: *This is the vowel digraph aw. A digraph is a pair of letters that makes a single sound that is different than the sound each letter makes.*

Say: *Remember, the vowel a has a short sound /a/ and a long sound /a/. The letter w makes the /w/ sound.*

Say: *Now listen to the sound the letters aw make when they are together in a word: /aw/. Say it with me: /aw/. Now say it on your own: /aw/.*

Repeat with the digraph **au**, and assess students' ability to recognize, name, and pronounce both digraphs.

Elicit Prior Knowledge

Display the Lesson 36 Practice Page. Prompt students to think about their primary language as you work together to complete section 1.

Ask: *What letters or symbols in your home language combine to make a sound similar to the digraph we are learning today?*

Say: *Think of a word in your home language that includes this sound.*

Model: Recognize Vowel Combinations aw, au

Direct students' attention to section 2 of the Lesson 36 Practice Page.

Say: *We will now look at words that have the vowel combinations aw and au.*

Have students echo read the words for each digraph, emphasizing /aw/ sound.

Sound	/aw/	
Vowel combination	aw	au
Words	jaw crawl	haul fault

Practice: Vowel Combinations aw, au

Read aloud section 3 of the Lesson 36 Practice Page in a fluent voice, emphasizing intonation and pronunciation of words and the targeted vowel sound. Invite students to echo read or chime on cue. Ensure comprehension by asking text dependent questions. Have students identify cognates.

Practice: Vowel Combinations aw, au

Complete section 4 of the Lesson 36 Practice Page with students.

Say: *We will now look at words with the digraphs we have studied.*

Have students echo read the words on the list, emphasizing the /aw/ sound. Allow time for students to fill in the chart.

Extend Language Knowledge

Practice: Use Words in Context

Complete section 5 of the Lesson 35 Practice Page with students.

Say: *Let's think about words with the vowel digraphs that make the /aw/ sound: aw and au. Complete each sentence using words from the word bank on the Practice Page. Take turns reading the completed sentences to your partner.*

1. The stale crackers taste **awful**.
2. Before you can walk, you learn to **crawl**.
3. The cat scratches with its sharp **claws**.
4. The puppy's **paws** left prints on the rug.
5. The audience stood up and **applauded** at the end of the show.
6. My favorite **author** writes mystery novels.
7. He likes spaghetti **sauce** on his **sausage**.
8. You need to mow to keep your **lawn** looking good.

Writing

Say: *Practice writing the sounds you hear as I say each word. Then write the word. I will also use the word in a sentence.*

Pronounce one word at a time from the Word List below, stretching each sound. Use the word in a sentence, and repeat it again after the sentence. For example, say the word **crawl**. Then say: *The baby can crawl across the room.* Repeat the word **crawl** after the sentence.

Help students as needed to form letters or recognize letters that form these words.

Sample words: **crawl, sausage, paw, because, fault**

Have students confirm their spelling with a partner, making corrections as needed.

Reflect and Review

Ask: *What did you learn today? Discuss with your partner.*

Have students work with their partners to complete the sentence frames at the end of the Lesson 36 Practice Page, assisting as needed.

Word Bank

Sound	/aw/	
Vowel combination	aw	au
Words	awful	cause
	claw	haul
	crawl	fault
	draw	author
	jaw	because
	law	sauce
	lawn	sausage
	paw	applause
	raw	
	yawn	

✔Formative Assessment

If the student completes each task correctly, precede to the next skill in the sequence.

Did the student…?	Intervention 2
Pronounce letter in isolation Pronounce letter in words	Use a mirror to show movement of mouth, tongue, and teeth as the sound is produced. Use hand over mouth to explore movement of air as the sound is produced.
Recognize meaning of words in context	Explain meaning of words before and after reading the text. Draw a quick sketch of the word.
Spell targeted sounds correctly	Use simple (CVC) words, practice sound segmentation and blending, use interactive and guided writing.

37 Vowel Combination oo

Lesson Objectives

- Identify and name the letters **oo**.
- Produce the sound of letters **oo**.
- Relate the sounds /ŏŏ/ and /ōō/ to the letters **oo**.
- Recognize vowel combination **oo** in words.
- Read common high frequency words.

Metacognitive Strategy

Selective auditory attention, imagery, auditory representation

Academic Language

letter name, letter sound, vowel, combination, digraph

Materials

- Frieze Card Vowel Digraph oo
- Phonics Lesson 37 Practice Page

Pre-Assess

- Recognition of the vowel sound represented by the digraph **oo**
- Identification of letters that represent the vowel sounds /ŏŏ/ and /ōō/

Transfer Notes:

English learners need explicit instruction to recognize and spell vowel digraphs because they must recognize the two letters together, rather than a one-to-one letter-sound correspondence. Reinforce the meaning of words, letter patterns, as well as the articulation of sounds.

Introduce the Lesson

Say: *Today we will recognize and identify the sounds /ŏŏ/ and /ōō/ made by the vowel combination, or digraph, oo. We will read texts with words that include this vowel digraph.*

Sound-Spelling Correspondence

Show the /oo/ frieze card

Say: *This is the vowel digraph oo. A digraph is a pair of letters that makes a single sound that is different than the sound each letter makes.*

Say: *Remember, the vowel o has a short sound /o/ and a long sound /ō/.*

Say: *Now listen to the one of the sounds the letters oo make when they are together in a word: /ŏŏ/. Say it with me: /ŏŏ/. Now say it on your own: /ŏŏ/.*

Repeat with the other sound digraph **oo** makes (ōō) and assess students' ability to recognize, name, and pronounce the digraph.

Elicit Prior Knowledge

Display the Lesson 37 Practice Page. Prompt students to think about their primary language as you work together to complete section 1.

Ask: *What letters or symbols in your home language combine to make sounds similar to the digraph we are learning today?*

Say: *Think words in your home language that include these sounds.*

Model: Recognize Vowel Combination oo

Direct students' attention to section 2 of the Lesson 37 Practice Page.

Say: *We will now look at words that have the vowel combination oo.*

Have students echo read the words for each sound, emphasizing the target digraph.

Sound	/ŏŏ/	/ōō/
Vowel combination	oo	oo
Words	book look	moon noon

Practice: Vowel Combination oo

Read aloud section 3 of the Lesson 37 Practice Page in a fluent voice, emphasizing intonation and pronunciation of words and the targeted vowel sound. Invite students to echo read or chime on cue. Ensure comprehension by asking text dependent questions. Have students identify cognates.

Practice: Recognize Vowel Combination oo

Complete section 4 of the Lesson 37 Practice Page with students.

Say: *We will now look at words with the digraph we have studied.*

Have students echo read the words on the list, emphasizing the /o͝o/ and /o͞o/ sounds. Allow time for students to fill in the chart.

Extend Language Knowledge

Practice: Make Meaning

Complete section 5 of the Lesson 37 Practice Page with students.

Say: *Let's read each clue together. Then work with a partner to find an answer from the word bank. Write the answer on the line.*

1. The foot part of a horse's leg (hoof)
2. They are good to eat with milk (cookies)
3. Where you can visit animals (zoo)
4. Opposite of "hello" (goodbye)
5. You can often see this in the night sky (moon)
6. Where you can go swimming (pool)

Writing

Say: *Practice writing the sounds you hear as I say each word. Then write the word. I will also use the word in a sentence.*

Pronounce one word at a time from the Word List below, stretching each sound. Use the word in a sentence, and repeat it again after the sentence. For example, say the word **pool**. Then say: *We splash each other in the pool.* Repeat the word **pool** after the sentence.

Help students as needed to form letters or recognize letters that form these words.

Sample words: **food, noon, stood, look, football, pool**

Have students confirm their spelling with a partner, making corrections as needed.

Reflect and Review

Ask: *What did you learn today? Discuss with your partner.*

Have students work with their partners to complete the sentence frames at the end of the Lesson 37 Practice Page, assisting as needed.

Word Bank

Sound	/o͝o/	/o͞o/
Vowel combination	oo	oo
Words	book hoof shook stood look wood cookie cookout football goodbye	zoo food moon noon pool root school scooter spoon balloon

✔Formative Assessment

If the student completes each task correctly, precede to the next skill in the sequence.

Did the student…?	Intervention 2
Pronounce letter in isolation Pronounce letter in words	Use a mirror to show movement of mouth, tongue, and teeth as the sound is produced. Use hand over mouth to explore movement of air as the sound is produced.
Recognize meaning of words in context	Explain meaning of words before and after reading the text. Draw a quick sketch of the word.
Spell targeted sounds correctly	Use simple (CVC) words, practice sound segmentation and blending, use interactive and guided writing.

38 Vowel Combinations ow, ou

Introduce the Lesson

Say: *Today we will recognize and identify the vowel sound /ou/ made by letter pairs, or digraphs, ow and ou. We will read texts with words that include these vowel digraphs.*

Phonemic Awareness and Sound-Spelling Correspondence

Show the **/ow/** frieze card

Say: *This is the vowel digraph ow. A digraph is a pair of letters that makes a single sound that is different than the sound each letter makes.*

Say: *Remember, the vowel o has a short sound /o/ and a long sound / /.The letter w makes the /w/ sound.*

Say: *Now listen to the sound the letters ow make when they are together in a word: / ou/. Say it with me: /ou/. Now say it on your own: /ou/.*

Repeat with the digraph ou, and assess students' ability to recognize, name, and pronounce the both digraphs.

Elicit Prior Knowledge

Display the Lesson 38 Practice Page. Prompt students to think about their primary language as you work together to complete section 1.

Ask: *What letters or symbols in your home language combine to make a sound similar to the digraphs we are learning today?*

Say: *Think of a word in your home language that includes this sound.*

Model: Recognize Vowel Combinations ow, ou

Direct students' attention to section 2 of the Lesson 38 Practice Page.

Say: *We will now look at words that have the vowel combinations ow and ou.*

Have students echo read the words for each digraph, emphasizing /ou/ sound.

Sound	/ou/	
Vowel combination	ow	ou
Words	how now	about shout

Practice: Vowel Combinations ow, ou

Read aloud section 3 of the Lesson 38 Practice Page in a fluent voice, emphasizing intonation and pronunciation of words and the targeted vowel sound. Invite students to echo read or chime on cue. Ensure comprehension by asking text dependent questions. Have students identify cognates.

Lesson Objectives

- Identify and name the letters **ow** and **ou**.
- Produce the sound of letters **ow** and **ou**.
- Relate the sound **/ou/** to the letters **ow** and **ou**.
- Recognize vowel combinations ow and ou in words.
- Read common high frequency words.

Metacognitive Strategy

Selective auditory attention, imagery, auditory representation

Academic Language

letter name, letter sound, vowel, combination, digraph

Materials

- Frieze Card Vowel Digraphs ow, ou
- Lesson 38 Practice Page

Pre-Assess

- Recognition of the vowel sound represented by the digraphs **ow** and **ou**
- Identification of letters that represent the vowel sound **/ou/**

Transfer notes:

English learners need explicit instruction to recognize and spell vowel digraphs because they must recognize the two letters together, rather than a one-to-one letter-sound correspondence. Reinforce the meaning of words, letter patterns, as well as the articulation of sounds.

Practice: Recognize Vowel Combinations ow, ou

Complete section 4 of the Lesson 38 Practice Page with students.

Say: *We will now look at words with the digraph we have studied.*

Have students echo read the words on the list, emphasizing the /ou/ sound. Allow time for students to fill in the chart.

Extend Language Knowledge

Practice: Use Words in Context

Complete section 5 of the Lesson 38 Practice Page with students.

Say: *Let's think about words with the vowel digraphs that make the /**ou**/ sound: ow and ou. Complete each sentence using words from the word bank on the Practice Page. Take turns reading the completed sentences to your partner.*

1. The farmer milks the cow.
2. We planted a garden of flowers all the way around house.
3. A crowd gathered to watch the clown.
4. The brown dog barked loudly.
5. The clouds were white and billowy.
6. The king wears a crown.

Writing

Say: *Practice writing the sounds you hear as I say each word. Then write the word. I will also use the word in a sentence.*

Pronounce one word at a time from the Word List below, stretching each sound. Use the word in a sentence, and repeat it again after the sentence. For example, say the word frown. Then say: *Most people frown when they're sad.* Repeat the word frown after the sentence.

Help students as needed to form letters or recognize letters that form these words.

Sample words: **clown, frown, found, house, flower, crown**

Have students confirm their spelling with a partner, making corrections as needed.

Reflect and Review

Ask: *What did you learn today? Discuss with your partner.*

Have students work with their partners to complete the sentence frames at the end of the Lesson 38 Practice Page, assisting as needed.

Word Bank

Sound	/ou/	
Vowel combination	ow	ou
Words	how	about
	now	cloud
	brown	couch
	clown	found
	crowd	hour
	crown	house
	flower	loud
	frown	mouth
	town	round
	towel	shout

✓Formative Assessment

If the student completes each task correctly, precede to the next skill in the sequence. If not, refer to suggested Intervention 2.

Did the student…?	Intervention 2
Pronounce letter in isolation Pronounce letter in words	Use a mirror to show movement of mouth, tongue, and teeth as the sound is produced. Use hand over mouth to explore movement of air as the sound is produced.
Recognize meaning of words in context	Explain meaning of words before and after reading the text. Draw a quick sketch of the word.
Spell targeted sounds correctly	Use simple (CVC) words, practice sound segmentation and blending, use interactive and guided writing.

39 Vowel Combinations oi, oy

Introduce the Lesson

Say: *Today we will recognize and identify the vowel sound /oi/ made by letter pairs, or digraphs, oi and oy. We will read texts with words that include these vowel digraphs.*

Phonemic Awareness and Sound-Spelling Correspondence

Show the **oi** frieze card.

Say: *This is the vowel digraph oi. A digraph is a pair of letters that makes a single sound that is different than the sound each letter makes.*

Say: *The vowels o and i each make long and short sounds. But listen to the new sound the vowels oi make when they are together in a word: /oi/. Say it with me: /oi/. Now say it on your own: /oi/.*

Repeat with the digraph **oy**, and assess students' ability to recognize, name, and pronounce both digraphs.

Elicit Prior Knowledge

Display the Lesson 39 Practice Page. Prompt students to think about their primary language as you work together to complete section 1.

Ask: *What letters or symbols in your home language combine to make a sound similar to the digraphs we are learning today?*

Say: *Think of a word in your home language that includes this sound.*

Model: Recognize Vowel Combinations oi, oy

Direct students' attention to section 2 of the Lesson 39 Practice Page.

Say: *We will now look at words that have the vowel combinations oi and oy.*

Have students echo read the words for each digraph, emphasizing /oi/ sound.

Sound	/oi/	
Vowel combination	oi	oy
Words	soil point	boy enjoy

Practice: Vowel Combinations oi, oy

Read aloud section 3 of the Lesson 39 Practice Page in a fluent voice, emphasizing intonation and pronunciation of words and the targeted vowel sound. Invite students to echo read or chime on cue. Ensure comprehension by asking text dependent questions. Have students identify cognates.

Lesson Objectives

- Identify and name the letters **oi** and **oy**.
- Produce the sound of letters **oi** and **oy**.
- Relate the sound **/oi/** to the letters oi and oy.
- Recognize vowel combinations **oi** and **oy** in words.
- Read common high frequency words.

Metacognitive Strategy

Selective auditory attention, imagery, auditory representation

Academic Language

letter name, letter sound, vowel, combination, digraph

Materials

- Frieze Cards: Vowel Digraphs oi, oy
- Phonics Lesson 39 Practice Page

Pre-Assess

- Recognition of the vowel sound represented by the digraphs **oi** and **oy**
- Identification of letters that represent the vowel sound **/oi/**

Transfer Notes:

English learners need explicit instruction to recognize and spell vowel digraphs because they must recognize the two letters together, rather than a one-to-one letter-sound correspondence. Reinforce the meaning of words, letter patterns, as well as the articulation of sounds.

Practice: Recognize Vowel Combinations oi, oy

Complete section 4 of the Lesson 37 Practice Page with students.

Say: *We will now look at words with the digraphs we have studied.*

Have students echo read the words on the list, emphasizing the **/oi/** sound. Allow time for students to fill in the chart.

Extend Language Knowledge

Practice: Make Meaning

Complete section 5 of the Lesson 38 Practice Page with students.

Say: *Let's read each clue together. Then work with a partner to find an answer from the word bank. Write the answer on the line.*

- You use it to talk (voice)
- It can make you sick or even kill you (poison)
- A trip (voyage)
- You plant flowers in it (soil)
- To bother someone (annoy)
- To hire someone to work for you (employ)

Writing

Say: *Practice writing the sounds you hear as I say each word. Then write the word. I will also use the word in a sentence.*

Pronounce one word at a time from the Word List below, stretching each sound. Use the word in a sentence, and repeat it again after the sentence. For example, say the word **toy**. Then say: *A yo-yo is my favorite toy.* Repeat the word **toy** after the sentence.

Help students as needed to form letters or recognize letters that form these words.

Sample words: **boy, employ, hoist, toy, enjoy**

Have students confirm their spelling with a partner, making corrections as needed.

Reflect and Review

Ask: *What did you learn today? Discuss with your partner.*

Have students work with their partners to complete the sentence frames at the end of the Lesson 39 Practice Page, assisting as needed.

Word Bank

Sound	/oi/	
Vowel combination	oi	oy
Words	avoid	toy
	foil	boy
	noise	annoy
	point	destroy
	poison	enjoy
	soil	royal
	voice	voyage
	moisture	employ
	hoist	decoy
	disappoint	royalty

✓Formative Assessment

If the student completes each task correctly, precede to the next skill in the sequence.

Did the student...?	Intervention 2
Pronounce letter in isolation Pronounce letter in words	Use a mirror to show movement of mouth, tongue, and teeth as the sound is produced. Use hand over mouth to explore movement of air as the sound is produced.
Recognize meaning of words in context	Explain meaning of words before and after reading the text. Draw a quick sketch of the word.
Spell targeted sounds correctly	Use simple (CVC) words, practice sound segmentation and blending, use interactive and guided writing.

Lesson Objectives

- Identify and name the letters **ea**.
- Produce the sound of letters **ea**.
- Relate the sound short **/e/** to the letters **ea**.
- Recognize vowel combination **ea** in words.
- Read common high frequency words.

Metacognitive Strategy

Selective auditory attention, imagery, auditory representation

Academic Language

letter name, letter sound, vowel, combination, digraph

Materials

- Frieze Card Digraph: ea
- Phonics Lesson 40 Practice Page

Pre-Assess

- Recognition of the vowel sound represented by the digraph **ea**
- Identification of letters that represent the vowel sounds short **/e/**

Transfer Notes:

English learners need explicit instruction to recognize and spell vowel digraphs because they must recognize the two letters together, rather than a one-to-one letter-sound correspondence. Reinforce the meaning of words, letter patterns, as well as the articulation of sounds.

40 Vowel Combination ea

Introduce the Lesson

Say: *Today we will recognize and identify the vowel sound short /e/ made by letter pair, or digraph, ea. We will read texts with words that include this vowel digraph.*

Phonemic Awareness and Sound-Spelling Correspondence

Show the **ea** frieze card.

Say: *This is the vowel digraph ea. A digraph is a pair of letters that makes a single sound that is different than the sound each letter makes.*

Say: *The vowel e has both a short and long vowel sound. But listen to the new sound the vowels ea make when they are together in a word: /e/. Say it with me: /e/. Now say it on your own: /e/.*

Elicit Prior Knowledge

Display the Lesson 40 Practice Page. Prompt students to think about their primary language as you work together to complete section 1.

Ask: *What letters or symbols in your home language combine to make a sound similar to the digraph we are learning today?*

Say: *Think of a word in your home language that includes this sound.*

Model: Recognize Vowel Combination ea

Direct students' attention to section 2 of the Lesson 40 Practice Page.

Say: *We will now look at words that have the vowel combination ea.*

Have students echo read the words, emphasizing the short **/e/** sound.

Sound	short /e/	
Vowel combination	ea	
Words	bread head	thread tread

Practice: Vowel Combination ea

Read aloud section 3 of the Lesson 40 Practice Page in a fluent voice, emphasizing intonation and pronunciation of words and the targeted vowel sound. Invite students to echo read or chime on cue. Ensure comprehension by asking text dependent questions. Have students identify cognates.

Practice: Recognize Vowel Combination ea

Complete section 4 of the Lesson 40 Practice Page with students.

Say: *We will now look at words with the digraph ea.*

Have students echo read the words on the list, emphasizing the short **/e/** sound. Allow time for students to fill in the chart.

Extend Language Knowledge

Practice: Use Words in Context

Complete section 5 of the Lesson 40 Practice Page with students.

Say: *Let's think about words with the vowel digraph ea that make the short /e/ sound. Complete each sentence using words from the word bank on the Practice Page. Take turns reading the completed sentences to your partner.*

I spread peanut butter on **bread** for **breakfast**.

She fell and hit her **head**.

Exercise and a good diet are important for your **health**.

When you run, you may **sweat**.

The **tread** on the tire was very thin.

I'll take the apple **instead** of the orange.

Writing

Say: *Practice writing the sounds you hear as I say each word. Then write the word. I will also use the word in a sentence.*

Pronounce one word at a time from the Word List below, stretching each sound. Use the word in a sentence, and repeat it again after the sentence. For example, say the word **read**. Then say: *I read a great book last week.* Repeat the word **read** after the sentence.

Help students as needed to form letters or recognize letters that form these words.

Sample words: **health, read, steady, threat, bread**

Have students confirm their spelling with a partner, making corrections as needed.

Reflect and Review

Ask: *What did you learn today? Discuss with your partner.*

Have students work with their partners to complete the sentence frames at the end of the Lesson 40 Practice Page, assisting as needed.

Word Bank

Sound	/ĕ/
Vowel combination	ea
Words	bread breath dead deaf death head health lead instead read spread stealth sweat threat tread

✔ Formative Assessment

If the student completes each task correctly, precede to the next skill in the sequence.

Did the student...?	Intervention 2
Pronounce letter in isolation Pronounce letter in words	Use a mirror to show movement of mouth, tongue, and teeth as the sound is produced. Use hand over mouth to explore movement of air as the sound is produced.
Recognize meaning of words in context	Explain meaning of words before and after reading the text. Draw a quick sketch of the word.
Spell targeted sounds correctly	Use simple (CVC) words, practice sound segmentation and blending, use interactive and guided writing.

41 R-Controlled Vowel Pattern ar

Introduce the Lesson

Say: *Today we will identify the name and sound that is made when a vowel is followed by the letter **r**. We will learn to recognize the sound of /**är**/ made by the vowel pattern **ar**. We will read texts with words that include this r-controlled vowel pattern.*

Phonemic Awareness and Sound-Spelling Correspondence

Show the r-controlled vowel **ar** frieze card

Say: *We know the letter **a** has a short sound /a/ and a long sound /a/. We also know that the letter **r** makes the /r/ sound. But when **r** follows the vowel **a**, the pair makes a new sound: /**är**/. Say it with me: /**är**/. Now say it on your own: /**är**/.*

Assess students' ability to recognize, name, and pronounce the letters and the r-controlled vowel pattern.

Elicit Prior Knowledge

Display the Lesson 41 Practice Page. Prompt students to think about their primary language as you work together to complete section 1.

Ask: *What letters or symbols in your home language combine to make a sound similar to the r-controlled sound /**är**/?*

Say: *Think of a word in your home language that includes this sound.*

Model: Recognize R-Controlled Vowel Pattern ar

Direct students' attention to section 2 of the Lesson 41 Practice Page.

Say: *Let's look at words that have the r-controlled vowel pattern **ar**.*

Have students echo read the words, emphasizing the /**är**/ sound.

Sound	/är/
R-controlled vowel pattern	**ar**
Words	arm bark cart hard

Practice: R-Controlled Vowel Pattern ar

Read aloud section 3 of the Lesson 41 Practice Page in a fluent voice, emphasizing intonation and pronunciation of words and the targeted vowel sound. Invite students to echo read or chime on cue. Ensure comprehension by asking text dependent questions. Have students identify cognates.

Practice: Recognize R-Controlled Vowel Pattern ar

Metacognitive Strategy

Selective auditory attention, imagery, auditory representation

Academic Language

letter name, letter sound, vowel, r-controlled, pattern

Materials

- Frieze Card: R-Controlled Vowel (ar)
- Phonics Lesson 41 Practice Page

Pre-Assess

- Recognition of the sound represented by r-controlled vowel **ar**
- Identification of r-controlled vowels that represent the vowel sound **/är/**

Complete section 4 of the Lesson 41 Practice Page with students.

Say: *Now let's look at words that have r-controlled vowel pattern ar.*

Have students echo read the words on the list, emphasizing the sound **/är/** sound. Allow time for students to fill in the chart.

Extend Language Knowledge

Practice: Make Meaning

Complete section 5 of the Lesson 41 Practice Page with students.

Say: *Let's read each clue together. Then work with a partner to find an answer from the word bank. Write the answer on the line.*

1. What dogs (bark)
2. Where you grow vegetables (garden)
3. Children play here (park)
4. Opposite of soft (hard)
5. Another name for lawn (yard)
6. Opposite of dull (sharp)

Writing

Say: *Practice writing the sounds you hear as I say each word. Then write the word. I will also use the word in a sentence.*

Pronounce one word at a time from the Word List below, stretching each sound. Use the word in a sentence, and repeat it again after the sentence. For example, say the word **garden**. Then say: *I plant flowers in the garden.* Repeat the word **garden** after the sentence.

Help students as needed to form letters or recognize letters that form these words.

Sample words: **bark, farm, garden, cart, party**

Have students confirm their spelling with a partner, making corrections as needed.

Reflect and Review

Ask: *What did you learn today? Discuss with your partner.*

Have students work with their partners to complete the sentence frames at the end of the Lesson 41 Practice Page, assisting as needed.

Word Bank

Sound	/är/
R-controlled vowel pattern	ar
Words	arm bark barn cart farm garden hard park sharp yard

✔Formative Assessment

If the student completes each task correctly, precede to the next skill in the sequence.

Did the student...?	Intervention 2
Pronounce letter in isolation Pronounce letter in words	Use a mirror to show movement of mouth, tongue, and teeth as the sound is produced. Use hand over mouth to explore movement of air as the sound is produced.
Recognize meaning of words in context	Explain meaning of words before and after reading the text. Draw a quick sketch of the word.
Spell targeted sounds correctly	Use simple (CVC) words, practice sound segmentation and blending, use interactive and guided writing.

42 R-Controlled Vowel Patterns er, ir, or, ur

Lesson Objectives

- Identify and name the letters **er, ir, or,** and **ur**
- Produce the sound of letters **er, ir, or,** and **ur**
- Relate the sounds **/ûr/** to the letters **er, ir, or,** and **ur**
- Recognize r-controlled vowel patterns **er, ir, or,** and **ur** in words.
- Read common high frequency words.

Metacognitive Strategy

Selective auditory attention, imagery, auditory representation

Academic Language

letter name, letter sound, vowel, r-controlled, pattern

Materials

- Frieze Card: R-Controlled Vowels er, ir, or and ur
- Phonics Lesson 42 Practice Page

Pre-Assess

- Recognition ofthe sound represented by r-controlled vowels er, ir, or, ur
- Identification of r-controlled vowels that represent the vowel sound **/ûr/**

Transfer Notes:

English learners need explicit instruction to recognize and pronounce R-controlled vowel patterns because most do not transfer to Spanish, Vietnamese, Hmong, Tagalog, Korean, Cantonese, Mandarin, Farsi, or Arabic. They must recognize the two letters together and that the vowel preceding the r is not voiced, rather than a one-to-one letter-sound correspondence. Reinforce the meaning of words, letter patterns, as well as the articulation of sounds.

Introduce the Lesson

Say: *Today we will identify the name and sound that is made when certain vowels are followed by the letter r. We will learn to recognize the sound of /ûr/ made by the vowel patterns er, ir, or, and ur. We will read texts with words that include these r-controlled vowel patterns.*

Phonemic Awareness and Sound-Spelling Correspondence

Show the R-Controlled Vowels (**er, ir, or** and **ur**) Frieze Card

Say: *We know the letter e has a short sound /e/ and a long sound /ē/. We also know that the letter r makes the /r/ sound. But when r follows the vowel e, the pair makes a new sound: /ûr/. Say it with me: /ûr/. Now say it on your own: /ûr/.*

Repeat with **ir, or,** and **ur,** and assess students' ability to recognize, name, and pronounce each letter and r-controlled vowel pattern.

Elicit Prior Knowledge

Display the Lesson 42 Practice Page. Prompt students to think about their primary language as you work together to complete section 1.

Ask: *What letters or symbols in your home language combine to make a sound similar to the r-controlled sound /ûr/?*

Say: *Think of a word in your home language that includes this sound.*

Model: Recognize R-Controlled Vowel Patterns **er, ir, or, ur**

Direct students' attention to section 2 of the Lesson 42 Practice Page.

Say: *Let's look at words that have the r-controlled vowel patterns er, ir, or, and ur.*

Have students echo read the words for each vowel pattern, emphasizing the **/ûr/** sound.

Sound	/ûr/			
R-controlled vowel pattern	er	ir	or	ur
Words	her were	bird shirt	word favor	fur turn

Practice: R-Controlled Vowel Patterns **er, ir, or, ur**

Read aloud section 3 of the Lesson 42 Practice Page in a fluent voice, emphasizing intonation and pronunciation of words and the targeted vowel sound. Invite students to echo read or chime on cue. Ensure comprehension by asking text dependent questions. Have students identify cognates.

Practice: Recognize R-Controlled Vowel Patterns er, ir, or, ur

Complete section 4 of the Lesson 42 Practice Page with students.

Say: *Now let's look at words that have r-controlled vowel patterns **er, ir, or, ur.***

Have students echo read the words on the list, emphasizing the sound **/ûr/** sound. Allow time for students to fill in the chart.

Extend Language Knowledge

Practice: Use Words in Context

Complete section 5 of the Lesson 42 Practice Page with students.

Say: *Let's think about words with the r-controlled vowel patterns that make the /ûr/ sound. Complete each sentence using words from the word bank on the Practice Page. Take turns reading the completed sentences to your partner.*

My **brother** and **sister** are twins.

Please don't **burn** my toast.

The **nurse** and doctor both **work** at the hospital.

Today is the baby's **first birthday**.

The **tailor** fixes the **shirt** using a sewing machine.

The **waiter works** at the café and **serves** us lunch.

Writing

Say: *Practice writing the sounds you hear as I say each word. Then write the word. I will also use the word in a sentence.*

Pronounce one word at a time from the Word List below, stretching each sound. Use the word in a sentence, and repeat it again after the sentence. For example, say the word **work**. Then say: *I work hard at school.* Repeat the word **work** after the sentence.

Help students as needed to form letters or recognize letters that form these words.

Sample words: **her, father, purple, swirl, after, work, her, birthday**

Have students confirm their spelling with a partner, making corrections as needed.

Reflect and Review

Ask: *What did you learn today? Discuss with your partner.*

Have students work with their partners to complete the sentence frames at the end of the Lesson 42 Practice Page, assisting as needed.

Word Bank

Sound	/ûr/	
R-controlled vowel pattern	er	ir
Words	after	bird
	brother	birthday
	dinner	dirt
	father	firm
	germ	first
	her	girl
	mother	shirt
	person	skirt
	serve	squirt
	sister	swirl
	under	twirl
R-controlled vowel pattern	or	ur
Words	word	fur
	work	curl
	color	hurt
	cursor	burn
	doctor	turn
	favor	church
	tailor	hurray
	world	hurry
	worm	nurse
	worse	purple
	worth	purse

✓Formative Assessment

If the student completes each task correctly, precede to the next skill in the sequence.

Did the student…?	Intervention 2
Pronounce letter in isolation Pronounce letter in words	Use a mirror to show movement of mouth, tongue, and teeth as the sound is produced. Use hand over mouth to explore movement of air as the sound is produced.
Recognize meaning of words in context	Explain meaning of words before and after reading the text. Draw a quick sketch of the word.
Spell targeted sounds correctly	Use simple (CVC) words, practice sound segmentation and blending, use interactive and guided writing.

Lesson 1 Practice Page

Continuous Sounding Consonants l, m, and n

1. Compare Sounds

My home language is _____.

Today's letters compared to my home language:

Today's letters	Does this sound exist in your language?	Is it represented by this letter?	Home language word example
l	YES __NO__	YES __NO__	
m	YES __NO__	YES __NO__	
n	YES __NO__	YES __NO__	

2. Read and Identify Words with Continuous Sounding Consonants

Have you ever run in a race? Running in a race is fun! If you run fast you could be a winner! Running is also good for your health. Many people enjoy running outside just after the sun sets. However I would rather run when the sun is shining and the birds are singing.

3. Classify Words

Letter	Initial (Beginning)	Medial (Middle)	Final (Ending)
l			
m			
n			

4. Your Turn

Letter	Initial (Beginning)	Medial (Middle)	Final (Ending)
l			
m			
n			

lunch woman swim nap make number salad brain manner ball next tomato

Today I learned that _____.This is important because _____. I now know _____.

Lesson 2 Practice Page
Continuous Sounding Consonants f, r, s

1. Compare Sounds

My home language is _____.

Today's letters compared to my home language:

Today's letters	Does this sound exist in your language?	Is it represented by this letter?	Home language word example
f	YES __NO__	YES __NO__	
r	YES __NO__	YES __NO__	
s	YES __NO__	YES __NO__	

2. Read and Identify Words with Continuous Sounding Consonants

Have you ever run in a race? Running in a race is fun! If you run fast you could be a winner! Running is also good for your health. Many people enjoy running outside just after the sun sets. However I would rather run when the sun is shining and the birds are singing.

3. Classify Words

Letter	Initial (Beginning)	Medial (Middle)	Final (Ending)
f			
r			
s			

4. Your Turn

1. Pigs, cows, and horses live on a _____.
2. When the sun _____, it gets _____ outside.
3. I like to go down the _____ at the _____.
4. Bananas are mushy when they are too _____.
5. Our _____ stayed in for recess because of the _____.
6. I do my homework _____school.

ripe   park   class   slide   after   sets   farm   rain   dark

Today I learned that _____. This is important because _____. I now know _____.

Lesson 3 Practice Page

Identify and Name Continuous Sounding Consonants
v, w, y, z

1. Prior Knowledge and Home Language Connections

My home language is _____.

Today's letters compared to my home language:

Today's letters	Does this sound exist in your language?	Is it represented by this letter?	Home language word example
v	YES __NO__	YES __NO__	
w	YES __NO__	YES __NO__	
y	YES __NO__	YES __NO__	
z	YES __NO__	YES __NO__	

2. Shared Reading Text

Have you ever run in a race? It can be a lot of fun to run in races with your family! Running is good exercise and can be an important part of your regular physical fitness regimen. Although many people enjoy running outside after the sun sets I would rather run my five miles when the sun shines and the birds sing.

3. Recognize Letter Position in Words

Letter	Initial (Beginning)	Medial (Middle)	Final (Ending)
v			
w			
y			
z			

4. Extend Language: Use words in context

1. There are many different countries in the _____.
2. _____ have black and white stripes.
3. Have you _____ seen a shooting star?
4. We _____ to the store after school.
5. I got a 100% on the math _____.
6. Cakes have a _____ of frosting.
7. A _____ lives on a farm.
8. I'm too _____ to get up today!

went cow lazy layer quiz zebras world ever

Today I learned that _____.This is important because _____. I now know _____.

Lesson 4 Practice Page

Stop Sound Consonants b, t, g

1. Compare Sounds

My home language is _____.

Today's letters compared to my home language:

Today's letters	Does this sound exist in your language?	Is it represented by this letter?	Home language word example
b	[YES __NO__	[YES __NO__	
t	[YES __NO__	[YES __NO__	
g	[YES __NO__	[YES __NO__	

2. Read and Identify Words with Stop Sound Consonants

Have you ever <u>been</u> to a <u>baseball</u> game?
The players work hard <u>to</u> win the <u>game</u>.
Some players <u>rub</u> pine tar on their <u>bat</u> in the <u>dugout</u>.
This gives them a <u>better</u> grip when they <u>go</u> to <u>slug</u> the <u>ball</u>.
It is fun <u>to</u> cheer for your favorite <u>team</u>.
If you <u>go</u> to a <u>game</u>, <u>take</u> a <u>baseball</u> glove <u>to</u> catch a <u>ball</u> that may come flying your way.

3. Classify Words

Letter	Initial (Beginning)	Medial (Middle)	Final (Ending)
b			
t			.
g			

4. Your Turn

1. The _____ house had lots of rooms.
2. My favorite sport is _____.
3. I _____ when you say something funny.
4. You should drink lots of _____ on hot days.
5. Worms _____ in the dirt.
6. The _____ _____ will win the _____ today.

team big water baseball wiggle giggle better game sport

Today I learned that _____. This is important because _____. I now know _____.

Lesson 5 Practice Page
Stop Sound Consonants p, h, j

1. Compare Sounds

My home language is _____.

Today's letters compared to my home language:

Today's letters	Does this sound exist in your language?	Is it represented by this letter?	Home language word example
p	YES __NO__	YES __NO__	
h	YES __NO__	YES __NO__	
j	YES __NO__	YES __NO__	

2. Read and Identify Words with Stop Sound Consonants

Most kids enjoy the park. They hop, skip, and jump, which is great for their health. However, they must be careful not to step behind the swings. If they do, they could get hit. Does your park have a basketball hoops? Many kids get great joy from shooting hoops at their neighborhood park.

3. Classify Words

Letter	Initial (Beginning)	Medial (Middle)	Final (Ending)
p			
h			
j			

4. Your Turn

1. I like _____ with extra cheese.
2. Some _____ like to _____ rope.
3. We were _____ about winning the soccer game.
4. I _____ playing basketball.
5. My brother likes to _____ me with my homework.
6. I hide _____ the big tree when I play _____ and seek.

enjoy happy pizza help behind hide jump kids

Today I learned that _____.This is important because _____.I now know _____.

Lesson 6 Practice Page

Stop Sound Consonants k, q, x

1. Compare Sounds

My home language is _____.

Today's letters compared to my home language:

Today's letters	Does this sound exist in your language?	Is it represented by this letter?	Home language word example
k	[YES __NO__	[YES __NO__	
q	[YES __NO__	[YES __NO__	
z	[YES __NO__	[YES __NO__	

2. Read and Identify Words with Stop Sound Consonants

You've read many stories with kings and queens. But did you know that some countries are still ruled by royalty? It is very exciting to meet a king or queen! When you talk to a king you call him "Your Excellency" and you call the queen "Your Majesty." If you ever get to meet a king or queen in person ask them questions about their lives. You may discover that they're not as different from you as you thought!

3. Classify Words

Letter	Initial (Beginning)	Medial (Middle)	Final (Ending)
k			
q			
z			

4. Your Turn

1. I _____ my money in a safe place.
2. The _____ and _____ live in a castle.
3. The _____ machine _____ a skilled worker to operate.
4. My _____ is due at the library today.
5. There is a _____ living in the woods near my house.
6. I _____ the door with a _____ so no one can get inside.

key   queen   book   lock   required   king   keep   fox   x-ray

Today I learned that _____.This is important because _____. I now know _____.

Lesson 7 Practice Page

Initial Consonant L-Blends bl-, cl-, fl-, gl-, pl-, sl-.

1. Compare Sounds

My home language is _____.

Today's letters compared to my home language:

What are some examples in your home language of two letters or symbols that combine to make a new sound?What are some words in your home language that have these combinations or blends of letters or symbols?

Letter or Symbol	+	Letter or Symbol	Example Words in Home Language
	+		

2. Recognize Initial Consonant Blends

bl-	cl-	fl-	gl-	pl-	sl-
black	class	flag	glove	play	slip
blade	clap	flower	glad	please	slope

3. Read and Identify Words with Initial Consonant L-Blends

Have you ever seen a blackbird? If you're not sure, here's a clue: its feathers look like steel blue glass as it glides through the sky. A blackbird flies slowly, only slightly flapping its wings to stay in flight. Suddenly, it swoops down into the deep grass, clamping onto its prey. Then it flies back up into the trees to eat it. Blackbirds like to eat fruit, especially yummy plums.

4. Classify Words

bl-	cl-	fl-	gl-	pl-	sl-

5. Your Turn

1. A color : _____
2. Opposite of quickly: _____
3. A compound word:_____
4. You can see them in the sky: _____
5. What birds can do: _____
6. Some windows are made out of this material _____

fly black bird glass blue slowly clouds

Something I learned today was _____.This knowledge helps me _____.I like _____.

Lesson 8 Practice Page

Initial Consonant R-Blends br-, cr-, dr-, fr-, gr-, pr-, and tr-

1. Prior Knowledge and Home Language Connections

My home language is _____.

Today's letters compared to my home language:

What are some examples in your home language of two letters or symbols that combine to make a new sound? What are some words in your home language that have these combinations or blends of letters or symbols?

Letter or Symbol	+	Letter or Symbol	Example Words in Home Language
	+		

2. Recognize Initial Consonant Blends

br-	cr-	dr-	fr-	gr-	pr-	tr-
brand	crab	drag	frame	green	price	trace
brow	crowd	drop	frog	grass	prank	truck

3. Shared Reading Text

Have you ever seen animals in the wild? Often they visit a brook of running water. You can hear brown crickets and green frogs from a distance as other animals wander down to take a drink. You might even see groups of young animals prancing around, getting into trouble as they play tricks on each other, while their mothers stands by, ready to cry out at the first sight of a predator.

4. Recognize Initial Consonant R-Blends

br-	cr-	dr-	fr-	gr-	pr-	tr-

5. Extend Language Knowledge: Make Meaning

1. Children color with it _____
2. It grows in a yard _____
3. The color of dirt _____
4. A salty snack _____
5. Water goes down it _____
6. Opposite of back _____
7. A path in the woods _____

grass pretzel brown drain crayon front trail

Something I learned today was _____. This knowledge helps me _____. I like _____.

Lesson 9 Practice Page
Initial Consonant S-Blends sc-, sk-, sn-, sp-, st-, sw-

1. Compare Sounds

My home language is _____.

Today's letters compared to my home language: What are some examples in your home language of two letters or symbols that combine to make a new sound? What are some words in your home language that have these combinations or blends of letters or symbols?

Letter or Symbol	+	Letter or Symbol	Used in a word or concept
	+		

2. Recognize Initial Consonant Blends

sc	sk	sn	sp	st	sw
score	skirt	snail	special	storm	swing
scale	skull	snow	sport	sting	sweet

3. Read and Identify Words with Initial Consonant S-Blends

Have you ever seen a live skunk? It can be a scary experience especially if it sneaks up on you! If you see one, don't stop and scream, or it might lift its tail and spray you with its smelly scent. Try to walk away quietly and swiftly.

4. Classify Words

sc-	sk-	sn-	sp-	st-	sw-

5. Your Turn

1. The water ran _____ in the river.
2. A weigh the apples on a _____.
3. I wear _____ to gym class.
4. We can _____ when the pond is frozen.
5. My favorite _____ is pretzels.
6. The little boy uses the _____ to reach the high shelf.
7. I use a _____ to stir the batter.
8. He likes to _____ in the ocean.

stool swiftly swim scale snack spoon sneakers skate

Something I learned today was _____. This knowledge helps me _____. I like _____.

Lesson 10 Practice Page

3-Letter Initial Consonant Blends scr-, spl-, spr-, squ-, str-

1. Prior Knowledge and Home Language Connections

My home language is _____.

Today's letters compared to my home language:

What are some examples in your home language of three letters or symbols that combine to make a new sound?What are some words in your home language that have these combinations or blends of letters or symbols?

Letter or Symbol	+	Letter or Symbol	Used in a word or concept
	+		

2. Recognize 3-Letter Initial Consonant Blends

scr-	spl-	spr-	squ-	str-
screen	splash	spring	squad	strict
scratch	splice	sprain	square	straw

3. Shared Reading Text

A visit to the beach is lots of fun, but be sure to put on sunscreen. You will enjoy splashing in the waves and squishing your toes in the sand. If you're lucky, you might spot some cool ocean creatures, like a squid or starfish, but don't scream if you see them--they won't hurt you! At the snack bar, you might enjoy a large ice cream cone with sprinkles! Take some pictures of the day to keep in your scrapbook.

4. Recognize 3-Letter Initial Consonant Blends

scr-	spl-	spr-	squ-	str-

5. Extend Language Knowledge: Make Meaning

1. Children like to _____ on paper with crayons.
2. If you're not careful you can get a _____ from touching something wooden.
3. Every morning, I _____ butter on my toast.
4. The pigs _____ with delight as they roll in the mud.
5. A _____ is a shape with four equal sides.
6. A ruler can help you make a _____ line.
7. When you have an itch, you _____ it to feel better.

spread straight square scribble scratch splinter squeal

Something I learned today was _____.This knowledge helps me _____.I like _____.

Lesson 11 Practice Page

Ending Consonant Blends -ct, -ft

1. Compare Sounds

My home language is _____.

Today's letters compared to my home language:

What are some examples in your home language of three letters or symbols that combine to make a new sound?What are some words in your home language that have these combinations or blends of letters or symbols?

Letter or Symbol	+	Letter or Symbol	Used in a word or concept
	+		

2. Recognize Ending Consonant Blends

-ct	-ft
act	raft
fact	left

3. Read and Identify Words with Ending Consonant Blends

To craft a sculpture of an object, you first create a draft, or a sketch. Next, you use clay to craft an exact replica of the object. Finally, you can give your project to someone as a gift.

4. Classify Words

-ct	-ft

5. Your Turn

1. Opposite of right(left)
2. A boat may do this(drift)
3. Something that is true(fact)
4. To move from one thing to another(shift)
5. A rough copy(draft)
6. Something you give to someone(gift)
7. You have to give this to get this(respect)
8. It floats(raft)

fact respect draft left raft gift drift shift

Something I learned today was _____.This knowledge helps me _____.I like _____.

Lesson 12 Practice Page

Ending Consonant Blends -ld, -lf, -lk, -lt, -lp

1. Compare Sounds

My home language is _____.

Today's letters compared to my home language:

What are some examples in your home language of three letters or symbols that combine to make a new sound? What are some words in your home language that have these combinations or blends of letters or symbols?

Letter or Symbol	+	Letter or Symbol	Used in a word or concept
	+		

2. Recognize Ending Consonant Blends

-ld	-lf	-lk	-lt	-lp
old	elf	milk	salt	gulp
told	gulf	silk	belt	yelp

3. Read and Identify Words with Ending Consonant Blends

What's your favorite snack? Is it a glass of cold milk with cookies? Or do you prefer popcorn with lots of butter and salt? Eating these snacks, however, won't have a good result. You'll need to loosen your belt! Instead of sugary drinks, gulp down lots of water. If you need help finding healthy snacks, take a look at the health food shelf at your local market.

4. Classify Words

-ld	-lf	-lk	-lt	-lp

5. Your Turn

1. The _____ is learning to read.
2. The blouse is made of a _____.
3. The ice cream will _____ in the sun.
4. I need _____ answering the question.
5. We like _____ on our popcorn.
6. I wear a sweater when it is _____.
7. She looks at _____ in the mirror.
8. The big men _____ heavy weights at the gym.

cold belt lift child melt salt silk help

Something I learned today was _____. This knowledge helps me _____. I like _____.

Lesson 13 Practice Page
Ending Consonant Blends -mp, -pt

1. Compare Sounds

My home language is _____.

Today's letters compared to my home language:

What are some examples in your home language of three letters or symbols that combine to make a new sound?What are some words in your home language that have these combinations or blends of letters or symbols?

Letter or Symbol	+	Letter or Symbol	Used in a word or concept
	+		

2. Recognize Ending Consonant Blends

-mp	-pt
pump	script
swamp	except

3. Read and Identify Words with Ending Consonant Blends

The dump is a great place to explore. What other people have thrown away, I've kept as my own treasures. I once discovered an old lamp that was great except that it didn't light up. Another time, I found a stamp collection. Even when I don't find anything, I have fun. For example, I attempt to jump from one pile of junk to another. One time, I crept inside an old camp tent and fell fast asleep! I slept for two hours! What do I do when I get bored with the dump? I head over to the swamp!

4. Classify Words

-mp	-pt

5.Your Turn

1. Moist
2. A place for junk
3. To have moved slowly
4. You sleep in tents
5. You do this on a trampoline
6. To try
7. What you did last night
8. You put this on an envelope to mail it

slept camp stamp crept damp attempt dump jump

Something I learned today was _____.This knowledge helps me _____.I like _____.

Lesson 14 Practice Page
Ending Consonant Blends -nd, -nk, -nt

1. Compare Sounds

My home language is _____.

Today's letters compared to my home language:

What are some examples in your home language of three letters or symbols that combine to make a new sound? What are some words in your home language that have these combinations or blends of letters or symbols?

Letter or Symbol	+	Letter or Symbol	Used in a word or concept
	+		

2. Recognize Ending Consonant Blends

-nd	-nk	-nt
find	bank	plant
land	sink	spent

Read and Identify Words with Ending Consonant Blends

Traffic jams stink! All you hear is Honk! Honk! But don't get too angry or you could have an accident. If you're patient, you won't end up with a dent in your car, or worse! When stuck in traffic, try to take your mind off of it and think of other things. Don't honk your horn or blink your lights because it won't help. Hopefully your tank is full and before you know it, you'll find yourself on your way.

4. Classify Words

-nd	-nk	-nt

5. Your Turn

1. You can get a _____ from the _____ if you are thirsty.
2. The flute _____ the trumpet are part of a _____.
3. Let's _____ the _____ man for his help.
4. We _____ crops in the _____.
5. Red and white _____ to make _____.
6. It is _____ to vote for the _____.
7. The _____ _____ to class.
8. You need a _____ to open a _____ account if you're a child.

important blend parent kind band thank sink bank land pink and student went plant president drink

Something I learned today was _____. This knowledge helps me _____. I like _____.

Lesson 15 Practice Page

Ending Consonant Blends -sk, -sp, -st

1. Compare Sounds

My home language is _____.

Today's letters compared to my home language:

Are two letters or symbols combined to make a new sound in your home language? Can you think of a word that has any of these sounds, letters, or symbols blended together in your home language?

Letter or Symbol	+	Letter or Symbol	Used in a word or concept

2. Recognize Ending Consonant Blends

-sk	-sp	-st
mask	crisp	must
dusk	wasp	rest

3. Read and Identify Words with Ending Consonant Blends

If you've been stung by a pest, like a wasp, you need to act fast to reduce the risk of a bad reaction. First, you must wash the sting area with water and soap. Next, apply a cold pack to the wound site to resist swelling and pain. It is most important to keep the wound clean and dry to prevent infection. And, it is in your best interest NOT to go looking for the wasp nest.

4. Classify Words

-sk	-sp	-st

5. Your Turn

1. Opposite of slow
2. Where you sit at school
3. Opposite of first
4. The outer covering of an ear of corn
5. To hold on to
6. What you do when you sleep
7. A flying insect that stings
8. Another word for right after sunset

husk fast wasp desk rest dusk last grasp

Something I learned today was _____. This knowledge helps me _____. I like _____.

Lesson 16 Practice Page

Initial Consonant Diagraphs wh-

1. Compare Sounds

My home language is _____.

Today's letters compared to my home language:

What are some examples in your home language of three letters or symbols that combine to make a new sound? What are some words in your home language that have these combinations or blends of letters or symbols?

Letter or Symbol	+	Letter or Symbol	Used in a word or concept
	+		

2. Recognize Initial Consonant Diagraphs

wh-		
what	whale	white
where	wheat	whisper

Read and Identify Words with Ending Consonant Blends

Have you ever gone whale watching? What an adventure it can be! When you arrive at the wharf to get on the boat, you wait until the captain blows the whistle to signal the start of the trip. Try to get a seat near the captain who will be at the wheel so that you can easily see the whales when you come upon them. Whoa! Hold on when the waves come!

4. Classify Words

wh-		

5. Your Turn

1. _____ are my keys?
2. A _____ is a big ocean animal.
3. Children sometimes _____ when they don't get what they want.
4. Please _____ in the library
5. The bread was made from _____ flour.
6. The kitten has long _____ on it face.

whine   wheat   where   whale   whiskers   whisper

Something I learned today was _____. This knowledge helps me _____. I like _____.

Lesson 17 Practice Page

Initial, Medial, and Final Consonant Digraphs sh, ch

1. Compare Sounds

My home language is _____.

Today's letters compared to my home language:

What are some examples in your home language of three letters or symbols that combine to make a new sound? What are some words in your home language that have these combinations or blends of letters or symbols?

Letter or Symbol	+	Letter or Symbol	Used in a word or concept
	+		

2. Recognize Consonant Digraphs

	Initial (Beginning)	Medial (Middle)	Final (Ending)
sh	sheet	wishes	dish
ch	chair	inches	which

3. Read and Identify Words with Consonant Digraphs

Many families enjoy spending the day at the beach. Children run in the sunshine and splash in the ocean. Others play in the sand, sharing pails and shovels. Meanwhile, parents enjoy sitting in their beach chairs, chatting with each other, as they watch their children play. Other people stand on the seashore trying to catch a fish. Lunch at the beach might include sandwiches and peaches from home or a milkshake from the snack bar. To stay safe at the beach, everyone should put on sunscreen, and you should not go in the ocean after you eat!

4. Classify Words

	Initial (Beginning)	Medial (Middle)	Final (Ending)
sh			
ch			

5. Your Turn

1. Opposite of tall
2. The meal you eat at noon
3. It has scales and lives in water
4. What happens when you jump in water
5. To talk with someone
6. Where the ocean meets land

splash   lunch   beach   chat   short   fish

Something I learned today was _____. This knowledge helps me _____. I like _____.

Lesson 18 Practice Page
Initial, Medial, and Final Consonant Digraph th

1. Compare Sounds

My home language is _____.

Today's letters compared to my home language:

What are some examples in your home language of three letters or symbols that combine to make a new sound? What are some words in your home language that have these combinations or blends of letters or symbols?

Letter or Symbol	+	Letter or Symbol	Used in a word or concept
	+		

2. Recognize Consonant Digraphs

	Initial (Beginning)	Medial (Middle)	Final (Ending)
th	thumb thing	mother panther	bath teeth

3. Read and Identify Words with Consonant Digraphs

My father is a thin man with very white teeth. He married my beautiful and thoughtful mother when he was twenty-three. They got married on Friday, March thirteenth during a huge thunderstorm. Thick grey cloud started to gather during the ceremony. When the rain started, guests threw their jackets over their heads without thinking and ran for cover. That's what happens when you marry on Friday the thirteenth!

4. Classify Words

	Initial (Beginning)	Medial (Middle)	Final (Ending)
th			

5. Your Turn

1. The _____ was very loud during the storm.
2. We ate lots of cake at the _____ party.
3. A _____ flew through a window and into _____ house.
4. The _____ wore running _____ for the race.
5. I gave my dog a _____ in the _____.
6. My _____ the _____ are the greatest parents.
7. I have lots of _____ in my _____!

moth   mother   teeth   birthday   thunder   clothes   bath   athlete   the   mouth   bathtub   father

Something I learned today was _____. This knowledge helps me _____. I like _____.

Lesson 19 Practice Page

Initial, Medial, and Final Consonant Digraph ph

1. Compare Sounds

My home language is _____.

Today's letters compared to my home language:

What are some examples in your home language of three letters or symbols that combine to make a new sound? What are some words in your home language that have these combinations or blends of letters or symbols?

Letter or Symbol	+	Letter or Symbol	Used in a word or concept
	+		

2. Recognize Consonant Digraphs

	Initial (Beginning)	Medial (Middle)	Final (Ending)
ph	phone photo	orphan elephant	autograph graph

3. Read and Identify Words with Consonant Digraphs

Animal photographers have a cool job! Imagine going on safari and photographing elephants in the wild. Or, picture taking underwater shots of dolphins as they swim by. Some people even capture underwater sounds with special microphones. Photographs of animals, such as pheasants, may not seem as exciting, but it's still challenging to get the perfect shot. Who knows, maybe one day you'll be a famous photographer and everyone will want your autograph!

4. Classify Words

	Initial (Beginning)	Medial (Middle)	Final (Ending)
ph			

5. Your Turn

1. You take it with a camera
2. The son of your brother or sister
3. In English, there are 26 letters in this
4. Singers use this so we can hear them
5. Your signature
6. You use it to make calls

microphone   alphabet   telephone   nephew   autograph   photograph

Something I learned today was _____. This knowledge helps me _____. I like _____.

Lesson 20 Practice Page

Initial, Medial, and Final Consonant Digraph gh

1. Compare Sounds

My home language is _____.

Today's letters compared to my home language:

What are some examples in your home language of three letters or symbols that combine to make a new sound?What are some words in your home language that have these combinations or blends of letters or symbols?

Letter or Symbol	+	Letter or Symbol	Used in a word or concept
	+		

2. Recognize Consonant Digraphs

	Initial (Beginning)	Medial (Middle)	Final (Ending)
gh	ghost	afghan laughing right	laugh though

3. Read and Identify Words with Consonant Digraphs

Sometimes when things are tough, the best thing you can do is laugh. Today, for example, was a rough one for me. It began when I overslept. I thought I turned on my alarm clock last night, but I didn't go off. I must have been quite a sight as I leapt out of bed and dressed in a hurry. As though that wasn't enough, I burnt my toast and fought my brother for the last doughnut! Luckily I got to my bus stop right before the driver was about to leave. My friends laughed when they saw me. I hadn't had time to brush my hair and my shirt was on backward. I must've been quite a sight!

4. Classify Words

	Initial (Beginning)	Medial (Middle)	Final (Ending)
gh	(/gh/)	(/gh/ like /f/) (silent /gh/)	(/gh/ like /f/) (silent /gh/)

5. Your Turn

1. The sandpaper feels _____ against my skin.
2. I _____ when someone tickles me.
3. I would be very scared if I saw a _____.
4. Sometimes we borrow sugar from our next door _____.
5. We like _____ with powdered sugar.
6. You should cover your mouth when you _____.

ghost   doughnuts   rough   cough   laugh   neighbor

Something I learned today was _____.This knowledge helps me _____.I like _____.

Lesson 21 Practice Page
Final Consonant Digraph -ng

1. Compare Sounds

My home language is _____.

Today's letters compared to my home language:

What are some examples in your home language of three letters or symbols that combine to make a new sound?What are some words in your home language that have these combinations or blends of letters or symbols?

Letter or Symbol	+	Letter or Symbol	Used in a word or concept
	+		

2. Recognize Final Consonant Digraph -ng

Final (Ending) -ng	
long	bang
strong	swing
song	king

3. Read and Identify Words with Final Consonant Digraph -ng

In a musical, the lines are sung in a song. Musicals are often long because of all the songs. Actors need to have strong voices and be able to sing loud enough for all to hear! Some musicals include sound effects, such as the bang of a drum, the clang of a bell, or the ring of a phone.

4. Classify Words

Final (Ending) -ng	

5. Your Turn

1. What some birds do _____
2. The sound you hear when a drum is hit _____
3. The royal head of government _____
4. Bats like to do this upside-down _____
5. The organ in your body that you use to breathe(lung)
6. Opposite of weak _____

king lung sing strong hang bang

Something I learned today was _____.This knowledge helps me _____.I like _____.

Lesson 22 Practice Page
Silent Consonant Digraphs dge, gn

1. Compare Sounds

My home language is _____.

Today's letters compared to my home language:

What are some examples in your home language of sounds, letters, or symbols that when combined one letter is silent?

Letter or Symbol	+	Letter or Symbol	Used in a word or concept
	+		

2. Recognize Consonant Digraphs dge, gn

Medial (middle) dge	Initial (beginning) gn	Medial (middle) gn	Final (ending) gn
bridge	gnu	cologne	sign
nudge	gnome	assignments	assign

3. Read and Identify Words with Silent Consonant Digraphs dge, gn

Building a bridge is a lot of work. The workers have to dodge traffic on the street as they work to nudge the large beams into place, making sure that they follow design of the bridge. They then have to make sure the edge of the bridge is not too close to any hedge or gnarly trees that may be on either side. The workers have to trudge the materials up to the construction site, because often there is not enough room to budge with a truck. Finally, they have to watch the budget, as they pledged to build the bridge for a certain cost. It's certainly a lot of work to build a bridge!

4. Classify Words

Medial (middle) dge	Initial (beginning) gn	Medial (middle) gn	Final (ending) gn

5. Your Turn

1. _____ who had made the best _____.
2. The _____ was small and cute.
3. Our teacher _____ too much homework.
4. The police officer wears a _____.
5. A _____ is a kind of bird.
6. The _____ are buzzing in my ear.

badge judged partridge gnats gnome fudge assigns

Something I learned today was _____.This knowledge helps me _____.I like _____.

Lesson 23 Practice Page

Initial Silent Consonant Digraphs kn-, wr-

1. Compare Sounds

My home language is _____.

Today's letters compared to my home language:

What are some examples in your home language of sounds, letters, or symbols that when combined one letter is silent?

Letter or Symbol	+	Letter or Symbol	Used in a word or concept
	+		

2. Recognize Consonant Digraphs kn-, wr-

	kn-	wr-
Initial (beginning)	knot knock	write wrap

3. Read and Identify Words with Silent Consonant Digraphs kn-, wr-

If your wrist hurts when you write you might be holding your pen the wrong way. The right way to hold your pen is to rest it on the bottom knuckle on your index finger. Once you get the knack of it, you'll be in less pain and your handwriting will improve.

4. Classify Words

	kn-	wr-
Initial (beginning)		

5. Your Turn

1. What you do to a gift before you give it
2. What you turn to open a door
3. What you do to a door to see if anyone is home
4. Where your hand is connected to your arm
5. In medieval times, he often wore a suit of armor
6. You use this to cut food

knock wrist knife knob knight wrap

Something I learned today was _____.This knowledge helps me _____.I like _____.

Lesson 24 Practice Page

Final Silent Consonant Digraphs -ld, -lf, -lk

1. Compare Sounds

My home language is _____.

Today's letters compared to my home language:

What are some examples in your home language of sounds, letters, or symbols that when combined one letter is silent?

Letter or Symbol	+	Letter or Symbol	Used in a word or concept
	+		

2. Recognize Final Silent Consonant Digraphs -ld, -lf, -lk

	-ld	-lf	-lk
Final (ending)	could should	calf half	walk folk

3. Read and Identify Words with Silent Consonant Digraphs -ld, -lf, -lk

Have you ever seen a live calf? It is about half the size of its full-grown mother. Shortly after birth, the calf can stand and walk to be able to drink the mother cow's milk. There are times when the mother cow will balk at letting the calf drink. If that is the case, then the farmer has to help the calf get the necessary nutrition from its mother. But you should be careful when you walk in the corral with the mother and calf…the mother can be very protective!

4. Classify Words

	-ld	-lf	-lk
Final (ending)			

5. Your Turn

1. I ___ like to ___ with you.
2. You ___ get at least 8 hours of sleep each night.
3. I'll split my cookie in ___ to share with you.
4. I ___ ride my bike or ___ to school.
5. The teacher writes on the board with ___.
6. A ___ is a baby cow.

walk   should   calf   would   could   chalk   half   talk

Something I learned today was _____.This knowledge helps me _____.I like _____.

Lesson 25 Practice Page

Medial and Final Silent Consonant Digraphs lm, mb, mn

1. Compare Sounds

My home language is _____.

Today's letters compared to my home language:

What are some examples in your home language of sounds, letters, or symbols that when combined one letter is silent?

Letter or Symbol	+	Letter or Symbol	Used in a word or concept
	+		

2. Recognize Silent Consonant Digraphs -lm, -mb, -mn

	lm	mb	mn
Medial (middle)	salmon	n/a	n/a
Final (ending)	calm palm	comb lamb	column autumn

3. Read and Identify Words with Silent Consonant Digraphs lm, mb, mn

The best salmon fishing is in the autumn. The water is very cold, so be sure to wear wading boots so that your feet don't get numb. You may have to climb on some rocks, so be careful. As you are casting your line out into the water, look out for low-hanging tree limbs. If you get your line caught on a limb, stay calm and ask someone to help you untangle it. Once you get your line in the water, you'll need to hold the fishing pole in the palm of one hand and the line with your thumb on the other so you can tell when you have a fish on the hook. Happy fishing!

4. Classify Words

	lm	mb	mn
Medial (middle)			
Final (ending)			

5. Your Turn

1. The season right before winter _____
2. A song sung in a church _____
3. Where one is buried _____
4. A type of fish _____
5. The opposite of worried _____
6. An arm or a leg _____

tomb calm autumn limb hymn salmon

Something I learned today was _____. This knowledge helps me _____. I like _____.

Lesson 26 Practice Page

Initial Silent Consonant Digraph rh-

1. Compare Sounds

My home language is _____.

Today's letters compared to my home language:

What are some examples in your home language of sounds, letters, or symbols that when combined one letter is silent?

Letter or Symbol	+	Letter or Symbol	Used in a word or concept
	+		

2. Recognize Initial Silent Consonant Digraphs rh-

	rh-	
Initial (beginning)	rhinoceros rhyme	rhythm rhumba

3. Read and Identify Words with Silent Consonant Digraphs rh-

Have you ever heard of a dance called the "rhumba"? It's a fun dance to watch, but challenging to learn. With its Afro-Cuban roots, the dancers move to the rhythm of the music. At times, their movements rhyme with each other; at other times they're more like a rhapsody of emotion. With their rhinestone-studded dance costumes, the dancers sparkle as they move across the floor. All in all, the rhumba is as beautiful to watch as it is challenging to learn!

4. Recognize Words

	rh-	
Initial (beginning)		

5. Your Turn

1. The ____ lives in the grasslands.
2. A ____ has four equal sides.
3. The words how and now ____.
4. I danced to the ____ of the drum.
5. I love my grandmother's ____ pie.
6. Here tiara was covered in ____.

rhyme   rhubarb   rhinoceros   rhinestones   rhombus   rhythm

Something I learned today was _____. This knowledge helps me _____. I like _____.

Lesson 27 Practice Page

Silent Consonant Digraph bt

1. Compare Sounds

My home language is _____.

Today's letters compared to my home language:

What are some examples in your home language of sounds, letters, or symbols that when combined one letter is silent?

Letter or Symbol	+	Letter or Symbol	Used in a word or concept
	+		

2. Recognize Silent Consonant Digraph bt

	bt
Medial (middle)	subtle debtor
Final (ending)	debt doubt

3. Read and Identify Words with Silent Consonant Digraph bt

Has anyone ever owed you something, like money? If so, what they owe you is considered a debt, even if it's not money. There's a subtle difference between a monetary debt and a debt of owing someone a favor to repay something the person did for you. Doubtless, both are still considered a debt, and often debtors – those who owe the debt – are held accountable for their debts by the person to whom the debt is owed, even if in a subtle way. It is always good for you to pay your debts, just as you would want your debtors to pay what they owe you!

4. Classify Words

	bt
Medial (middle)	
Final (ending)	

5. Your Turn

1. The opposite of obvious_____
2. Someone who owes you money _____
3. To not believe something_____
4. When you owe something to someone_____
5. When there is likely that something is true_____
6. When it is unlikely that something is true _____

doubt doubtless debtor subtle debt doubtful

Something I learned today was _____.This knowledge helps me _____.I like _____.

Lesson 28 Practice Page
Medial (CVC) Short Vowels (a, e, i, o, u)

1. Compare Sounds

My home language is _____.

Today's letters compared to my home language:

What letters or symbols in your home language have two different sounds? What is an example of a word in your home language with letters or symbols that have two different sounds?

Letter or Symbol: One sound	Letter or Symbol: Second sound	Used in a word or concept

2. Recognize Medial Short Vowels

	ă	ĕ	ĭ	ŏ	ŭ
	CVC	CVC	CVC	CVC	CVC
Medial (middle)	bat mat	bet met	bit hit	cot hot	cut hut

3. Read and Identify Words with Medial Short Vowels

Playing the mud with a pal is a lot of fun. You may want to ask permission first, as your clothes will get very wet and dirty. But if you hop, skip, or jump in the mud, be careful: It is very slippery! Did you know that a pig or hog will roll around in the mud in its pen to cool off on a hot day? Just like a kid, a pup often likes to run and dig in the mud, and you may have to get a pan of water and use a rag to rub all the mud off you and the pup's paws!

4. Classify Words

	ă	ĕ	ĭ	ŏ	ŭ
	CVC	CVC	CVC	CVC	CVC
Medial (middle)					

5. Your Turn

1. The _____ took a _____ to their _____.
2. The _____ has _____ out of ink.
3. The sick _____ went to _____.
4. My _____ and _____ are the best parents.
5. He _____ the ball hard with a _____.
6. The _____ rolled in the _____ to get cool on the _____ day.

dog pig vet pen hit men run mud cab dad job bat mom hot

I never knew that _____. This is interesting to me because _____. I will use this _____.

Lesson 29 Practice Page

Medial (CVC) Short Vowels (a, e, i, o, u) in Multisyllabic Words

1. Compare Sounds

My home language is _____ .

Today's letters compared to my home language:

What letters or symbols in your home language have two different sounds?What is an example of a word in your home language with letters or symbols that have two different sounds?

Letter or Symbol: One sound	Letter or Symbol: Second sound	Used in a word or concept

2. Recognize Medial (CVC) Short Vowels in Multisyllabic Words

Medial Position (middle)	ă	ĕ	ĭ	ŏ	ŭ
	CVC	CVC	CVC	CVC	CVC
	dragon capital	pencil reject	winter kitten	hotdog confirm	number justify

3. Read and Identify Multisyllabic Words with Medial (CVC) Short Vowels

Have you ever imagined what a dragon might look like? Many people have. Some picture a dragon as a monster, standing with a flipper like a dolphin, and scales that shimmer. Some of their dragons slumber, others lumber around. Each person's vision of a dragon is different, some quite fantastic and others frightening. How do you envision a dragon?

4. Classify Words

Medial Position (middle)	ă	ĕ	ĭ	ŏ	ŭ
	CVC	**CVC**	**CVC**	**CVC**	**CVC**

5. Your Turn

1. A baby cat_____
2. An instrument in a band_____
3. Almost the same_____
4. Upper case letter_____
5. Opposite of accept_____
6. A place for sick people_____

similar   reject   hospital   trumpet   capital   kitten

Something I learned today was _____.This knowledge helps me _____.I like _____.

Lesson 30 Practice Page

(CVCe) Long Vowels a, i, o, u

1. Compare Sounds

My home language is _____ .

Today's letters compared to my home language:

What letters or symbols in your home language have two different sounds?What letter or symbol in your home language has a long vowel sound? What is an example of a word in your home language that has a long vowel sound?

Letter or Symbol: Similar sound	Used in a word or concept

2. Recognize (CVCe) Long Vowels a, i, o, u

ā	ī	ō	ū
CVCe	CVCe	CVCe	CVCe
cake face tale	bike dice tile	joke robe role	mute tube rule

3. Read and Identify (CVCe) Long Vowels a, i, o, u

Pet mice are very cute and can be quite nice. First, you need to have a cage to keep them in. You need a small box they can use as their home. They may chew a hole in the box to get inside. Mice are nocturnal, so you don't want to poke them during the day, as they might not like being woken up! If you want a lot of mice, then make sure there's a mate, and before you know it, you will have more mice galore!

4. Classify Words

ā	ī	ō	ū
CVCe	CVCe	CVCe	CVCe
cake face tale	bike dice tile	joke robe role	mute tube rule

5. Your Turn

1. The ___ took two hours to ___ .
2. I ___ the bus ___after school every day.
3. Kittens are so ___ !
4. The ___ bear was asleep in the ___.
5. It took a long ___ to ___all the leaves in the yard.
6. The man whistles a happy ___ as he works.

home tune cake ride cute bake rake cave time huge

I never knew that _____.This is interesting to me because _____.I will use this _____.

Lesson 31 Practice Page

Long Vowel a Combinations ai, ay, ea, eigh

1. Compare Sounds

My home language is _____.

Today's letters compared to my home language:

What are some examples of letters or symbols in your home language that make a sound similar to the long a sound?
What are some words in your home language that have a sound similar to the long a sound?

Letter or Symbol: Similar sound	Used in a word or concept

2. Recognize Long Vowel a Combinations ai, ay, ea, eigh

Sound	ā			
Letters	ai	ay	ea	eigh
Words	aim gain	day play	break great	eight sleigh

3. Read and Identify Words with Long Vowel a Combinations ai, ay, ea, eigh

Riding on a train can be a great adventure. You watch scenery go by as the train travels toward your destination. There are many great ways to engage your brain as you ride on a train. You can work with a neighbor on the train to try to find eight different landmarks as you travel across the country. In many states, the terrain is rather plain, but your mind should not stray as you challenge yourself and your neighbor to use your brain on the train!

4. Classify Words

Sound	ā			
Letters	ai	ay	ea	eigh
Words				

5. Your Turn

1. You use it to think_____
2. The land _____
3. Opposite of fancy _____
4. To not follow an agreed upon path _____
5. The product of 2 x 4 _____
6. Animal that hibernates in a cave_____

stray terrain eight bear brain plain

Something I learned today was _____.This knowledge helps me _____.I like _____.

Lesson 32 Practice Page

Long Vowel e Combinations ea, ee, ei, ie, ey, y

1. Compare Sounds

My home language is _____.

Today's letters compared to my home language:

What are some examples of letters or symbols in your home language that make a sound similar to the long e sound?

What are some words in your home language that have a sound similar to the long e sound?

Letter or Symbol: Similar sound	Used in a word or concept

2. Recognize Long Vowel e Letter Combinations ea, ee, ei, ie, ey, y

Sound	ē					
Letters	ea	ee	ei	ie	ey	y
Words	weak beach	green three	receive deceit	grief piece	monkey hockey	funny happy

3. Read and Identify Words with Long Vowel e Letter Combinations ea, ee, ei, ie, ey, y

Have you ever seen a beetle up close? It's a really neat bug! Some are green and black, and they vary in size. Beetles eat either leaves, seeds, fruit, or wood. Some fly, which some people think is creepy. Some people believe that beetles are dangerous, so they scream in fear when they see or get near a beetle. Most people just leave beetles alone or sweep them gently aside when they see them. Beetles can be found in a valley as well as in fields, gardens, and homes. The next time you see a beetle, take a moment to appreciate its beauty and its role in our ecosystem.

4. Classify Words

Sound	ē					
Letters	ea	ee	ei	ie	ey	y
Words						

5. Your Turn

1. The king and _____ live in a castle.
2. We were _____ and _____ after the long uphill hike.
3. The _____ for the branch.
4. I _____ because I like to _____ the kitchen _____.
5. When you _____ the crumbs get everywhere!
6. The _____ took my, _____ !
7. The _____ _____ won the game.
8. I once had a _____ that I sailed across the seven _____ .

keep weak sweep team hungry queen monkey clean thief reaches cookies money seas eat hockey dream

I never knew that _____.This is interesting to me because _____.I will use this _____.

Lesson 33 Practice Page
Long Vowel i Combinations ie, igh, ind, ild, y

1. Compare Sounds

My home language is _____.

Today's letters compared to my home language:

What are some examples of letters or symbols in your home language that make a sound similar to the long e sound?
What are some words in your home language that have a sound similar to the long i sound?

Letter or Symbol: Similar sound	Used in a word or concept

2. Recognize Long Vowel i Letter Combinations ie, igh, ind, ild, y

Sound	ī				
Letters	ie	igh	ind	ild	y
Words	pie lie	high right	find kind	wild child	by dry

3. Read and Identify Words with Long Vowel i Letter Combinations ie, igh, ind, ild, y

Have you ever flown in an airplane? It is really wild! You fly high in the sky, and the sun is really bright, especially when you fly above the clouds. The flight attendants are very kind, and if a child asks, they may be able to find a deck of cards for the child to play with. Some people are afraid they will die if they fly. However, research has shown that air travel is much safer than traveling in a car. So the next time you are flying in an airplane, you can relax a bit and enjoy the flight knowing that you are safer than if you were in a car!

4. Classify Words

Sound	ī				
Letters	ie	igh	ind	ild	y
Words					

5. Your Turn

1. It happens during a storm_____
2. A pastry dish made with a shell and filling _____
3. Opposite of "in front of" _____
4. Sneaky _____
5. Opposite of tame_____
6. We are all a part of this _____

behind human kind lightning wild sly pie

Something I learned today was _____. This knowledge helps me _____. I like _____.

Lesson 34 Practice Page

Long Vowel o Combinations oa, oe, ow,

1. Compare Sounds

My home language is _____.

Today's letters compared to my home language:

What are some examples of letters or symbols in your home language that make a sound similar to the long o sound?
What are some words in your home language that have a sound similar to the long o sound?

Letter or Symbol: Similar sound	Used in a word or concept

2. Recognize Long Vowel e Letter Combinations oa, oe, ow

Sound	ō		
Letters	oa	oe	ow
Words	boat load	toe foe	mow grow

3. Read and Identify Words with Long Vowel e Letter Combinations oa, oe, ow

Have you ever seen a meadow out in the forest? It often is filled with animals such as does, bucks, and rabbits, coming to soak up the sun and eat some of the wild grasses and oats that grow there. Many times there is water that flows in a creek or brook nearby, complete with a resident toad. The animals are wary of what might lurk in the shadows, though. They don't want to be eaten by their foes! There is no cover in the meadow, so they must be very cautious. If you get to visit a meadow in the forest, be sure to enjoy its beauty, but you, too, should beware of what might lurk in the shadows!

4. Classify Words

Sound	ō		
Letters	oa	oe	ow
Words			

5. Your Turn

1. The _____ sailed along the _____ .
2. The walked _____ across the _____ .
3. The grass _____ so fast that we have to _____ it every week.
4. The mother had to _____ out of the sleeping baby's room.
5. Out on the ocean, the water _____ and the wind _____ .
6. The _____ ate grass in the _____ .

road blows doe mow coast tiptoe flows meadow boat slowly grows

I never knew that _____.This is interesting to me because _____.I will use this _____.

Lesson 35 Practice Page
Long Vowel u Combinations ue, ew

1. Compare Sounds

My home language is _____.

Today's letters compared to my home language:

What are some examples of letters or symbols in your home language that make a sound similar to the long o sound?
What are some words in your home language that have a sound similar to the long u sound?

Letter or Symbol: Similar sound	Used in a word or concept

2. Recognize Long Vowel u Letter Combinations ue, ew

Sound	ū	
Letters	ue	ew
Words	due true	new blew

3. Read and Identify Words with Long Vowel e Letter Combinations oa, oe, ow

Have you ever seen a swimmer distress? The first clue that there is trouble when he or she is flailing around in the water. The lifeguard crew is always scanning the water, prepared to jump in and rescue those in distress. If the water is really cold, the person may turn blue by the time the lifeguard gets there. Sometimes, the swimmer in distress will be disoriented and argue with the rescuer, which makes the rescue even more challenging. If you go swimming, always be sure there is a lifeguard on duty, in case you need to be rescued!

4. Classify Words

Sound	ū	
Letters	ue	ew
Words		

5. Your Turn

1. The opposite of old_____
2. Use this to connect two pieces of metal_____
3. To save someone _____
4. Opposite of false _____
5. Past tense of throw _____
6. To disagree_____

rescue argue screw threw new true

Something I learned today was _____.This knowledge helps me _____.I like _____.

Lesson 36 Practice Page
Vowel Combinations aw, au

1. Compare Sounds

My home language is _____ .

Today's letters compared to my home language:

What are some examples of letters or symbols in your home language that make a sound similar to the short /e/ sound?
What are some words in your home language that have a sound similar to the short /e/ sound

Letter or Symbol: Similar sound	Used in a word or concept

2. Recognize Vowel Combinations aw, au

Sound	/aw/	
Vowel combination	aw	au
Words	jaw crawl	haul fault

3. Read and Identify Words with Vowel Combinations aw, au

Have you ever seen animals at a zoo entertain themselves? They do some very crazy things! Some lie on the lawn and yawn as if they are bored! Others swipe their paws and claws at each other playfully. The seals have learned how to open their jaws and beg for their favorite food, raw fish, from the zoo visitors. They make an awful ruckus, which often draws the visitor's applause, as they haul in the food. If you go to the zoo, be sure to take some time to see what the animals do to pass the time.

4. Classify Words

Sound	/aw/	
Vowel combination	aw	au
Words		

5. Your Turn

1. The stale crackers taste _____ .
2. Before you can walk, you learn to _____ .
3. The cat scratches with its sharp _____ .
4. The puppy's _____ left prints on the rug.
5. The _____ stood up and _____ at the end of the show.
6. My favorite _____ writes mystery novels.
7. He likes spaghetti _____ on his _____ .
8. You need to mow to keep your _____ looking nice.

paws   author   crawl   sauce   lawn   awful   claws   applauded   sausage   audience

I never knew that _____ .This is interesting to me because _____ .I will use this _____ .

Lesson 37 Practice Page
Vowel Combination oo

1. Compare Sounds

My home language is _____.

Today's letters compared to my home language:

What are some examples of letters or symbols in your home language that make a sound similar to the /o͝o/ and /o͞o/ sounds? What are some words in your home language that have a sound similar to the /o͝o/ and /o͞o/ sounds?

Letter or Symbol: Similar sound	Used in a word or concept

2. Recognize Vowel Combination oo

Sound	/o͝o/	/o͞o/
Vowel combination	oo	oo
Words	book look	moon noon

3. Read and Identify Words with Vowel Combination oo

Cookouts can be a lot of fun! There is usually a lot of good food, including cookies for dessert. You can decorate the picnic area with balloons so that your family and friends will be able to find your group easier. Some parks have a place where you can barbeque your food or a fire pit where you can burn wood to make a fire cook over. There are usually some games going on, such as football, baseball, or volleyball. If you get there around noon, you can even bring your bicycle or scooter and ride around the park while it is still light out!

4. Classify Words

Sound	/o͝o/	/o͞o/
Vowel combination	oo	oo
Words		

5. Your Turn

1. The foot part of a horse's leg _____
2. They are good to eat with milk _____
3. Where you can visit animals _____
4. Opposite of "hello" _____
5. You can often see this in the night sky _____
6. Where you can go swimming _____

zoo hoof pool cookies goodbye moon

Something I learned today was _____. This knowledge helps me _____. I like _____.

Lesson 38 Practice Page
Vowel Combinations ow, ou

1. Compare Sounds

My home language is _____.

Today's letters compared to my home language:

What are some examples of letters or symbols in your home language that make a sound similar to the /ou/ sound?
What are some words in your home language that have a sound similar to the /ou/ sound?

Letter or Symbol: Similar sound	Used in a word or concept

2. Recognize Vowel Combinations ow, ou

Sound	/ou/	
Vowel combination	ow	ou
Words	how now	about shout

3. Read and Identify Words with Vowel Combinations ow, ou

Have you ever seen a clown perform? It can be very entertaining! The clown may have a round red nose and wear big brown shoes. Sometimes he will have a flower in his hat. His mouth may be painted like a frown or like a big, bright smile. The clown may like to "play" the crowd, or try to get people in the audience to participate in the gag jokes that he plays. You can hire a clown to come to your house or to wherever the party is going to be held. You usually have to pay the clown by the hour, so save up your money so you can have a great time at your next party!

4. Classify Words

Sound	/ou/	
Vowel combination	ow	ou
Words		

5. Your Turn

1. The farmer milks the _____ .
2. We planted a garden of _____ all the way around _____ .
3. A _____ gathered to watch the _____ .
4. The _____ dog barked _____ .
5. The _____ were white and billowy.
6. The king wears a _____ .

> clown clouds crown cowflowers brown crowd loudly house

I never knew that _____. This is interesting to me because _____. I will use this _____.

Lesson 39 Practice Page

Vowel Diagraphs oi, oy

1. Compare Sounds

My home language is _____.

Today's letters compared to my home language:

What are some examples of letters or symbols in your home language that make a sound similar to the /oi/ sound? What are some words in your home language that have a sound similar to the /oi/ sound?

Letter or Symbol: Similar sound	Used in a word or concept

2. Recognize Vowel Combinations oi, oy

Sound	/oi/	
Vowel combination	oi	oy
Words	soil point	boy enjoy

3. Read and Identify Words with Vowel Combinations oi, oy

People enjoy gardening, but it takes a lot of hard work. First you need to till the soil and avoid using poisons because they will destroy your plants. Next, the new plants need plenty of moisture and you must keep out the weeds and bugs. Before long, you will have a garden full of great things to eat. But beware – as soon as the fruits and vegetables in your garden get ripe, you may have to use a decoy, like a scarecrow, to keep the birds and critters away! All in all though, gardening can bring you great joy!

4. Classify Words

Sound	/oi/	
Vowel combination	oi	oy
Words		

5. Your Turn

1. You use it to talk_____
2. It can make you sick or even kill you _____
3. A trip _____
4. You plant flowers in it _____
5. To bother someone _____
6. To hire someone to work for you _____

voyage   annoy   voice   employ   poison   soil

Something I learned today was _____.This knowledge helps me _____.I like _____.

Lesson 40 Practice Page
Vowel Combination ea

1. Compare Sounds

My home language is _____ .

Today's letters compared to my home language:

What are some examples of letters or symbols in your home language that make a sound similar to the short /e/ sound?
What are some words in your home language that have a sound similar to the short /e/ sound?

Letter or Symbol: Similar sound	Used in a word or concept

2. Recognize Vowel Combination ea

Sound	short /e/	
Vowel combination	ea	
Words	bread head	thread tread

3. Read and Identify Words with Vowel Combination ea

Have you ever had the opportunity to learn how to skydive? It is exhilarating! You may have read some interesting stories about people who skydive as a hobby. They often recommend that you learn the safety rules before you go so that you don't endanger your health. You will wear a helmet to protect your head, and a harness to hold the parachute on your back. A plane takes you high up into the sky, and when you are ready, you jump out into the heavens, arms spread wide, with the wind blowing so hard in your face that it takes your breath away! You won't have time to break out in a sweat, as your skydive will be over before you know it, and you'll be back on the ground, ready to go again!

4. Classify Words

Sound	short /e/
Vowel combination	ea
Words	

5. Your Turn

1. I _____peanut butter on _____for _____ .
2. She fell and hit her _____ .
3. Exercise and a good diet are important for your _____ .
4. When you run, you may _____ .
5. The _____on the tire was very thin.
6. I'll take the apple _____of the orange.

sweat health spread instead bread head breakfast tread

I never knew that _____.This is interesting to me because _____.I will use this _____ .

Lesson 41 Practice Page

R-Controlled Vowel Pattern ar

1. Compare Sounds

My home language is _____.

Today's letters compared to my home language:

What are some examples of letters or symbols in your home language that make a sound similar to the /är/ sound?

What are some words in your home language that have a sound similar to the /är/sound?

Letter or Symbol: Similar sound	Used in a word or concept

2. Recognize R-Controlled Vowel Pattern ar

Sound	/är/
R-controlled vowel pattern	ar
Words	arm bark cart hard

3. Read and Identify Words with R-Controlled Vowel Pattern ar

Most farms have a barn, where animals live along with food and farm equipment. Nearby, you might find a garden, where food is grown. You need a strong arm to work in a garden, to till the soil, and plant the vegetables. When you're ready to harvest the vegetables, you'll need a cart to put them in. The farmers may share some with their family and friends or even sell some from a stand in their front yard!

4. List Words

Sound	/är/
R-controlled vowel pattern	ar
Words	

5. Your Turn

1. What dogs do_____
2. Where you grow vegetables_____
3. Children play here_____
4. Opposite of soft _____
5. Another name for lawn_____
6. Opposite of dull_____

park yard hard bark sharp garden

Something I learned today was _____.This knowledge helps me _____.I like _____.

Lesson 42 Practice Page

R-Controlled Vowel Patterns er, ir, or, ur

1. Compare Sounds

My home language is _____.

Today's letters compared to my home language:

What are some examples of letters or symbols in your home language that make a sound similar to the /ûr/sound? What are some words in your home language that have a sound similar to the /ûr/sound?

Letter or Symbol: Similar sound	Used in a word or concept

2. Recognize R-Controlled Vowel Patterns er, ir, or, ur

Sound	/ûr/			
R-controlled vowel pattern	er	ir	or	ur
Words	her were	bird shirt	word favor	fur turn

3. Read and Identify Words with R-Controlled Vowel Patterns er, ir, or, ur

Have you ever had a big birthday party? It can be really fun, especially if your mother, father, sisters, and brothers are there, along with all your friends. Sometimes the party includes dinner, and you may be able to cut and serve your birthday cake to everyone! If there are a lot of family members and friends, you may have to find a bigger place to hold the party, such as a park or a church. Some people like to give out party favors to everyone who comes. If you go to a park, be careful: the birds may try to take off with some of your food and birthday cake!

4. Classify Words

Sound	/ûr/			
R-controlled vowel pattern	er	ir	or	ur
Words				

5. Your Turn

1. My _____ and _____ are twins.
2. Pleas don't _____ my toast.
3. The _____ and the _____ both work at the hospital.
4. Today is the baby's _____ .
5. The _____ fixes the _____ using a sewing machine.
6. The _____ works at the café and _____ us lunch.

shirt burn sister waiter birthday doctors serves brother nurses tailor first

I never knew that _____.This is interesting to me because _____.I will use this _____.

Word Study

1 Plural Noun Inflectional Endings -s, -es

Metacognitive Strategy

Selective auditory attention, Use deductive thinking

Academic Language

singular, plural, nouns, ending

Materials

Word Study Lesson 1 Practice Page

Pre-Assess

- Recognition of **singular** as meaning **one** and **plural** as **more than one**

Transfer Notes:

There is no use of plural nouns in Vietnamese, Hmong, Tagalog, Korean, and Cantonese Reinforce the meaning of nouns in the lesson as well as their grammatical function.

Introduce the Lesson

Say: *Today we will form plural nouns by adding the inflectional ending -s or -es. We will also read text that includes words with these inflectional endings*

Recognize Inflectional Endings -s and -es

Say: *Nouns are words that name people, places, things and animals. Singular means one and plural means more than one. To form a plural noun in English, we add -es to words that end in ch, sh, x, or z. Most other words we add an -s.*

Say: *To change a singular noun, such as pen, to plural, I add -s to the end, forming the plural pens.*

Say: *To change the singular noun box to plural, I add -es to the end, forming the plural boxes.*

Elicit Prior Knowledge

Display the Lesson 1 Practice Page. Prompt students to think about their primary language as you work together to complete section 1.

Ask: *How do you change a word in your home language from singular to plural? Sketch a drawing and label one and more than one in your home language.*

Model: Recognize and Form Plurals

Direct students' attention to section 2 of the Lesson 1 Practice Page.

Say: *Practice changing singular nouns to plural by adding either the inflectional ending -s or -es. Then identify the meaning of the new, plural word.*

Singular Noun	Add -s or -es to make it plural	New meaning
book		
bus		
fox		

Practice: Singular and Plural Nouns

Read aloud section 3 of the Lesson 1 Practice Page in a fluent voice emphasizing intonation and pronunciation of words and inflectional endings. Invite students to echo read or chime on cue. Ensure comprehension by asking text dependent questions. Have students identify cognates. Then instruct students to identify the singular and plural nouns in the passage, and write them in the correct columns in section 4.

Practice: Recognize Plurals with Inflectional Endings -s and -es

Complete section 4 of the Lesson 1 Practice Page with students.

Say: *Look at words that you have identified from the reading passage. Change singular words to plural and change plural words to singular.*

Extend Language Knowledge

Practice: Use Words in Context

Complete section 5 of the Lesson 1 Practice Page with students.

Say: *Let's think about plural nouns with inflectional endings -s and -es. Complete each sentence using words from the word bank on the Practice Page. Take turns reading the completed sentences to your partner.*

1. People borrow **books** from the library.
2. We packed our things in **boxes** when we moved.
3. We sat on the **couches** in the living room.
4. I like to wear **jeans** and t-shirts.
5. My sister and I both wear **eyeglasses** to see.
6. I wear **gloves** in the winter to keep my hands warm.

Writing

Say: *Practice writing the words you hear me say. I will pronounce the word, use it in a sentence and repeat it one more time.*

Pronounce one word at a time from the Word List below, stretching each sound. Use the word in a sentence, and repeat it again after the sentence. For example, say the word **glasses**. Then say: *I drank two glasses of water because I was thirsty.* Repeat the word **glasses** after the sentence.

Sample words: **books, bags, pens, socks, boxes, brushes, glasses**

Have students confirm their spelling with a partner, making corrections as needed.

Reflect and Review

Ask: *What did you learn today? Discuss with your partner.*

Have students work with their partners to complete the sentence frames at the end of the Lesson 1 Practice Page, assisting as needed.

Word Bank

-s	-ss	sh
bus	class	ash
gas	glass	fish
cactus	dress	brush
iris	grass	dish
walrus	boss	wish
	cross	peach
ch	x	
arch	lockbox	
beach	flax	
church	fox	
inch	lynx	
witch	index	
sandwich	annex	

✓Formative Assessment

If the student completes each task correctly, proceed to the next skill in the sequence.

Did the student...?	Intervention
Pronounce –s or –es in isolation Pronounce –s or –es in words	Use a mirror to show movement of mouth, tongue, and teeth as the sound is produced. Use hand over mouth to explore movement of air as the sound is produced.
Understand the academic term singular and plural	Use concrete objects to show one and more than one Use math symbol for more or greater than >1
Do they recognize meaning of words in context	Explain meaning of words before reading the text and discuss after reading text. Sketch briefly and label

2 Plural Noun Inflectional Endings -s, -ies

Lesson Objectives

- Recognize and form singular and plural nouns.
- Generalize the meaning of inflectional endings.
- Apply rule for forming plurals for nouns ending in **y**.

Metacognitive Strategy

Selective auditory attention, Use deductive thinking

Academic Language

singular, plural, nouns, ending

Materials

Word Study Lesson 2 Practice Page

Pre-Assess

- Recognition of **singular** as meaning **one** and **plural** as **more than one**

Transfer Notes:

There is no use of plural nouns in Vietnamese, Hmong, Tagalog, Korean, and Cantonese Reinforce the meaning of nouns in the lesson as well as their grammatical function.

Introduce the Lesson

Say: *Today we will form the plural of singular nouns that end in y using inflectional endings -s or -ies. We will also read text that includes words with these inflectional endings.*

Recognize Inflectional Endings -s and -ies

Say: *Nouns are words that name people, places, things and animals. Singular means one and plural means more than one.*

Say: *To form the plural of a noun ending in y, add -s if the letter before the y is a vowel. For example, we make the singular noun key plural by adding the letter -s to the end: keys.*

Say: *If the letter before the y is a consonant, such as the singular noun baby, we replace the y with ies, to form the plural babies.*

Elicit Prior Knowledge

Display the Lesson 2 Practice Page. Prompt students to think about their primary language as you work together to complete section 1.

Say: *Today we are learning a language rule. What is a rule in your home language?*

Model: Recognize and Form Plurals

Direct students' attention to section 2 of the Practice Page.

Say: *Practice changing singular nouns to plural by adding either the inflectional ending -s or replacing the y with -ies.*

Nouns ending in y	If the letter before y is a vowel add -s	If the letter before the y is a consonant add -ies
boy		
lady		
guy		

Practice: Singular and Plural Nouns

Read aloud section 3 of the Practice Page in a fluent voice emphasizing intonation and pronunciation of words and inflectional endings. Invite students to echo read or chime on cue. Ensure comprehension by asking text dependent questions. Have students identify cognates. Then instruct students to identify the singular and plural nouns in the passage, and write them in the correct columns in section 4.

Practice: Recognize Plurals with Inflectional Endings -s and -ies

Complete section 4 of the Practice Page with students.

Say: *Look at words that you have identified from the reading passage. Change singular words to plural and change plural words to singular.*

Extend Language Knowledge

Practice: Make Meaning

Complete section 5 of the Lesson 2 Practice Page with students.

Say: *Let's read each clue together. Then work with a partner to find an answer from the word bank. Write the answer on the line.*

Animals that swing from trees (monkeys)

Places where things are made (factories)

Books are full of these (stories)

They may be in a bouquet (daisies)

1. They cry when their hungry (babies)

Writing

Say: *Practice writing the words you hear me say. I will pronounce the word, use it in a sentence and repeat it one more time.*

Pronounce one word at a time from the Word List below, stretching each sound. Use the word in a sentence, and repeat it again after the sentence. For example, say the word **stories**. Then say: *I read two stories to the children.* Repeat the word **stories** after the sentence.

Sample words: **pony, ponies; story, stories; fly, flies; day, days; boy, boys**

Have students confirm their spelling with a partner, making corrections as needed.

Reflect and Review

Ask: *What did you learn today? Discuss with your partner.*

Have students work with their partners to complete the sentence frames at the end of the Lesson 2 Practice Page, assisting as needed.

Word Bank

ivy	jay
baby	key
pony	Guy
lady	boy
body	monkey
factory	tray
country	holiday
story	bay
party	valley
belly	birthday
jelly	chimney

✔Formative Assessment

If the student completes each task correctly, proceed to the next skill in the sequence.

Did the student…?	Intervention
Pronounce –s or –ies in isolation Pronounce –s or –ies in words	Use a mirror to show movement of mouth, tongue, and teeth as the sound is produced. Use hand over mouth to explore movement of air as the sound is produced.
Understand the academic term singular and plural	Use concrete objects to show one and more than one Use math symbol for more or greater than >1
Do they recognize meaning of words in context	Explain meaning of words before reading the text and discuss after reading text. Sketch briefly and label

3 Plural Noun Inflectional Endings f/v + -es

Lesson Objectives

- Recognize and form singular and plural nouns.
- Generalize the meaning of inflectional endings.
- Apply rule for forming plurals for nouns by changing **f** to **v** and adding **-es.**

Metacognitive Strategy

Selective auditory attention, use deductive thinking

Academic Language

singular, plural, nouns, ending

Materials

Word Study Lesson 3 Practice Page

Pre-Assess

- Recognition of **singular** as meaning **one** and **plural** as **more than one**

Transfer Notes:

There is no use of plural nouns in Vietnamese, Hmong, Tagalog, Korean, and Cantonese Reinforce the meaning of nouns in the lesson as well as their grammatical function.

Introduce the Lesson

Say: *Today we will form the plural nouns by replacing the letters **f** and **fe** with the inflectional ending **v + -es**. We will also read text that includes words with this inflectional ending.*

Recognize Inflectional Ending f/v and -es

Say: *Nouns are words that name people, places, things and animals. Singular means one and plural means more than one.*

Say: *To form the plural of a noun ending in **f**, replace the **f** with **v** and add **-es**. For example, the singular noun **loaf** becomes **loaves**.*

Say: *To form the plural of a noun ending in **fe**, replace the **fe** with **v** and add **-es**. For example, the singular noun **wife** becomes **wives**.*

Elicit Prior Knowledge

Display the Lesson 3 Practice Page. Prompt students to think about their primary language as you work together to complete section 1.

Say: *We are learning how inflectional endings change the meaning of a word. How do letters or symbols placed at the end of a word change its meaning in your home language?*

Model: Recognize and Form Plurals

Direct students' attention to section 2 of the Practice Page. Remind students of the rules for forming plurals of words that end in f or fe.

Say: *Practice changing singular nouns to plural*

For nouns ending in f	Change the f to a v and add -es	For nouns ending in -fe, change the -fe to v and add -es
knife		
self		
life		

Practice: Singular and Plural Nouns

Read aloud section 3 of the Practice Page in a fluent voice emphasizing intonation and pronunciation of words and inflectional endings. Invite students to echo read or chime on cue. Ensure comprehension by asking text dependent questions. Have students identify cognates. Then instruct students to identify singular nouns that end in **f** or **fe** and plural nouns with inflectional ending **-es** in the passage, and write them in the correct columns in section 4.

Practice: Recognize Plurals with Inflectional Endings f/v and -es

Complete section 4 of the lesson practice page with students.

Say: *Look at the words that follow the rule we learned today and change singular to plural or plural to singular.*

Extend Language Knowledge

Practice: Make Meaning

Complete section 5 of the Lesson 1 Practice Page with students.

Say: *Let's read each clue together. Then work with a partner to find an answer from the word bank. Write the answer on the line.*

People who take things that are not their own (thieves)

Place where books are kept (shelves)

They say cats have nine of them (lives)

You buy them at a bakery (loaves)

Magical story characters that live in the woods (elves)

Writing

Say: *Practice writing the words you hear me say. I will pronounce the word, use it in a sentence and repeat it one more time.*

Pronounce one word at a time from the Word List below, stretching each sound. Use the word in a sentence, and repeat it again after the sentence. For example, say the word **lives**. Then say: *Cats have nine lives.* Repeat the word **lives** after the sentence.

Sample words: **life, lives, wolf, wolves, elf, elves, wife, wives**

Reflect and Review

Ask: *What did you learn today? Discuss with your partner.*

Have students work with their partners to complete the sentence frames at the end of the Lesson 3 Practice Page, assisting as needed.

Word Bank

elf	knife
calf	life
wolf	wife
shelf	jackknife
myself	pocketknife
thief	

✔ Formative Assessment

If the student completes each task correctly, proceed to the next skill in the sequence.

Did the student…?	Intervention
Pronounce f, v, -ves in isolation Pronounce f, v, -ves in words	Use a mirror to show movement of mouth, tongue, and teeth as the sound is produced. Use hand over mouth to explore movement of air as the sound is produced.
Understand the academic term singular and plural	Use concrete objects to show one and more than one Use math symbol for more or greater than >1
Recognize meaning of words in context	Explain meaning of words before reading the text and discuss after reading text. Sketch briefly and label

4 Irregular Plural Nouns

Lesson Objectives

- Recognize and form singular and plural nouns.
- Apply rule for forming plurals for irregular plurals.

Metacognitive Strategy

Selective auditory attention, use deductive thinking

Academic Language

singular, plural, nouns, irregular

Materials

Word Study Lesson 4 Practice Page

Pre-Assess

- Student's ability to recognize **singular** to mean **one** and **plural** as **more than one**

Transfer Notes:

There is no use of plural nouns in Vietnamese, Hmong, Tagalog, Korean, and Cantonese Reinforce the meaning of nouns in the lesson as well as their grammatical function. English Learners need to learn meaning of nouns in addition to learning how to make them plural.

Introduce the Lesson

Say: *Today we will learn that some words that have irregular plural forms.*

Recognize Irregular Plural Forms

Say: *Nouns are words that name people, places, things and animals. Singular means one. Plural means more than one. In English there are words that have irregular plural forms. These words do not follow the usual grammatical rules for making a singular noun plural by adding inflectional endings -s, -es, or -ies.*

Ask: *What does singular mean? (Singular means one.)*

Ask: *What does plural mean? (Plural means more than one.)*

Say: *Today we will look at words with irregular plurals. We learn these by remembering them.*

Elicit Prior Knowledge

Display and/or distribute the Practice Page and complete section 1 with students.

Ask: *Most languages have rules that help people learn and remember how to speak or write in that language. However, in most languages there are exceptions to the rules. This means a word that does not follow the usual language rule. Are there any exceptions to a language rule in your home language?*

Model: Recognize and Form Irregular Plural Nouns

Refer to section 2 of the Practice Page with students. Create chart on board and add words as each example is given.

Say: *Some nouns are made plural by changing the vowels. For example: **foot** becomes **feet**. Some nouns are made plural by changing most of the word. For example: **mouse** becomes **mice**. Some nouns are made of plural by keeping their Latin plural form. For example: **cactus** becomes **cacti**.*

Changing the vowels	Change the word	Keep their Latin plural form
foot- feet	mouse - mice	cactus - cacti
goose - geese	child - children	antenna - antennae

Practice: Identify Singular and Plural Nouns

Read aloud section 3 of the Practice Page in a fluent voice emphasizing intonation and pronunciation of words and targeted sounds. Invite students to echo read or chime on cue. Discuss content of text by asking text dependent questions to ensure comprehension. Ask students to recognize and call out cognates.

Ask: *What words do you see that are irregular plurals? Work with a partner to underline and read the words you identify.*

Practice: Recognize Plurals in Context

Complete section 4 of the Practice Page with students.

Say: *We will now look at words that you have identified. If they are plural, change them to plural, if they are plural, write their singular form*

Singular	Plural		Singular	Plural		Singular	Plural

Say: *Next, we are going to practice pronunciation by breaking up the words into syllables. We will clap out the syllables as we say each word then annotate syllables with a slash. When done annotating, read each word aloud to your partner.*

Extend Language Knowledge: Making Meaning

Complete section 4 of the Practice Page with students.

Say: *We will now look at irregular plurals and use them in context. Read and complete each sentence with the word from the word bank that makes most sense. Take turns reading the completed sentences to your partner.*

1. The opposite of man: **woman**
2. A desert plant: **cacti**
3. Ants use these to smell: **antennae**
4. They love to play: **children**
5. These fall out and new ones grow: **teeth**

Spelling/Writing

Say: *Now we can practice writing plurals we hear in each word. I will pronounce each word and you will write it down.*

Pronounce one word at a time, stretching each sound.

Sample words: **men, women, cactus, cacti, foot, feet, mouse, mice, tooth, teeth.**

Sample sentence: *Men, women, children and people of all ages, are welcomed here!*

Say: *Check your spelling with your partner. Verify the correct spelling and rewrite as needed.*

Reflect and Review

Ask: *What did you learn today? Discuss with your partner.*

Provide sentence frames: Something new I learned today was _____.

I now know that _____. I will use this when _____.

Word Bank

woman - women	child-children	cactus- cacti
man- men	person - people	fungus-fungi
foot-feet	mouse-mice	vertebra-vertebrae
goose-geese	tooth-teeth	antenna-antennae

✔Formative Assessment

If the student completes each task correctly, precede to the next skill in the sequence.

Did the student…?	Intervention
Pronounce irregular plurals in isolation Pronounce irregular plurals in context	Use mirrors to show movement of mouth, tongue, and teeth as the sound is produced. Use hand over mouth to explore movement of air as the sound is produced.
Understand the academic term singular and plural	Use concrete objects to show one and more than one Use math symbol for more or greater than >1
Do they recognize meaning of words in context	Explain meaning of words before reading the text and discuss after reading text. Sketch briefly and label.

Lesson Objectives

- Identify inflectional endings in verbs **-s**, **-ing**, **-ed**
- Recognizethat **-s** ending means third person in singular present tense
- Recognizethat **-ing** ending means action in happening now
- Recognizethat **-ed** ending means the action is in the past.

Metacognitive Strategy

Selective auditory attention, use deductive thinking

Academic Language

verb, action word, past, present, future, tense, ending, base word

Materials

Word Study Lesson 5 Practice Page

Pre-Assess

- Student's ability to identify a verb, a word that denotes action and a sense of time.

Transfer Notes:

There verb to be can be omitted in Vietnamese Hmong, Tagalog, Korean, and Cantonese

The verb to be has a permanent (ser) and temporary (estar) form in Spanish.

English Learners need to learn the meaning of the verbs as well as their grammatical function.

5 Inflectional Endings in Verbs -s, -ing, -ed

Introduce the Lesson

Say: *Today we will learn when to add inflectional ending* **-s**, **-ing** *and* **-ed** *at the end of verbs to show who is doing the action and when.*

Recognize inflectional ending -s and -es to Form Plural Nouns

Say: *A verb is a word that describe an action and tells when the action. An action can happen in the present, in the past or in the future.*

Ask: *What does present mean? It means that an action happens now, in the present. What does past mean? It means that an action already happened. What does future mean? It means that the action will happen later, at a future time.*

Say: *Today we will learn to add* **-s**, **-ing** *and* **-ed** *at the end of verbs to show or notice who is doing the action and when.*

Elicit Prior Knowledge

Display and/or distribute the Practice Page and complete section 1 with students.

Ask: *Do you know how to say past, present and future in your home language? Can you tell what past, present and future means? How will you remember what it means?*

Model: Recognize and Form Plural by Adding Inflectional Ending -s, -ing, -ed

Refer to section 2 of the Practice Page with students. Create a chart like the one below, write the word jump in each column adding endings as you explain using gestures and movement.

Say: *This is the word* **jump**. *It is a verb. It tells about an action. I can jump. I add* **-s**. *It reads* **jumps**. *It means he or she jumps now, in the present. I add* **-ing**. *It reads* **jumping**. *It means he or she is jumping continuously. I add* **-ed.** *It reads* **jumped**. *It means he or she already jumped.*

Present	Present Progressive	Past
action is now	action is continuous	action has already happened
jumps	jumping	jumped

Practice: Identify Singular and Plural Verbs

Read aloud section 3 of the Practice Page in a fluent voice emphasizing intonation and pronunciation of words and targeted sounds. Invite students to echo read or chime on cue. Discuss content of text by asking text dependent questions to ensure comprehension. Ask students to recognize and call out cognates.

Ask: *What words do you see that include inflectional ending* **-ing** *or* **-ed** *to show action? Work with a partner to underline and read the words you identify.*

Practice: Recognize Inflectional Endings in Verbs

Complete section 4 of the Practice Page with students.

Say: *Referencing the shared reading above, add the inflectional endings to change verb tense.*

Verb	+ s	+ ing	+ed
walk			
play			
listen			
cook			
watch			

Say: *Next, we are going to practice pronunciation by breaking up the words into syllables. We will clap out the syllables as we say each word then annotate syllables with a slash. When done annotating, read each word aloud to your partner.*

Extend Language Knowledge: Making Meaning

Complete section 4 of the Practice Page with students.

Say: *We will now use verbs in sentences. Notice if the action takes place in the past or in the present. Read and complete each sentence with the word from the word bank that makes most sense. Take turns reading the completed sentences to your partner.*

1. *He **cooks** dinner for his family.*
2. *She is **jumping** all the time.*
3. *Yesterday, he **helped** his friend.*
4. *He is always **reading** books.*
5. *We **wanted** to go to the park yesterday.*

Spelling/Writing

Say: *Now we can practice writing verbs in past and present tense. I will pronounce each word and you will write it down.*

Pronounce one word at a time, stretching each sound, emphasizing inflectional endings.

Sample words: w**alk, walking, walked, cook, cooking, cooked, play, playing, played**

Sample sentence: *Men, women, children and people of all ages, are welcomed here!*

Say: *Check your spelling with your partner. Verify the correct spelling and rewrite as needed.*

Reflect and Review

Ask: *What did you learn today? Discuss with your partner.*

Provide sentence frames: Something new I learned today was _____.

I now know that _____. I will use this when _____.

Word Bank

-t	-d	-ed
looked	opened	started
worked	learned	painted
talked	lived	toasted
liked	played	needed
stopped	studied	ended
laughed	tried	wanted

✔Formative Assessment

If the student completes each task correctly, precede to the next skill in the sequence.

Did the student…?	Intervention
Pronounce-ed in isolation Pronounce –ed in words	Use mirrors to show movement of mouth, tongue, and teeth as the sound is produced. Use hand over mouth to explore movement of air as the sound is produced. Practice with a list of –ed classified by it's three different pronunciations :/t/ /ed/ /d/
Understand past, present, future	Use simple illustrations or calendar to show time. Use time words yesterday= past, today= present Tomorrow = future.

6 Adjective Inflectional Endings -ful, -less

Introduce the Lesson

Say: *Today we will form adjectives by adding the inflectional endings -ful and -less to base or root words, and recognize how the suffixes modify a word's meaning. We will also read text that includes adjectives with these inflectional endings.*

Recognize Adjective Inflectional Endings -ful and -less

Say: A suffix is a word ending that changes, or modifies, the meaning of the word. For example, it can change a noun to an adjective –– a word that describes something or someone. The suffixes **-ful** and **-less** have opposite meanings. The suffix **-ful** means to have a certain characteristic, and **-less** means to lack it.

Elicit Prior Knowledge

Display the Lesson 6 Practice Page. Prompt students to think about their primary language as you work together to complete section 1.

Say: *In the English language, a suffix changes a word's meaning.*

Ask: *What letters or symbols in your home language change the meaning of words? How do they change the meaning?*

Model: Recognize and Form Adjective Inflectional Endgings -ful and -less

Direct students' attention to section 2 of the Practice Page.

Write the word **color** on the board. Then add the suffix **-ful** and explain how it changed the word's meaning.

Say: *Practice changing the base words to opposite meaning adjectives by adding the suffixes -ful and -less.*

Base Word	-ful changes the word to an adjective that describes that characteristic	-less changes the word to an adjective that describes a lack
color		
care		
help		

Practice: Adjectives Inflectional Endings -ful and -less

Read aloud section 3 of the Practice Page in a fluent voice emphasizing intonation and pronunciation of words and inflectional endings. Invite students to echo read or chime on cue. Ensure comprehension by asking text dependent questions. Ask students to recognize and call out cognates. Then have students identify adjectives with the suffix **-ful** or **-less**, and write them in the correct columns in section 4. Also ask students to identify cognates.

Practice: Recognize Adjective Inflectional Endings -ful, -less

Complete section 4 of the Practice Page with students.

Say: *Let's look at the adjectives you identified in the shared reading. We will form opposite meaning adjectives by changing the **-ful** suffixes to **-less** and the **-less** ones to **-ful**. Extend Language Knowledge*

Practice: Make Meaning

Complete section 5 of the Practice Page with students.

Say: *Let's read each clue together. Then work with a partner to find an answer from the word bank. Write the answer on the line.*

1. Someone who helps **helpful**
2. Someone who has no hope **hopeless**
3. Someone who feels happy **cheerful**
4. Someone who loves to play **playful**
5. Something that is of a lot of value to you **priceless**

Writing

Say: *Practice writing the words you hear me say. I will pronounce the word, use it in a sentence and repeat it one more time.*

*Pronounce one word at a time from the Word List below, stretching each sound. Use the word in a sentence, and repeat it again after the sentence. For example, say the word **thankful**. Then say:* I am thankful for my wonderful family. *Repeat the word **thankful** after the sentence.*

Sample words: **thankful, thankless, helpful, helpless, colorful, colorless**

Have students confirm their spelling with a partner, making corrections as needed.

Reflect and Review

Ask: *What did you learn today? Discuss with your partner.*

Have students work with their partners to complete the sentence frames at the end of the Lesson 6 Practice Page, assisting as needed.

Word Bank

+ -ful	+-less
faithful	wordless
flavorful	worthless
hateful	meaningless
peaceful	aimless
purposeful	expressionless
restful	guiltless
v	heartless

✓Formative Assessment

If the student completes each task correctly, proceed to the next skill in the sequence.

Did the student…?	Intervention
Pronounce –ful and -less in isolation Pronounce –full and -less in words	Use a mirror to show movement of mouth, tongue, and teeth as the sound is produced. Use hand over mouth to explore movement of air as the sound is produced.
Understand the academic terms base word, adjective, suffix	Review the function of adjectives: to describe. Point out that adding a –less or –full suffix to a base noun makes it an adjective. Use several –less or –ful words to describe. Have students segment and blend the base word and suffixes.
Recognize meaning of words in context	Explain meaning of words before reading the text and discuss after reading text. Sketch briefly and label

7 Comparative and Superlative Suffixes -er, -est

Introduce the Lesson

Say: *Today we will form comparative adjectives by adding the inflectional endings -er and -est to base or root words, and recognize how the suffixes modify a word's meaning. We will also read text that includes comparative adjectives.*

Recognize Comparative and Superlative Suffixes -er, -est

Say: *A suffix is a word ending which changes, or modifies, the meaning of the word. The suffixes -er and -est modify an adjective by forming comparisons. We add the suffix -er to compare two people or things. We use the suffix -est to compare more than two people or things.*

Elicit Prior Knowledge

Display the Lesson 7 Practice Page. Prompt students to think about their primary language as you work together to complete section 1.

Say: *In the English language, we use comparative suffixes to make comparisons.*

Ask: *What letters or symbols in your home language do you use to compare? For example, how do you say:* The blue car is faster than the red car *in your language? What words do you use to make comparisons?*

Model: Recognize Comparative and Superlative Suffixes -er, -est

Direct students' attention to section 2 of the Practice Page.

Write the word **fast** on the board. Then add the suffix **-er** and explain how it changes the word's meaning.

Adjective	Comparative use -er to compare two things	Superlative use -est to compare more than two
fast		
long		
heavy		
easy		

Note: When the adjective ends in **y**, change the **y** to and **i** and then add **-er** or **-est**.

Practice: Comparative and Superlative Suffixes -er, -est

Read aloud section 3 of the Lesson 7 Practice Page in a fluent voice emphasizing intonation and pronunciation of words and inflectional endings. Invite students to echo read or chime on cue. Ensure comprehension by asking text dependent questions. Ask students to recognize and call out cognates.

Lesson Objectives

Recognize inflectional endings in adjectives and decode common suffixes **-er** and **-est**. Recognize that suffixes placed at the end of a root/base word modify the meaning of the word.
Recognize that suffixes **-er** and **-est** are used for forming comparisons.

Metacognitive Strategy

Selective auditory attention, use deductive thinking

Academic Language

word ending, word meaning, adjective, base word, comparison

Materials

Word Study Lesson 7 Practice Page

Pre-Assess

• Ability to use suffix as a clue to word meaning
• Recognition of a base or root word as a word part that contains meaning and can stand-alone

Transfer Notes:

In Spanish, Hmong, Vietnamese and Farsi adjectives follow the noun they modify.

In Spanish adjectives reflect the gender and number of noun modified.

Reinforce the meaning of adjectives in the lesson as well as their grammatical function.

Practice: Recognize Comparative and Superlative Suffixes -er and -est

Complete section 4 of the Practice Page with students.

Say: *Let's look at comparative and superlative adjectives you identified in the shared reading. We will recognize the base adjective word and form the comparative or superlative of each word.*

Extend Language Knowledge

Practice: Use Words in Context

Complete section 5 of the Lesson 7 Practice Page with students.

Say: *Let's think about comparative and superlative adjectives. Complete each sentence using words from the word bank on the Practice Page. Take turns reading the completed sentences to your partner.*

The girl's legs are **shorter** than her older brother's legs.

I ate more pizza because I'm **hungrier** than you.

He is the **funniest** kid in the whole class.

My puppy is the **cutest** pet in the world.

The **fastest** runner won the race.

Writing

Say: *Practice writing the adjectives you hear me say. I will pronounce the word, use it in a sentence and repeat it one more time.*

Pronounce one word at a time from the Word List below, stretching each sound. Use the word in a sentence, and repeat it again after the sentence. For example, say the word **tallest**. Then say: *The tallest player on the team was almost seven feet.* Repeat the word **tallest** after the sentence.

Sample words: **short, shorter, shortest, tall, taller, tallest**

Have students confirm their spelling with a partner, making corrections as needed.

Reflect and Review

Ask: *What did you learn today? Discuss with your partner.*

Have students work with their partners to complete the sentence frames at the end of the Lesson 7 Practice Page, assisting as needed.

Adjective Word Bank

wise	dirty	pretty
kind	soft	hard
empty	calm	quick
clean	fine	rich
quiet	fresh	cool
fancy	lovely	cold
smooth	brave	smart

✔Formative Assessment

If the student completes each task correctly, proceed to the next skill in the sequence.

Did the student...?	Intervention
Pronounce –er and -est in isolation Pronounce –er and-est in words	Use a mirror to show movement of mouth, tongue, and teeth as the sound is produced. Use hand over mouth to explore movement of air as the sound is produced.
Understand the academic terms base word, adjective, comparative, superlative	Review the function of adjectives – to describe Point out that comparative means to compare – look up in bilingual dictionary. Point out the prefix super in superlative to denote the highest and best of all.
Recognize meaning of words in context	Explain meaning of words before reading the text and discuss after reading text. Model using context clues. Sketch briefly and label.

Lesson Objectives

Recognize common Latin suffixes.

Recognize that suffixes placed at the end of a root/base word modify the meaning of the word.

Generalize meaning of suffixes and use to determine meaning of words.

Metacognitive Strategy

Selective auditory attention

Use deductive thinking

Academic Language

word ending, word meaning, modify, derivative

Materials

Word Study Lesson 8 Practice Page

Pre-Assess

- Ability to use suffix as a clue to word meaning
- Recognition of a base or root word as a word part that contains meaning and can stand-alone

Transfer Notes:

Latin suffixes transfer into Spanish and usually create cognates. English Learners from other than Romance languages will need more practice internalizing the meaning of each suffix.

8 Common Latin Suffixes -al -ial, -able -ible, -tion

Introduce the Lesson

Say: *Today we will form new words by adding common Latin suffixes to the end of root words. These are called derivations, meaning words that derive their basic meaning from the root word.*

Recognize Common Latin Suffixes

Say: *A suffix is a word ending which changes, or modifies, the meaning of the word. Most suffixes in the English language come from Latin or Greek languages. Today we will learn the meaning of some common Latin suffixes. We use our knowledge of suffixes to learn the meaning of new words.*

Elicit Prior Knowledge

Display the Lesson 8 Practice Page. Prompt students to think about their primary language as you work together to complete section 1. Remind students that a derivation is a word that is derived from another, such as **nation** and **national**.

Ask: *How do you say the word **nation** in your home language? How do you say **national**?*

Model: Recognize Latin Suffixes -al -ial, -able -ible, -tion

Direct students' attention to section 2 of the Practice Page.

Say: *Read the word with me: nation. Say the suffix with me: -al. The suffix -al means "relating to." So **national** means "relating to the nation."*

Repeat with examples below.

Root Word	Suffix	Meaning	Example
nation	-al	Relating to	National flags are meaningful.
response	-able -ible	Able to, can do	I am responsible,
educate	-tion	The process of	I am getting an education

Practice: Latin Suffixes

Read aloud section 3 of the Practice Page in a fluent voice emphasizing intonation and pronunciation of words and inflectional endings. Invite students to echo read or chime on cue. Ensure comprehension by asking text dependent questions. Ask students to recognize and call out cognates.

Practice: Recognize Latin Suffixes

Complete section 4 of the Practice Page with students.

Say: *Look at words that you have identified. We will recognize the root word by segmenting it from the root word. Think how the suffix modifies the root word and creates a new word that derives its meaning from the root word.*

Extend Language Knowledge

Practice: Make Meaning

Complete section 5 of the Practice Page with students.

Say: *Let's read each clue together. Then work with a partner to find an answer from the word bank. Write the answer on the line.*

1. The process of educating **education**
2. The giving or receiving of knowledge or intelligence **information**
3. The characteristic of someone who meets their obligations **responsible**
4. Someone you can rely on **reliable**
5. Someone who knows two languages **bilingual**

Say: *Practice writing the words you hear me say. I will pronounce the word, use it in a sentence and repeat it one more time.*

Pronounce one word at a time from the Word List below, stretching each sound. Use the word in a sentence, and repeat it again after the sentence. For example, say the word **educate**. Then say: *The teacher's job is to educate her students.* Repeat the word **educate** after the sentence.

Sample words: **form, formal, response, responsible, educate, education, person, personable**

Have students confirm their spelling with a partner, making corrections as needed.

Reflect and Review

Ask: *What did you learn today? Discuss with your partner.*

Have students work with their partners to complete the sentence frames at the end of the Lesson 8 Practice Page, assisting as needed.

Word Bank

-al	-able	-ible	-tion
critical	available	collectible	animation
cultural	debatable	predictable	competition
dimensional	consumable	comprehensible	multiplication
emotional	detachable	convincible	reaction
institutional	likable	detectible	translation
magical	accountable	invincible	prevention

✔ Formative Assessment

Did the student…?	Intervention
Pronounce –al, able, ible and -tion in isolation or in words	Use a mirror to show movement of mouth, tongue, and teeth as the sound is produced. Use hand over mouth to explore movement of air as the sound is produced.
Understand the academic terms root word, derivative, modify	Review terms by looking them up in dictionary. Derivative means to derive, to come from, Modify means to change slightly, to change a little Root word is the word that provide the basic meaning
Recognize meaning of words in context	Explain meaning of words before reading the text and discuss after reading text. Model using context clues. Sketch briefly and label. Use bilingual dictionaries to negotiate meaning.

Lesson Objectives

Recognize common Greek suffixes.
Recognize that suffixes placed at the end of a root/base word modify the meaning of the word.
Generalize meaning of suffixes and use to determine meaning of words.

Metacognitive Strategy

Selective auditory attention
Use deductive thinking

Academic Language

word ending, word meaning, modify, derivative

Materials

Word Study Lesson 9 Practice Page

Pre-Assess

- Ability to use suffix as a clue to word meaning
- Recognition of a base or root word as a word part that contains meaning and can stand-alone

Transfer Notes:

Greek suffixes transfer into Spanish and usually create cognates. English Learners from other than Romance languages will need more practice internalizing the meaning of each suffix.

9 Common Greek Suffixes -ist, -graph, -logy

Introduce the Lesson

Say: *Today we will form new words by adding common Greek suffixes to the end of root words. These are called derivations, meaning words that derive their basic meaning from the root word.*

Recognize Common Greek Suffixes

Say: *A suffix is a word ending which changes, or modifies, the meaning of the word. Most suffixes in the English language come from Latin or Greek languages. Today we will learn the meaning of some common Greek suffixes. We use our knowledge of suffixes to learn the meaning of new words.*

Elicit Prior Knowledge

Display the Lesson 9 Practice Page. Prompt students to think about their primary language as you work together to complete section 1. Remind students that a derivation is a word that is derived from another, such as **art** and **artist**. *Ask: How do you say the word art in your home language? How do you say artist?*

Model: Recognize Greek Suffixes -ist, -graph, -logy

Direct students' attention to section 2 of the Practice Page.

Say: *Read the word with me:* ***art.*** *Say the suffix with me:* ***-ist.*** *The suffix* ***-ist*** *means "one who specializes in." So an artist is a person who specializes in creating art.*

Repeat with examples below.

Root Word	Suffix	Meaning	Example
art	-ist	one who specializes in	Picasso was a great artist.
photograph	-graphy	picture or writing	This is a photograph of my dog.
biology	-logy	the study of	I study living things during biology.

Practice: Greek Suffixes

Read aloud section 3 of the Practice Page in a fluent voice emphasizing intonation and pronunciation of words and inflectional endings. Invite students to echo read or chime on cue. Ensure comprehension by asking text dependent questions. Ask students to recognize and call out cognates.

Practice: Recognize Greek Suffixes

Complete section 4 of the lesson practice page with students.

Say: *We will now look at words that you have identified. We will recognize the root word by segmenting it from the word.*

Extend Language Knowledge

Practice: Make Meaning

Complete section 5 of the Practice Page with students.

Say: *Let's read each clue together. Then work with a partner to find an answer from the word bank. Write the answer on the line.*

1. The study of ecosystems **ecology**
2. Someone who studies living organisms **biologist**
3. The study of dance **choreography**
4. The study of earth **geology**
5. The art of reproducing images with a camera **photography**

Writing

Say: *Practice writing the words you hear me say. I will pronounce the word, use it in a sentence and repeat it one more time.*

Pronounce one word at a time from the Word List below, stretching each sound. Use the word in a sentence, and repeat it again after the sentence. For example, say the word **scientist**. Then say: *The scientist works in a lab.* Repeat the word **scientist** after the sentence.

Sample words: **biologist, artist, scientist, biology, ecology, geology, photography**

Have students confirm their spelling with a partner, making corrections as needed.

Reflect and Review

Ask: *What did you learn today? Discuss with your partner.*

Have students work with their partners to complete the sentence frames at the end of the Practice Page, assisting as needed.

Word Bank

-ist	-logy	-graphy
activist	morphology	calligraphy
dentist	chronology	oceanography
pharmacist	ideology	videography
tourist	sociology	autobiography
guitarist	histology	cartography
cartoonist	psychology	logography

✔Formative Assessment

If the student completes each task correctly, proceed to the next skill in the sequence.

Did the student...?	Intervention
Pronounce **-ist**, **-logy** **-graphy** in isolation or in words	Use a mirror to show movement of mouth, tongue, and teeth as the sound is produced. Use hand over mouth to explore movement of air as the sound is produced.
Understand the academic terms root word, derivative, modify	Review terms by looking them up in dictionary. Derivative means to derive, to come from, Modify is to change slightly, to change a little Root word is the word that provide the basic meaning
Recognize meaning of words in context	Explain meaning of words before reading the text and discuss after reading text. Model using context clues. Sketch briefly and label. Use bilingual dictionaries to negotiate meaning.

10 Common Latin Prefixes

Introduce the Lesson

Say: *Today we will practice adding a prefix at the beginning of a root word to form derivations of the root word. A derivation means that the new word derives or gets its basic meaning from the root word to which the prefix is added. A prefix modifies or changes the meaning of a word.*

Recognize Common Latin prefixes

Say: *A prefix is a group of letters added at the beginning of a word that modifies the meaning of the root word. Most of the prefixes used in English come from the Latin or Greek languages. Today we are going to learn the meaning of some common Latin prefixes. Latin prefixes have their own meaning. When you learn the meaning of a prefix you can use that knowledge to learn the meaning of words.*

Ask: *Where do we add a prefix? (We add the prefix at the beginning of a word.)*

Ask: *What do prefixes do to a word? (Prefixes modify the meaning of the root word).*

Ask: *Do Latin prefixes have their own meaning? (Yes, they do).*

Elicit Prior Knowledge

Display and/or distribute the lesson practice page and complete section 1 with students.

Ask: *Are there letters or symbols placed at the beginning of a word that changes or modify the meaning or form derivations? A derivation is a word that is derived from another, for example:* **justice** *and* **injustice***. How do you say* **justice** *in your home language? How do you say* **injustice***?*

Model: Recognize and generalize the meaning of Latin prefixes re-, anti-, in-, un-, de-

Refer to section 2 of the Practice Page with students. Write the word **justice** on the board. As you add the prefix **in-** point to the word beginning.

Say: *This word is* **justice***. Read it with me:* **justice***. This is the prefix* **in-***. Say it with me:* **in-***. Prefix* **in-** *means* **not***. I will add the prefix* **in-** *at the beginning of the word* **justice***. It now says:* **injustice***. Read it with me:* **injustice***. It means not just, not fair. For example: An injustice is an act that is not fair. Heroes fight against injustice.*

Repeat with examples below.

Root Word	Prefix	Meaning	Example
write	re-	to do again	We had to **rewrite** the paragraph.
Atlantic	trans-	across	It was a huge **transatlantic** ship.
justice	in-	not	He worked to stop social **injustice**.
pleasant	un-	not	It was an **unpleasant** situation.

Practice: Identify Latin Prefixes

Read aloud section 3 of the Practice Page in a fluent voice emphasizing intonation and pronunciation of words and targeted sounds. Invite students to echo read or chime on cue. Discuss content of text by asking text dependent questions to ensure comprehension. Ask students to recognize and call out cognates.

Lesson Objective

Recognize common Latin prefixes
Recognize that prefixes placed at the beginning of a root/base word modify the meaning of the word.
Generalize meaning of prefixes and use to determine meaning of words.

Metacognitive Strategy:

Selective auditory attention. Use deductive thinking.

Academic Language:

word ending, word meaning, modify, prefix

Materials

Word Study Lesson 10 Practice Page

Pre-Assess:

Student's ability to recognize the end of a word as a clue to word meaning. Student's ability to recognize or root word as the part of the word that contains meaning and can stand-alone.

Transfer Notes:

Latin prefixes transfer into Spanish and usually create cognates. English Learners from other than Romance languages will need more practice internalizing the meaning of each prefix.

Ask: *What words do you see that include Latin prefixes? Work with a partner to underline and read the words you identify.*

Practice: Deconstruct Prefixes and Root Words

Complete section 4 of the Practice Page with students.

Say: *We will now look at words that you have identified. We will recognize the root word by segmenting it from the main word. As you do so, lets think how the prefix modifies the root word and creates a new word that derives its meaning from the root word.*

re-	in-	un-	trans-
re+write	in+appropriate	un+welcomed	trans+portation
re+place	in+capable		
re+ produce	in+effective		
re+trace	in+ validated		
	in+separable		

Say: *Next, we are going to practice pronunciation by breaking up the words into syllables. We will clap out the syllables as we say each word then annotate syllables with a slash. When done annotating, read each word aloud to your partner.*

Extend Language Knowledge: Making Meaning

Complete section 4 of the Lesson 1 practice page with students.

Say: *We will now look at common Latin prefix words context. Read and complete each sentence with the word from the word bank that makes most sense. Take turns reading the completed sentences to your partner.*

1. To move across (**transport**)
2. To not be effective (**ineffective**)
3. To produce again (**reproduce**)
4. To return or put something back (**replace**)
5. To not be capable (**incapable**)

Spelling/Writing

Say: *Now we can practice writing these words that contain Latin prefixes. I will pronounce each word and you will write it down. Pronounce one word at a time, stretching each sound. Use guided writing as needed.*

Sample words: **call, recall, use, reuse, start, restart, form, inform, fit, unfit**

Sample sentence: I will recall the message, translate, rewrite and resend it.

Say: *Check your spelling with your partner. Verify the correct spelling and re-write as needed.*

Reflect and Review

Ask: *What did you learn today? Discuss with your partner.*

Say: *Provide sentence frames: Something new I learned today was _____.*

Say: *I now know that _____. I will use this when _____.*

Word Bank

re-	in-	un-	trans-
reapply	inappropriate	unwelcome	transform
retrace	incapable	unfit	translate
reproduce	ineffective	unchain	transborder
recall	inform	unpleasant	transmedia
replace	invalidate	unannounced	transcellular
resend	inseparate	unstuck	transport
restart	immovable	uncork	transcontinental
reuse	insensitive	uninvited	transmarine

✓ Formative Assessment

If the student completes each task correctly, precede to the next skill in the sequence.

Did the student...?	Intervention
Pronounce re-, in-, un- and trans- in isolation or in words	Use mirrors to show movement of mouth, tongue, and teeth as the sound is produced. Use hand over mouth to explore movement of air as the sound is produced.
Understand the academic terms root word, derivative, modify	Review terms by looking them up in dictionary. Derivative means to derive, to come from, Modify is to change slightly, to change a little Root word is the word that provide the basic meaning
Do they recognize meaning of words in context	Explain meaning of words before reading the text and discuss after reading text. Model using context clues. Sketch briefly and label. Use bilingual dictionaries to negotiate meaning.

11 Common Greek Prefixes

Introduce the Lesson

Say: *Today we will practice adding a prefix at the beginning of a root word to form derivations of the root word. A derivation means that the new word derives or gets its basic meaning from the root word to which the prefix is added. A prefix modifies or changes the meaning of a word.*

Recognize Common Greek Prefixes

Say: *A prefix is a group of letters added at the beginning of a word that modifies the meaning of the root word. Most of the prefixes used in English come from the Greek or Latin languages. Today we are going to learn the meaning of some common Greek prefixes. Greek prefixes have their own meaning. When you learn the meaning of a prefix you can use that knowledge to learn the meaning of words.*

Ask: *Where do we add a prefix? (We add the prefix at the beginning of a word.)*

Ask: *What do prefixes do to a word? (Prefixes modify the meaning of the root word).*

Ask: *Do Greek prefixes have their own meaning? (Yes, they do).*

Elicit Prior Knowledge

Display and/or distribute the Practice Page and complete section 1 with students.

Ask: *Are there letters or symbols placed at the beginning of a word that changes or modify the meaning or form derivations? A derivation is a word that is derived from another, for example: **war** and **antiwar**. How do you say **war** in your home language? How do you say **antiwar**?*

Model: Recognize Greek Prefixes pro-, anti-, hyper-, en-

Refer to section 2 of the Practice Page with students. Write the word **speed** on the board. As you add the prefix **hyper-** point to the word beginning.

Say: *This word is **speed**. Read it with me: **speed**. This is the prefix **hyper-**. Say it with me **hyper-**. Prefix **hyper-** means "excessive". I will add the prefix **hyper-** at the beginning of the word **speed**. It now says: **hyper-speed**. Read it with me: **hyper-speed**. It means excessive **speed**. For example:A spacecraft travels at **hyper-speed**.*

Repeat with examples below.

Root Word	Prefix	Meaning	Example
proactive	pro-	before, in front of	She is **proactive**, always thinking ahead.
antibacterial	anti-	against, opposite	The **antibacterial** fights harmful bacteria.
hyperlink	hyper	over, excessive	The **hyperlink** gave us lot of information.
joy	en	in, into, on	I actually **enjoy** studying words.

Practice: Identify Comparative Prefixes

Read aloud section 3 of the lesson Practice Page in a fluent voice emphasizing intonation and pronunciation of words and targeted sounds. Invite students to echo read or chime on cue. Discuss content of text by asking text dependent questions to ensure comprehension. Ask students to recognize and call out cognates.

Ask: *What words do you see that include Greek prefixes? Work with a partner to underline and read the words you identify.*

Lesson Objectives

Recognize common Greek prefixes
Recognize that prefixes placed at the beginning of a root/base word modify the meaning of the word.
Generalize meaning of prefixes and use to determine meaning of words.

Metacognitive Strategy:

Selective auditory attention. Use deductive thinking.

Academic Language:

word ending, word meaning, modify, prefix

Materials

Word Study Lesson 11 Practice Page

Pre-Assess:

Student's ability to recognize the end of a word as a clue to word meaning. Student's ability to recognize or root word as the part of the word that contains meaning and can stand-alone.

Transfer Notes:

Greek prefixes transfer into Spanish and usually create cognates. English Learners from other than Romance languages will need more practice internalizing the meaning of each prefix.

Practice: Deconstruct Prefixes and Root Words

Complete section 4 of the Practice Page with students.

Say: *We will now look at words that you have identified. We will recognize the root word by segmenting it from the root word. As you do so, lets think how the prefix modifies the root word and creates a new word that derives its meaning from the root word.*

pro-	anti-	hyper-	en-
proactive	antibacterial	hypercomplex	enable
pronoun	anticrime	hyperactive	enjoy
probability	antiwar	hyperconfident	enlarge
problematic	antifungal	hyperclean	entrap
protagonist	antihero	hypergrowth	encase
proclaim	antibiotic	hyperlink	enlist

pro-	anti-	hyper-	en-
Pro+active	anticrime	Hyper+gowth	En+list
Pro+claiming		Hyper+compex	
Pro+test			
Prot + agonist			

Say: *Next, we are going to practice pronunciation by breaking up the words into syllables. We will clap out the syllables as we say each word then annotate syllables with a slash. When done annotating, read each word aloud to your partner.*

Extend Language Knowledge: Making Meaning

Complete section 4 of the Practice Page with students.

Say: *We will now look at common Greek prefix words context. Read and complete each sentence with the word from the word bank that makes most sense. Take turns reading the completed sentences to your partner.*

1. The students protested against the war during a peaceful **antiwar** demonstration.
2. We were **hyper-confident,** however we lost the game.
3. The **antibiotic** medicine made her feel better.
4. They provide the tools that **enable** us to work.
5. The **probability** of rain for tomorrow is 100%.

Spelling/Writing

Say: *Now we can practice writing these words that contain Greek prefixes.*

I will pronounce each word and you will write it down.

Pronounce one word at a time, stretching each sound. Use guided writing as needed.

Sample words: **war, antiwar, active, proactive, noun, pronoun, joy, enjoy, active, hyperactive**

Sample sentence: T*he child was so hyperactive it became difficult for one person to care for him.*

Say: *Check your spelling with your partner.*

Reflect and Review

Ask:*What did you learn today? Discuss with your partner.*

Provide sentence frames: Something new I learned today was _____.

I now know that _____. I will use this when _____.

✔Formative Assessment

If the student completes each task correctly, precede to the next skill in the sequence.

Did the student…?	Intervention
Pronounce pro- anti- hyper-en- in isolation or in words	Use mirrors to show movement of mouth, tongue, and teeth as the sound is produced. Use hand over mouth to explore movement of air as the sound is produced.
Understand the academic terms root word, derivative, modify	Review terms by looking them up in dictionary. Derivative means to derive, to come from, Modify is to change slightly, to change a little Root word is the word that provide the basic meaning
Do they recognize meaning of words in context	Explain meaning of words before reading the text and discuss after reading text. Model using context clues. Sketch briefly and label. Use bilingual dictionaries to negotiate meaning.

Lesson Objectives

Recognize common Latin roots.
Recognize that many different words are made from the same root.
Use root to learn meaning of unfamiliar words.

Metacognitive Strategy

Selective auditory attention. Use deductive thinking.

Academic Language

word ending, word meaning, modify, prefix, suffix, root

Materials

Word Study Lesson 12 Practice Page

Pre-Assess

• Ability to use word parts (e.g., prefix, suffix, root) as a clue to word meaning
• Recognition of a base or root word as a word part that contains meaning and can stand-alone

Transfer Notes:

Latin roots transfer into Spanish and usually create cognates. English Learners from other than Romance languages will need more practice internalizing the meaning of each suffix.

12 Common Latin Roots

Introduce the Lesson

Say: *Today we will learn about roots. A root is the basic element of a word upon which the meaning of a word is built. Many words in the English language have a Greek or Latin root. Recognizing common Greek and Latin roots helps us understand the meaning of new words.*

Prefix	Root	Suffix
trans	forma	tion

Elicit Prior Knowledge

Display the Lesson 12 Practice Page. Prompt students to think about their primary language as you work together to complete section 1.

Ask: *In your home language, what letters or symbols appear at the beginning, middle or end of a word that change or modify its meaning? What words in your home language come from other languages?*

Model: Recognize Common Latin Roots

Direct students' attention to section 2 of the Practice Page. Write the word form on the board.

Say: *This word is **form**. Read it with me: **form**. It's a Latin root that means shape or structure.*

Say: *When we add a prefix or a suffix to the root word **form**, we modify its meaning.*

As you add a prefix and/or suffix to the root **form**, read the new word and have students repeat.

Prefix	Root	Suffix	Meaning
re to do again	**forma** shape/structure	**tion** the process of	Reformation -the process of structuring again.
trans move across	**forma** shape/structure	**able** the ability to	Transformable -the ability to change structure
de opposite	**forma** shape/structure	**tion** the process of	Deformation -the process of distorting form or structure

Practice: Common Latin Roots

Read aloud section 3 of the Practice Page in a fluent voice emphasizing intonation and pronunciation of words and inflectional endings. Invite students to echo read or chime on cue. Ensure comprehension by asking text dependent questions. Ask students to recognize and call out cognates.

Ask: *Which words include a Latin root word? Work with a partner to underline and read the words you identify*

Practice: Recognize Common Latin Roots

Complete section 1 of the Practice Page with students.

Say: *Let's look at words that you identified. We will recognize the root word by segmenting it from its prefixes and suffixes. We will associate the root words with its derivatives to understand or get a clue for what each word means.*

ami	aqua	flect	corps

Extend Language Knowledge

Practice: Making Meaning

Complete section 5 of the Practice Page with students.

Say: *Let's read each clue together. Then work with a partner to find an answer from the word bank. Write the answer on the line.*

1. Bendable **flexible**
2. Place where fish can live **aquarium**
3. Friendly person **amiable**
4. System for transporting water **aqueduct**
5. A mirror provides this **reflection**

Writing

Say: *Practice writing the words you hear me say. I will pronounce the word, use it in a sentence and repeat it one more time.*

Pronounce one word at a time from the Word List below, stretching each sound. Use the word in a sentence, and repeat it again after the sentence. For example, say the word **aquarium**. Then say: *We saw many different kinds of fish at the aquarium.* Repeat the word **aquarium** after the sentence.

Sample words: **aquatic, corporal, corporation, aquarium, reflect.**

Reflect and Review

Ask: *What did you learn today? Discuss with your partner.*

Have students work with their partners to complete the sentence frames at the end of the Practice Page, assisting as needed.

✓**Formative Assessment**

If the student completes each task correctly, precede to the next skill in the sequence.

Did the student…?	Intervention
Pronounce re-, in-, un- and trans- in isolation or in words	Use a mirror to show movement of mouth, tongue, and teeth as the sound is produced. Use hand over mouth to explore movement of air as the sound is produced.
Understand the academic terms root word, derivative, modify	Review terms by looking them up in dictionary. Derivative means to derive, to come from, Modify is to change slightly, to change a little Root word is the word that provide the basic meaning
Do they recognize meaning of words in context	Explain meaning of words before reading the text and discuss after reading text. Model using context clues. Sketch briefly and label. Use bilingual dictionaries to negotiate meaning.

13 Common Greek Roots

Introduce the Lesson

Say: *Today we will learn about roots. A root is the basic element of a word upon which the meaning of a word is built. Many words in the English language have a Greek or Latin root. Recognizing common Greek and Latin roots helps us understand the meaning of new words.*

Prefix + Root+Suffix		
mono	graph	ic

prefix+root	
phono	graph

Root +suffix	
graph	ology

Elicit Prior Knowledge

Display the Lesson 12 Practice Page. Prompt students to think about their primary language as you work together to complete section 1.

Ask: *In your home language, what letters or symbols appear at the beginning, middle or end of a word that change or modify its meaning? What words in your home language come from other languages?*

Model: Recognize Common Greek Roots

Direct students' attention to section 2 of the Practice Page. Write the word **graph** on the board.

Say: *This word is **graph**. Read it with me: **graph**. It's a Greek root that means write, or record. When we add a prefix or a suffix to the root word form, we modify its meaning.*

As you add a prefix and/or suffix to the root **graph**, read the new word and have students repeat.

Prefix	Root	Suffix	Meaning
photo light	**graph** write or record	er one who	photographer one who records using light
bio life	**graph** write or record	ic relating to	biographic related to recording/writing about life
demo people	**graph** write or record	ical relating to	demographical relating to recording/writing about people

Practice: Common Greek Roots

Read aloud section 3 of the Practice Page in a fluent voice emphasizing intonation and pronunciation of words and inflectional endings. Invite students to echo read or chime on cue. Ensure comprehension by asking text dependent questions. Ask students to recognize and call out cognates.

Ask: *Which words include a Greek root word? Work with a partner to underline and read the words you identify.*

Lesson Objectives

- Recognize common Greek roots.
- Recognize that many different words are made from the same root.
- Use root to learn meaning of unfamiliar words.

Metacognitive Strategy

Selective auditory attention. Use deductive thinking.

Academic Language

word ending, word meaning, modify, prefix, suffix, root

Materials

Word Study Lesson 13 Practice Page

Pre-Assess

- Ability to use word parts (e.g., prefix, suffix, root) as a clue to word meaning
- Recognition of a base or root word as a word part that contains meaning and can stand-alone

Transfer Notes:

Latin roots transfer into Spanish and usually create cognates. English Learners from other than Romance languages will need more practice internalizing the meaning of each suffix.

Practice: Recognize Common Greek Roots

Complete section 4 of the Practice Page with students.

Say: *Let's look at words that you identified. We will recognize the root of each word by segmenting it from its prefix and suffix. We will associate the root with its derivatives to understand what the word means.*

Root	Meaning	Words
carto	map	cartology, cartographer, cartography
geo	earth	geographical
photo	light	photography
astro	star, space	Astronomical, astrophotography
techno	art, science, skill	technology
meta	greathuge	metamorphosing
morph	change	metamorphosing
demo	people, human	demographical

Word Bank

Root	Meaning	Example
cycle	ring, circle	bicycle
phon	sound	telephone
scope	see, vision	telescope
therm	heat	thermometer
arch	most important	monarch, archetype
chron	time	chronological order
tele	from far away, distance	television
hydr	water	dehydrate, hydration

Extend Language Knowledge

Practice: Making Meaning

Complete section 5 of the Practice Page with students.

Say: *Let's read each clue together. Then work with a partner to find an answer from the word bank. Write the answer on the line.*

1. The art of capturing images through light **photography**
2. The study of objects in space **astronomy**
3. A great change **metamorphosis**
4. Relating to recording human population **demography**
5. The art of creating maps and charts **cartology**

Writing

Say: *Practice writing the words you hear me say. I will pronounce the word, use it in a sentence and repeat it one more time.*

Pronounce one word at a time from the Word List below, stretching each sound. Use the word in a sentence, and repeat it again after the sentence. For example, say the word **photographer**. Then say: *The photographer adjusted her camera before taking pictures.* Repeat the word **photographer** after the sentence.

Sample words: **photo, photography, photographer, astronomy, astronomer, technology**

Have students confirm their spelling with a partner, making corrections as needed.

Reflect and Review

Ask: *What did you learn today? Discuss with your partner.*

Have students work with their partners to complete the sentence frames.

✔Formative Assessment

If the student completes each task correctly, precede to the next skill in the sequence.

Did the student…?	Intervention
Pronounce Greek roots in isolation or in words	Use a mirror to show movement of mouth, tongue, and teeth as the sound is produced. Use hand over mouth to explore movement of air as the sound is produced.
Understand the academic terms root word, derivative, modify	Review terms by looking them up in dictionary. Derivative means to derive, to come from, Modify is to change slightly, to change a little Root word is the word that provide the basic meaning
Do they recognize meaning of words in context	Explain meaning of words before reading the text and discuss after reading text. Model using context clues. Sketch briefly and label. Use bilingual dictionaries to negotiate meaning.

14 Derivatives

Introduce the Lesson

Say: *Today we will learn about Greek and Latin roots and their derivatives. A root is the basic element of a word upon which the meaning of a word is built. Many words in the English language have a Greek or Latin root. Recognizing common Greek and Latin roots helps us understand the meaning of new words.*

Recognize Word Parts

Say: *A derivative is a word formed from another word, or root, and usually has a meaning related to the root. For example, the word **childish** is a derivative of **child**. We form derivatives by attaching prefixes and/or suffixes to roots. Each part of a word –– prefix, root, and suffix –– has its own meaning which changes, or modifies, the meaning of the new word.*

Elicit Prior Knowledge

Display the Lesson 14 Practice Page. Prompt students to think about their primary language as you work together to complete section 1.

Ask: *What words or symbols in your home language derive or come from other languages or other words?*

Model: Recognize Derivatives

Direct students' attention to section 2 of the Practice Page. Write the each root on the board: **mar, memor, simil**. Explain the meaning of each. Read the derivative of each root. Point to the root embedded in each derivative. Read, echo read and discuss meaning.

Say: *Remember, derivatives are words that are derived or come from or contain the same root.*

Root	Meaning	Derivatives
mar	sea	**mar**ine, **mar**itime, sub**mar**ine, ultra**mar**ine
mem	memory	**mem**ory, re**mem**ber, com**mem**orate, **mem**oir, **mem**o
simil	same	**simil**arity, **simil**e, **simil**itude, assimilation, **simil**ar

Practice: Derivatives

Read aloud section 3 of the Practice Page in a fluent voice emphasizing intonation and pronunciation of words and inflectional endings. Invite students to echo read or chime on cue. Ensure comprehension by asking text dependent questions. Ask students to recognize and call out cognates. Point out that most Greek and Latin derivatives are Spanish-English cognates.

Ask: *Which words are derivatives? Work with a partner to underline the root in each derivative and read the words you identify.*

Lesson Objectives

Recognize common Greek and Latin roots.
Recognize that many different words are made from the same root.
Use root words and derivatives to learn meaning of unfamiliar words

Metacognitive Strategy

Selective auditory attention. Use deductive thinking.

Academic Language

word ending, word meaning, prefix, suffix, root, derivatives

Materials

Word Study Lesson 14 Practice Page

Pre-Assess

- Ability to use word parts (e.g., prefix, suffix, root) as a clue to word meaning
- Recognition of a base or root word as a word part that contains meaning and can stand-alone

Transfer Notes:

Both Greek and Latin roots, as well as their derivatives transfer into Spanish and usually create cognates. English Learners from other than Romance languages will need more practice internalizing the meaning of each root.

Practice: Recognize Derivatives

Complete section 4 of the Practice Page practice page with students.

Say: *Let's look at words that you identified. We will recognize the root of each word by segmenting it from its prefix and suffix. We will associate the root with its derivatives to understand what the word means. We will look up the words in dictionary to confirm and discuss their meanings.*

Root	Meaning	Words
gratus	thankful, free, pleasing	grateful, gracious, gratitude, gratification, gratis, gratuity
manus	hands	manuscript, manicure, manual, manage, manifest.
spec	to see	spectacular, spectacles, circumspect, inspection, introspect retrospect, spectators

Extend Language Knowledge

Practice: Use Words in Context

Complete section 5 of the Practice Page with students.

Say: *Let's look at derivatives in context. Read and complete each sentence using a word from the word bank on the Practice Page. Take turns reading the completed sentences to your partner.*

1. The mechanic did an **inspection** of our car to make sure it was safe to drive.
2. Her son's accomplishment gave her great **gratification**.
3. The **manual** provides instructions for how to assemble the toy.
4. The **spectators** clapped when the player scored.

Writing

Say: *Practice writing the words you hear me say. I will pronounce the word, use it in a sentence and repeat it one more time.*

Pronounce one word at a time from the Word List below, stretching each sound. Use the word in a sentence, and repeat it again after the sentence. For example, say the word **manual**. Then say: *The manual gives step-by-step instructions for how to assemble the chair.* Repeat the word **manual** after the sentence.

Sample words: **manual, manuscript, gratis, grateful, gratitude, spectacular, spectators**

Reflect and Review

Ask: *What did you learn today? Discuss with your partner.*

Have students work with their partners to complete the sentence frames at the end of the Lesson 14 Practice Page, assisting as needed.

Word Bank

Root	Meaning	Example
rupt	break	erupt, corrupt disrupt, interrupt
port	to carry	airport, carport, import, export
voc	voice	advocate, vocalize, vocabulary
scope	vision to see	bioscope, microscope, telescope
ology	the study of	biology, psychology, radiology
mono	one	monocle, monorail, monotone

✔Formative Assessment

If the student completes each task correctly, precede to the next skill in the sequence.

Did the student...?	Intervention
Pronounce the words	Use a mirror to show movement of mouth, tongue, and teeth as the sound is produced. Use hand over mouth to explore movement of air as the sound is produced. Segment by syllables and repeat and eco read.
Understand the academic terms root word, derivative, modify	Review terms by looking them up in dictionary. Derivative means to derive, to come from, Modify is to change slightly, to change a little Root word is the word that provide the basic meaning
Do they recognize meaning of words in context	Explain meaning of words before reading the text and discuss after reading text. Model using context clues. Sketch briefly and label. Use bilingual dictionaries to negotiate meaning.

Word Study Lesson 1 Practice Page

Word Recognition: Plural Noun Inflectional Endings -s and -es

1. Compare Words

My home language is _____.

Today's concept compared to my home language:

Draw and label examples of a singular and plural word from your home language.

SINGULAR (one)	PLURAL (more than one)

2. Recognize and Form Plural Nouns

Singular Noun	Add -s or -es to make it plural	New meaning
book		
bus		
fox		

3. Read and Identify Singular and Plural Nouns

Have you ever packed a suitcase? It is simple if you plan ahead. First you may want to think of things to wear, such as pants, shirts, coats, jackets, shoes, and socks. Then you may want to include personal items such as brushes, glasses, gloves and sandals. You may also need bottles of lotions, soap and toothpaste. Don't forget to pack a good book, your camera, and a delicious snack.

4. Classify Words

Singular	Plural

Singular	Plural

5. Your Turn

1. People borrow _____ from the library.
2. We packed our things in _____ when we moved.
3. We sat on the _____ in the living room.
4. I like to wear _____ and _____.
5. My sister and I both wear _____ to see.
6. I wear _____ in the winter to keep my _____ warm.

couches   hands   boxes   jeans   gloves   books   eyeglasses   t-shirts

Something new I learned was _____. I now know that _____. I will use this when _____.

Word Study Lesson 2 Practice Page
Plural Noun Inflectional Endings -s and -ies

1. Prior Knowledge and Home Language Connections

My home language is _____.

Today's concept compared to my home language:

What is a rule in your home language?

A language rule that you already know.	
Do not do this. This is wrong.	Do this. This is correct.

2. Recognize and Form Plural Nouns

How to form the plural of nouns ending in **y**.	If the letter before the **y** is a vowel (**a, e, i, o, u**) add **s** to make the plural.	If the letter before the **y** is a consonant take out the **y** and add **-ies.**
boy		
lady		
guy		
pony		

3. Read and Identify Singular and Plural Nouns

Have you ever visited a factory? Factories are buildings where things are made. A factory can make toys like a rag monkey or a soft pony. Other factories make food. A bread factory can make delicious cupcakes with daisies and berries. Before the holidays, factories are busy making things people will buy at the stores.

4. Classify Words

Singular	Plural

Singular	Plural

5. Your Turn

1. Animals that swing from trees_____
2. Places where things are made _____
3. Books are full of these _____
4. They may be in a bouquet_____
5. They cry when they are hungry_____

daisies   factories   monkeys   babies   stories

Something new I learned was _____. I now know that _____. I will use this when _____

Word Study Lesson 3 Practice Page
Plural Noun Inflectional Endings Nouns f/v + -es

1. Compare Words

My home language is _____.

Today's concept compared to my home language:

What letters or symbols placed at the end of a word change its meaning in your home language?

Letters or symbols placed at the end of a word to change its meaning.	How does it change its meaning? From: _____ to _____

2. Recognize and Form Plural Nouns

How to form the plural of nouns ending in **f** or **fe**.	If the word ends in **f**, change the **f** to a **v** and add **-es** to make the plural.	If the word ends in **-fe** change the **-fe** to a **v** and add **-es** to make the plural.
knife		
half		
self		
life		

3. Read and Identify Singular and Plural Nouns

What is your favorite book? One day, I got a book off the shelf, I thought it was about a thief, but it was about chef knives. It had pictures of carving knives and cheese knives, some of them were decorated with carvings of wolves and old bearded elves. I do not own a chef knife myself, but I know that some people spend their lives collecting them.

4. Classify Words

Singular	Plural

Singular	Plural

5. Your Turn

1. People who take things that are not their own _____
2. Place where books are kept _____
3. They say cats have nine of them _____
4. You buy them at a bakery _____
5. Magical story characters that live in the wood _____

elves   lives   loaves   thieves   bookshelves

Something new I learned was _____. I now know that _____. I will use this when _____.

Word Study Lesson 4 Practice Page

Word Recognition Irregular Plural Nouns

1. Prior Knowledge and Home Language Connections

My home language is _____.

Today's language concept of grammatical rules and exceptions in my home language:

How the rule usually is:	The exception to the rule:

2. Shared Reading Text

Some men and women like to work close to nature. They get jobs that most people do not think about. For example, working in botanical gardens where they make sure rare cacti plants do not get fungi or larvae on their stems. Others work with animals, outdoors counting the geese in a flock, checking the teeth on a horse, or indoors conducting experiments with mice. I imagine that as children they walked miles on their feet admiring the wonders of nature.

3. Recognize Irregular Plurals in Context

Singular	Plural

Singular	Plural

Singular	Plural

4. Extend Language: Make Meaning

1. The opposite of man: _____

2. A desert plant: _____

3. Ants use these to smell: _____

4. They love to play: _____

5. These fall out and new ones grow: _____

teeth   antennae   woman   cacti   children

Today I learned that _____. This is important because _____. I now know _____.

Word Study Lesson 5 Practice Page
Word Recognition: Inflectional Endings in Verbs

1. Prior Knowledge and Home Language Connections

My home language is _____.

Today's language concept of past, present, and future in my home language:

PAST	PRESENT	FUTURE

2. Shared Reading Text

Do you like to walk? I love walking with my friends. We like looking at the houses and smiling at the neighbors. Yesterday, we enjoyed ourselves a lot. We wanted to eat so we decided get ice-cream. We played in the park and listened to music and relaxed under the trees. Even though I wanted to stay longer, we started back home. When I got home, my mom was cooking dinner and my sister was watching TV. I looked for my backpack and started to do my homework.

3. Recognize Inflectional Endings in Verbs

Verb	+ ing	+ ed
walk		
play		
listen		
cook		
watch		

4. Extend Language: Make Meaning

1. He _____ dinner for his family.
2. She is _____ all the time.
3. Yesterday, he _____ his friend.
4. He is always _____ books.
5. We _____ to go to the park yesterday.

jumping   helped   reading   wanted   cooks

Today I learned that _____. This is important because _____. I now know _____.

Word Study Lesson 6 Practice Page
Adjective Inflectional Endings -ful, -less

1. Compare Words

My home language is _____.

Today's concept compared to my home language:

What are examples in your home language of letters or symbols that change the meaning of a word when placed at the end of a word? How does it change these words' meanings?

Letters or symbols placed at the end of a word to change its meaning.	How does it change its meaning? From: _____ to _____

2. Recognize and Form Adjectives

Base Word	-ful changes the base word to an adjective used to describe something that **has** that characteristic	-less changes the base word to an adjective used to describe something that **lacks** that characteristic
color		
care		
help		
joy		

3. Read and Identify Adjectives

How would you describe your best friend? Is she someone who always helps you? Then you would say she is helpful. Or maybe she is graceful and cheerful, too. A good friend does not always have to be playful or joyful. A good friend is priceless. It is someone who accepts you just the way you are. I am thankful that I have wonderful friends in my life.

4. Classify Words

- ful	-less

- ful	-less

5. Your Turn

1. Someone who helps _____
2. Someone who has no hope _____
3. Someone who feels happy _____
4. Someone who loves to play _____
5. Something that is of a lot of value to you _____

cheerful   priceless   helpful   playful   hopeless

Something new I learned was _____. I now know that _____. I will use this when _____.

Word Study Lesson 7 Practice Page
Comparative and Superlative Suffixes -er, -est

1. Compare Words

My home language is _____.

Today's concept compared to my home language:

In your home language, how do you say "The blue car is **faster** than the red car"? What words or word endings do you use to make comparisons?

Translate: The blue car is **faster** than the red car.	What words or word endings do you use to make comparisons?

2. Recognize and Form Comparative and Superlative Adjectives

Base Word Adjective	Comparative use **-er** to compare two things	Superlative use **-est** to compare more than two
big		
slow		
heavy		
easy		

3. Shared Reading Text

The other day I went to the store to buy a skateboard. I wasn't sure if I wanted the longer or shorter deck, if I should get a wider or narrower deck, or one with larger or smaller wheels. I knew I wanted the best truck, that is, the part that holds the wheels to the deck. I wanted the strongest, sturdiest truck and knew it had to be set at the lowest possible place on the deck to allow leverage for skating tricks.

4. Classify Words Create Comparative and Superlative Adjectives Using Suffixes

Base Word Adjective	Comparative use **-er** to compare two things	Superlative use **-est** to compare more than two
big		
slow		
heavy		
easy		

5. Your Turn

1. The girl's legs are _____ than her older brother's legs.
2. I ate more pizza because I'm _____ than you.
3. He is the _____ kid in the whole class.
4. My puppy is the _____ pet in the world.
5. The _____ runner won the race.

funniest cutest fastest brightest shorter hungrier

Something new I learned was _____. I now know that _____. I will use this when _____.

Word Study Lesson 8 Practice Page
Common Latin Suffixes

1. Compare Words

My home language is _____.

Today's concept compared to my home language:

How do you say **nation** in your home language?	How do you say **national** in your home language?

2. Recognize Common Latin Suffixes

Root Word	Suffix	Meaning	Example

3. Read and Identify Latin Suffixes

Have you ever thought about getting a job? First you fill out an application. Your application has information about your education, and your talents and experiences. It should give the reader the idea that you are a responsible, credible, and respectable person. After all, they are going to want someone who is reliable and capable. Then, you will get a call for a formal interview. During a professional interview you will be asked questions. The employer is usually looking for someone who is personable, sensible , bilingual, and has a great attitude!

4. Classify Words

-al	-tion	-ible	-able

5. Your Turn

1. The process of educating _____
2. The giving or receiving of knowledge or intelligence _____
3. The characteristic of someone who meets their obligations _____
4. Someone you can rely on_____
5. Someone who knows two languages _____

reliable   responsible   bilingual   education   information

Something new I learned was _____. I now know that _____. I will use this when____.

Word Study Lesson 9 Practice Page
Common Greek Suffixes

1. Compare Words

My home language is _____.

Today's concept compared to my home language:

How do you say **art** in your home language?	How do you say **artist** in your home language?

2. Recognize Common Greek Suffixes

Root Word	Suffix	Meaning	Example

3. Read and Identify Greek Suffixes

Do you have a favorite subject in school? My favorite subject is science. I like geology, biology, and ecology. I also like the arts, which includes photography, cinematography and even choreography. I am not sure if I want to be a scientist, biologist or an artist, but I know that whatever career I choose, I will be creative and do something that will help all mankind.

4. Classify Words

-ist	-graphy	-logy

5. Your Turn

1. The study of ecosystems _____
2. Someone who studies living organisms _____
3. The study of dance _____
4. The study of earth _____
5. The art of reproducing images with a camera _____

photography   biologist   geology   choreography   ecology

Something new I learned was _____. I now know that _____. I will use this when _____.

Word Study Lesson 10 Practice Page
Common Latin Prefixes

1. Prior Knowledge and Home Language Connections

My home language is _____.

Today's concept compared to my home language:

How do you say **justice** in your home language?	How do you say **injustice** in your home language?

2. Recognize and Generalize the Meaning of Latin Prefixes re-, in-, un-, trans-

Root Word	Prefix	Meaning	Example

3. Shared Reading Text

Did you ever have a backward day? Yesterday everything went wrong. Not only did we had to rewrite our paragraphs, we had to replace all the information that was inappropriate relating to our transportation project. Let me tell you, it was unwelcomed news when our teacher asked us to restart and retrace our planning. We felt so ineffective; we stood there incapable of believing that all our work was invalidated. Today we will reproduce our work; our group is hardworking and inseparable.

4. Deconstruct Prefixes and Root Words

re-	in-	un-	trans-

5. Extend Language: Make Meaning

1. To move across _____
2. To not be effective _____
3. To produce again _____
4. To return or put something back _____
5. To not be capable _____

incapable   transport   reproduce   ineffective   replace

Something new I learned was _____. I now know that _____. I will use this when ____.

Word Study Lesson 11 Practice Page
Common Greek Prefixes

1. Prior Knowledge and Home Language Connections

My home language is _____.

Today's concept compared to my home language:

How do you say **war** in your home language?	How do you say **antiwar** in your home language?

2. Recognize and Generalize the Meaning of Greek Prefixes pro-, anti-, hyper-, en-

Root Word	Prefix	Meaning	Example

3. Shared Reading Text

Have you ever felt proactive? Proactive means you act with positive intent. You probably feel strongly about injustice or crimes and begin a social justice or anticrime campaign. You may or enlist friends to join you in proclaiming the rights of animals. It may be that you protest against the hyper-growth of your town and the construction of hyper-complex buildings next to a lagoon. Your actions enable others to become aware of issues that affect us all. So, when you feel like a protagonist, move forward with courage.

4. Deconstruct Prefixes and Root Words

pro-	anti-	hyper-	en-

5. Extend Language: Make Meaning

1. The students protested against the war during a peaceful _____ demonstration.
2. We were _____, however we lost the game.
3. The _____ medicine made her feel better.
4. They provide the tools that _____ us to work.
5. The _____ of rain for tomorrow is 100%.

probability hyper-confident antibiotic enable antiwar

Something new I learned was _____. I now know that _____. I will use this when _____.

Word Study Lesson 12 Practice Page
Common Latin Roots

1. Compare Words

My home language is _____.

Today's concept compared to my home language:

What letters or symbols appear at the beginning, middle or end of a word that change or modify the meaning of the word?	What words come from other languages?

2. Recognize Common Latin Roots

Prefix	Root	Suffix	Meaning

3. Read and Identify Latin Roots

Did you ever wonder where words come from? Many words in the English language are of Greek and Latin origin. For example, **ami** in Latin means love, that is where the word **amiable, amity** and **amorous** come from. **Aqua** means **water**, which is where words like **aquarium, aquatic** and **aqueduct** derive from. The root **flect** means to **bend, reflect, reflection, reflective** and **flexible** all derive from that Latin root. The root **corps** means **body**, the words **corporal, corporation, corpse, corpulen**t and **incorporate** all have meaning related to **a body** or **group of bodies.**

4. Classify Words

ami	aqua	flect	corps

5. Your Turn

1. Bendable _____
2. Place where fish can live _____
3. Friendly person _____
4. System for transporting water _____
5. A mirror provides this _____

aquarium amiable reflection flexible aqueduct

Something new I learned was _____. I now know that _____. I will use this when ____.

Word Study Lesson 13 Practice Page
Common Greek Roots

1. Compare Words

My home language is _____.

Today's concept compared to my home language:

What letters or symbols appear at the beginning, middle or end of a word that change or modify the meaning of the word?	What words come from other languages?

2. Recognize Common Greek Roots

Prefix	Root	Suffix	Meaning

3. Read and Identify Greek Roots

Did you ever wonder how map-making has changed over the centuries? Cartology is the study of the creation of maps and charts based on geographical or demographical information. Long ago, a cartographer was more like an artist drawing the cartographic information with paper and ink. In the late 1800, the invention of photography contributed to the evolution of map-making. In modern times, astrophotography is used to map astronomical objects such as planets and nebulae million of light years away. Currently, digital technology is metamorphosing the mapping industry. I wonder how map-making will continue to evolve?

4. Classify Words

Root	Meaning	Word

5. Your Turn

1. The art of capturing images through light _____
2. The study of objects in space _____
3. A great change _____
4. Relating to recording human population _____
5. The art of creating maps and charts _____

metamorphosis   astronomy   demography   cartology   photography

Something new I learned was _____. I now know that _____. I will use this when _____.

Word Study Lesson 14 Practice Page
Derivatives

1. Compare Words

My home language is _____.

Today's concept compared to my home language:

What words or symbols in your home language derive or come from other languages or other words?

2. Recognize Derivatives

Root	Meaning	Derivatives

3. Read and Identify Derivatives

Did you know that by learning 10 root words you are able to learn the meaning of over 200 words? For example, if you know that **gratus** means **grateful** or **thankful**, you then can relate that meaning to the words **gratitude, gracious gratification, gratify, gratis** and **gratuity**. If you know that **manus** means **hands**, then you can relate that meaning to **manuscript, manicure, manual, manage** and **manifest**. I love the root **spec**, it means to **see**, as in: **spectacular, spectacles, circumspect, inspection, introspect** and **retrospect**. If you reference a dictionary, you will understand how their meaning relates. If you know Spanish, you will notice that all of these words are cognates.

4. Classify Words

Root	Meaning	Word

5. Your Turn

1. The mechanic did an _____ of our car to make sure it was safe to drive.
2. Her son's accomplishment gave her great _____.
3. The _____ provides instructions for how to assemble the toy.
4. The _____ clapped when the player scored a goal.

inspections spectators gratification manual

Something new I learned was _____. I now know that _____. I will use this when _____.